The Great Eastern Railway

The Great Eastern Railway

From the Grouping to the Elizabeth Line
1923–2023

Charles Philips

PEN & SWORD
TRANSPORT
AN IMPRINT OF PEN & SWORD BOOKS LTD.
YORKSHIRE – PHILADELPHIA

First published in Great Britain in 2024 by
Pen and Sword Transport
An imprint of
Pen & Sword Books Ltd.
Yorkshire - Philadelphia

ISBN 9781036103583

A CIP catalogue record for this book is available from the British Library.

Typeset in INDIA by IMPEC eSolutions
Printed and bound in the UK on paper from a sustainable source
by CPI Group (UK) Ltd., Croydon. CR0 4YY.

Pen & Sword Books Ltd. incorporates the imprints of Pen & Sword Books: After the Battle, Archaeology, Atlas, Aviation, Battleground, Discovery, Family History, History, Maritime, Military, Politics, Select, Transport, True Crime, Fiction, Frontline Books, Leo Cooper, Praetorian Press, Seaforth Publishing, Wharncliffe and White Owl.

For a complete list of Pen & Sword titles please contact

PEN & SWORD BOOKS LIMITED
George House, Beevor Street, Off Pontefract Road, Hoyle Mill, Barnsley, South Yorkshire, England, S71 1HN.
E-mail: enquiries@pen-and-sword.co.uk
Website: www.pen-and-sword.co.uk

or

PEN AND SWORD BOOKS
1950 Lawrence Rd, Havertown, PA 19083, USA
E-mail: uspen-and-sword@casematepublishers.com
website: www.penandswordbooks.com

FSC www.fsc.org
MIX
Paper | Supporting responsible forestry
FSC® C013604

Contents

Rear Cover – 100 Class 745 twelve car emus entered service with Greater Anglia in 2020 and have replaced the final locomotive propelled trains in East Anglia – the Liverpool Street to Norwich service. Here we see a unit on an up express at Margaretting on 19 May 2023.

Author

Front Cover – 36 British Railways' Standard 7MT 4 6 2s or Britannia's were the locomotives that transformed the G E section giving it for a short time the fastest train in Great Britain. No 70006 Robert Burns is seen entering Liverpool Street with the 11 49 up East Anglian on 6 May 1951. Note the dynamometer car in the formation.

Ken Nunn

Preface and Acknowledgements

This is a history of the lines of the former Great Eastern Railway (GER) from Grouping in 1923 to the complete opening of the Elizabeth Line in 2023.

The book covers such topics as the impact of the Grouping of the GER into the LNER and later into British Railways and its subsequent privatization; the impact of the Second World War on the railway; the Britannia Class locomotives and how they revolutionised the line's schedules; the modernisation of the railway including electrification and dieselisation; closures both before and after the publication of the Beeching Report; and the Elizabeth Line. I have also included shipping and preservation. Motive power is also included be it railway or maritime.

The book is a follow up to my two previous volumes on the history of the GER from 1811 to 1924.

I was a season ticket holder from Billericay to central London via Liverpool Street from June 1972 to March 2005 and so I observed some of the later events described in the book. Sometimes, particularly during times of industrial action, it was hard being a railway enthusiast and a season ticket holder. As a child and a teenager I had travelled on the GE Section including behind steam and also on the electric trains when they ran on 1,500 volts direct current.

I think compared to how things were when I started work there are good and bad things. On the good side, trains are gangwayed within sets. Non-gangwayed carriages, including compartments, are something I do not look back on with nostalgia. I regret the passing of guards, as trains do need someone other than the driver to man them and help passengers for a variety of reasons. Printed timetables are no longer available other than the European Rail Timetable which includes Britain, but not every service or every station. They have to be downloaded off the internet. I'm sorry, but there *are* people who do not know how to or do not have the internet or even wish to have it. Another wonderful advert for car travel! The people who think these things up do not live in the real world. I am not blaming front line railway staff or senior managers. They have to operate the system that has been imposed and they deserve courtesy and sympathy. It is the powers above senior managers that deserve criticism.

With the abolition of paper tickets and timetables, the job of future railway and other historians is going to be considerably more difficult. I am afraid that politicians have an awful lot to answer for.

The former GER today is a paradox. It is both more efficient compared to the past, but also less interesting. I cannot see a person getting excited over one of the latest electric multiple units (emus) compared to a Britannia or a Brush Type 4. I would suggest that the future of railway enthusiasm lies more in the study of the history of the railway and less in the study of the motive power. I would hope that railway preservation continues, despite the fact that those of us who knew everyday working steam and travelled behind it are declining in numbers. By the middle of the twenty-first century, there will be few alive who saw a steam locomotive in everyday service. Whether one likes it or not, both the steam locomotive and the diesel train are polluters and contributors towards global warming. The steam locomotive was incredibly dirty – as were diesel locomotives – if not well cleaned. One hopes a solution will be found. I believe that something needs to be done about climate change, but not by alienating the people whose support is needed.

I have used a number of sources in this book including previously published books, contemporary newspapers and magazines. I could not have written this book without the help of the members of the Great Eastern Railway Society. Thank you for putting up with my awkward questions. All efforts have been made to trace the owners of copyright material including photographs. The publishers and I apologise for any infringement that has occurred and will pay any outstanding reproduction fees. We also apologise for converting colour photographs to black and white for the sake of continuity of the illustrations in the book and will pay any fees that are necessary.

The Great Eastern Railway Society have produced CDs and/or downloads of the following magazines, some of which but not all were used in writing this book. They are: *The Great Eastern Railway Magazine, The London and North Eastern Railway Magazine, British Railways Eastern Region Magazine, Railway and Travel Monthly, The Locomotive, Railways.* Details of the magazines will be found in the Sales section of the Great Eastern Railway Society website, as can a dvd of the 8mm films mainly taken on the GE by the Society's founding President Bernard Walsh.

Charles Phillips

Chapter 1

From 1923 to the Outbreak of the Second World War

The London and North Eastern Railway (LNER), which was the second largest of the four railway companies created by the Railways Act 1921, was formed on 1 January 1923 by the amalgamation of the North Eastern (NER), North British (NBR), GER, Great Northern (GNR), Great Central (GCR) and Great North of Scotland (GNOSR) railways as well as a number of minor railways such as East and West Yorkshire Union (E&WUR) and London and Blackwall railways. To these companies was added on 1 July 1923 the Colne Valley and Halstead Railway (CV&HR) and on 1 July 1924 the Mid Suffolk Light Railway (MSLR). Of the minor companies, only the East and West Yorkshire Union, Colne Valley and Halstead and Mid Suffolk Light owned and operated their own lines. Other companies were worked by larger companies, such as in the case of the London and Blackwall Railway by the GER.

The LNER had 6,590 route miles. The Company operated train services in England, Scotland and Wales. There were shipping services to the Netherlands and Belgium. In the early days, it also operated some bus services in England and Scotland and in those two countries it also operated some tramways. There were a number of railways that were jointly owned with other railways. In the East of England these were the Midland and Great Northern Joint and Norfolk and Suffolk Joint railways which were jointly owned with the London, Midland and Scottish Railway (LMS) and in London the East London Joint Committee with the Southern and the Metropolitan and Metropolitan District railways and the Tottenham and Hampstead jointly with the LMS. In the East of England, the Great Northern and Great Eastern Joint became entirely part of the LNER. Not every railway in Britain was included in one of the four big new railway companies. The narrow gauge Southwold Railway in Suffolk was not included. The LNER was the only one of the new companies not to own a narrow gauge railway.

On 1 January 1925, the freehold of the East London Railway, which provided a connection between the GER and the railways south of the River Thames was vested in the Southern Railway. As this was subject to a perpetual lease to the Joint committee which then consisted of the Metropolitan, the Metropolitan District, the London and North Eastern and the Southern railways, there was no practical change in the day-to-day running of the Railway.

In the Eastern Counties of England, the LNER had a virtual monopoly of traffic to and from London. Only between Southend in Essex and London was there competition in the form of the LMS which included within in its constituents the Midland Railway which had acquired the London, Tilbury and Southend Railway (LT&SR) in 1912. The Midland and Great Northern Joint Railway (M&GNJTR) remained the joint responsibility of the LMS and LNER, but in 1935 the two owning companies agreed that the local administration of the Joint Railway should be taken over by LNER officials. This came into force on 1 October 1936. In many ways the GER did not easily fit into the LNER. In the sort of traffic that it carried it resembled the constituent companies of the Southern Railway. Its goods traffic was principally agricultural, whilst its passenger services were principally City workers, holiday makers and passengers for the continent. Its suburban service out of Liverpool Street station was the densest in the world – all operated by steam.

The last General Meeting of the GER took place on 20 February 1923. The first Ordinary General Meeting of the LNER took place on 14 March 1924 at the Hotel Great Central, Marylebone, London. Marylebone station was the head office of the new company.

The General Manager of the new LNER was Ralph Wedgewood, who was previously the General Manager of the North Eastern Railway. In the January 1923 edition of the *Great Eastern Railway Magazine*, Wedgewood wrote a letter:

> I should like to take the double opportunity of the New Year and the inauguration of the new London & North Eastern Railway to send my greetings to the staff of the old Great Eastern Railway, with whom I shall in future have the pleasure to be so closely associated.
>
> [It is my] earnest hope that the changes which are inseparable from the new order of things may be carried through smoothly, with fair and full consideration to all the varied interests involved, and that before all things the fine traditions of the Great Eastern Railway for mutual loyalty, devotion, and good feeling shall be passed forward to the new Company, so that in the days to come the name of the London & North Eastern Company shall be as much an object of pride to Great Eastern men as that of the Great Eastern Railway is to-day.

Four Directors of the GER joined the board of the new company. They were: The Rt. Hon. Lord Ailwyn, PC, KCVO, KBE (who had been the Deputy Chairman of the GER); Colonel William Johnson Galloway; Sir Eric Hambro, KBE; and Mr. Hubert

Thomas Bailey. The GER's last Chairman, Lord Claud Hamilton did not join the board of the new company.

The Chairman of the new company was William Whitelaw, who was previously the Chairman of the North British Railway. The Deputy Chairman was Lord Farringdon, who had been Chairman of the Great Central Railway.

A number of GER officers were appointed to posts in the LNER. The GER's last General Manager, Sidney Parnwell, was appointed Divisional General Manager, Southern Area. The Southern Area covered the lines of the former Great Eastern, Great Central and Great Northern railways. Sir Sam Fay the last General Manager of the Great Central Railway and Charles Dent the last General Manager of the Great Northern Railway both retired. Parnwell, who had only taken up his post on 1 December 1922, unfortunately had been handed a poisoned chalice. His predecessor as General Manager of the GER, Sir Henry Thornton, had resigned to take up the post of President of the newly formed Canadian National Railways. It is said that the choice for the post of General Manager of the LNER was between Thornton and the North Eastern Railway's General Manager Ralph Wedgewood and that Thornton's departure left the way clear for the latter. Thornton was right to take the job with Canadian National Railways. It is a pity, though, that someone else other than Parnwell and who had more experience was not appointed to the role of Divisional General Manager of the Southern Area of the LNER: even if they had been with one of the other existing pre-Grouping companies from another of the groups, and that Parnwell was not persuaded to retire early at the end of 1922. After all, Thornton's appointment as General Manager of the GER in 1914 was unprecedented. The Southern Area of the LNER had a total of 3,095 route miles, which was greater than the total of the smallest of the four groups – the Southern Railway whose total route mileage was 2,115½ miles and whose General Manager Sir Herbert Walker had been a General Manager of one of the constituent companies (the London and South Western Railway) since 1 January 1912. Rather longer than poor Parnwell's tenure as General Manager of the GER. He was replaced on 28 June 1924 by Alexander Wilson, Divisional General Manager, North Eastern Area of the LNER.

Other officers of the GER who had senior posts in the new company were: Thomas Chew, Solicitor of the GER who became Solicitor of the new company in charge of legal work of a particular nature; G.F. Thurston, Secretary of the Great Eastern; along with James McLaren, Secretary of the North British Railway who became Joint Secretaries of the LNER.

The *GER Magazine* as a separate entity survived until the end of 1926 when it was succeeded by the new *LNER Magazine* which embraced the whole of the LNER.

According to the *Locomotive Magazine* of January 1923:

> Early last month a train was on view at King's Cross terminus made up of freshly-painted bogie carriages belonging to each of the constituent railways forming the Eastern group. Vehicles were sent by the Great North of Scotland, North British, North-Eastern, Great Central, Great Eastern and Great Northern Railways for the inspection of the directors with a view to selecting a livery for the coaching stock of the new Company. The new North Eastern Ry. Pacific type engine No. 2400 and the electric passenger loco. No. 13 were also on view together at York Station a week or so later with locomotives from each of the railways in the group, in the pre-war colours.

The new Company decided that its livery would bright green for passenger tender locomotives and black for all goods and passenger tank locomotives.

According to the *Locomotive Magazine* of March 1923:

> At Marylebone terminus on 22 February 1923 twelve of the latest type of locomotives belonging to the principal railways forming the Eastern Group were on exhibition for the directors' inspection with a view to deciding the new standard style of painting. On the track alongside departure platform No. 4 were nine passenger engines, while three goods engines and four bogie carriages were on view at arrival platform No. 1. At the head of the line of passenger engines stood No. 1534 of the Great Eastern section, one of the standard 4-6-0 express passenger engines, painted bright green 'with black bands and white lining, chocolate framing with a-fine vermilion line above the footplate, and black below, with the motion painted vermilion. On the tender were the initials in 6-in. gilt block letters, with the engine number in 12-in. letters underneath.' The same magazine for May 1923 recorded under the heading G E Section that 'Claud Hamilton is the second Stratford engine to be painted green: goods and passenger tanks are being painted black'.

The LNER introduced a class system based on that of the GNR:

A 4-6-2
B 4-6-0
C 4-4-2
D 4-4-0
E 2-4-0
F 2-4-2

G 0-4-4
H 4-4-4
J 0-6-0
K 2-6-0
L 2-6-4
M 0-6-4
N 0-6-2
O 2-8-0
P 2-8-2
Q 0-8-0
R 0-8-2
S 0-8-4
T 4-8-0
U 2-8-8-2
V 2-6-2
W 4-6-4
X 4-2-2 & 2-2-4
Y 0-4-0
Z 0-4-2
Electrics ES, EF, EB, EE & EM

The LNER renumbered its locomotives as follows. Initially a letter suffix was given to the locomotive's number: D signifying Darlington for ex-NER and Hull; Barnsley locomotives (H&BR); C for ex-GCR; N for ex-GNR; E for ex-GER; B for ex-NBR; and S for ex-GNOSR.

In 1924 another renumbering took place. Ex-NER and H&BR locomotives retained their numbers; ex-GNR locomotives had 3000 added to their numbers; ex-GCR locomotives had 5000 added to their number except Duplicate List locomotives renumbered to 6402-6494 in order of age (youngest first); ex-GER had 7000 added to their numbers; ex-GNOSR had 6800 added to their numbers; ex-NBR had 9000 added to their numbers. The ex-CV&HR and MSLR as they were located in the ex-GER area took numbers 8312-8317, which were blank numbers in the GER series. The ex-E&WYUR being located in the ex-GNR area took numbers 3112-3115, which were blank numbers in the GNR series. The ex-M&GNJR, locomotives when the LNER took over responsibility for the railway in 1937 had a '0' added as a prefix to their numbers. The ex -Metropolitan Railway locomotives taken over by the LNER in 1937, being located in the ex-GCR operating area took numbers 6154-6163 and 6415-6422 in the GCR series.

Following the formation of the LNER all former GER locomotives were given an E suffix to their number. 1923 built D16/1 No 1787E is seen at Liverpool Street on 5 July 1924 with the 5.39pm train to Southend. *Ken Nunn*

Locomotives Nos 990E to 999E were the last locomotives to be built at Stratford works, in 1923-4. Here the penultimate member of the batch No 998E is seen at Stratford works on 12 July 1924. *Harold Hopwood*

In 1924 the LNER increased the numbers of the GER locomotives by 7000. F3 No 8040 formerly No 1040 is seen leaving Colchester with a local train for Clacton on 4 August 1933. *Pamlin Prints*

On 1 January 1923, the LNER inherited from the GER 1,317 locomotives. Of these, 1,314 were in service and three were awaiting to go into service. To these, a further thirty were added in 1923 and 1924.

To the aforementioned were added in the Great Eastern Section five locomotives from the Colne Valley and Halstead Railway on 1 July 1923 and three locomotives from the Mid Suffolk Light Railway on 1 July 1924.

The following GER classes with their GER and LNER class numbers were inherited by the LNER:

4-6-0 S69 – B12, 4-4-0, 4-4-0 T19-D13, S46-D14, D56-D15, H88 – D16, 2-4-0 T26 - E4, 0-6-0 N31 – J14, Y14 – J15, F48 – J16, G58 – J17, E72 – J18, T77 – J19, D81- J20, 0-6-2 tank locomotive - L77 – N7, 2-4-2 tank locomotive C32 – F3, M15 – F4, M15R – F5, G69 – F6, Y65- F7, 0-4-4 tank locomotive S44 – G4, 0-6-0 tank locomotive E22 – J65, T18 – J66, R24 – J67, C72 – J68, S56 and R24R – J69, C53 – J70, 0-4-0 tank locomotive B74 – Y4, G15 – Y6, 209 – Y5, 0-6-0 crane tank locomotive Z4 – later J92 petrol locomotive – Y11. 0-4-0 tank locomotive No A although in existence at the formation of the London and North Eastern Railway was not allocated a class.

> The following are the C, V& HR locomotives with their LNER classes: No 1 0 4 2 tank locomotive Z6, Nos 2, 3 and 4 2 4 2 tank locomotives F9 and No 5 0 6 2 tank locomotive N18.
>
> The three MSLR 0 6 0 tank locomotives were classed J64.

For passenger rolling stock, varnished teak was the livery adopted.

The *Great Eastern Railway Magazine* of July 1923 noted:

> One of the first fruits of Grouping, by the way, is that Great Northern 2-6-0 (H2/K1) express goods engines of the '1640' class were now working piped express goods trains between Spitalfields, March and Doncaster for which some of the locomotives were stationed at Stratford and Whitemoor.

The *Locomotive Magazine* of August 1923 reported that some of the former GCR (Class 8F/B4) 4-6-0s Nos 1100-4 were working over the Great Northern and Great Eastern Joint Line from March on fruit, fish and vegetable trains. These locomotives,

The LNER repainted all express passenger locomotives a rather attractive apple green livery. B12 No 8533 formerly 1533 is seen leaving Colchester with an express train for Clacton on 4 August 1933. *Pamlin Prints*

Starting in 1923 a number of locomotives from other sections of the LNER began appearing on the Great Eastern Section. Ex Great Northern K2 No 4681 is seen in about 1925 on an ordinary passenger train comprised of ex Great Eastern stock at Bow Junction. *Photomatic*

because they were not built to the GER loading gauge, would not have been able to work any further south over former GER metals.

Although of the six constituent companies that formed the LNER, four – the North Eastern, the North British, the Great Eastern and the Great North of Scotland – used the Westinghouse air brake and only two – the Great Northern and the Great Central – used the vacuum brake, the latter brake was decided on except for the Great Eastern suburban services which continued to use the Westinghouse brake.

1924 saw the first trial use of a diesel locomotive on the Great Eastern Section. The 0-4-0 locomotive ran tests between Tottenham and Cambridge. After the end of the tests nothing further was heard of the locomotive.

At the time of the formation of the LNER, the GER still operated one motor bus service. This service which ran from Harwich to Upper Dovercourt was withdrawn on 30 September 1923.

The early years of the LNER saw a number of changes on or relating to the former GER. Other than in the continental expresses and a set used for excursions and a Sunday Clacton Pullman train, Pullman Cars were withdrawn from the Great Eastern Section on 7 April 1924 and transferred to East Coast main line out of King's Cross.

The GER's line to Hertford received competition in the form of a more direct route from King's Cross to Hertford when the line known as the Hertford Loop was opened for passenger traffic on 2 June 1924. The Hertford Loop had started off as a branch line from Wood Green on the Great Northern main line to Enfield which had opened in 1871. In 1898, a plan was approved to extend the line north to Hertford and Stevenage, in order to relieve congestion on the main line without having to widen the Welwyn Viaduct from two to four tracks. Work had started in 1905 and Cuffley was reached on 4 April 1910. The construction of two major viaducts and the Ponsbourne Tunnel, at 2,684 yards the longest in the eastern counties of England and the last to be built by traditional methods, combined with First World War shortages of men and materials, delayed the opening of the route to Stevenage until 4 March 1918. Then it was single track and for goods services only. The line was doubled on 23 December 1920, but as mentioned was not opened to passengers until 2 June 1924. On that day the existing former Great Northern station in Hertford closed and trains from Hatfield were diverted to the new station.

In 1929 on the Tendring Hundred line the section between Frinton and Walton-on-the-Naze was resited due to fears of costal erosion on the original alignment. In 1938, Frinton became a crossing point. Another piece of new work was in January 1930 when, under the LNER Act of 1924, a connection was put in between the yard at Palace Gates station and Bounds Green depot on the Hertford Loop. Not only for the movement of suburban carriage stock, but even some east coast excursion trains from former Great Northern Railway suburban stations during the summer of 1939.

The principle new construction carried out during the period of this chapter was the quadrupling of the Ipswich main line from Romford to Gidea Park in 1931 and to Shenfield in 1934. This involved rebuilding the stations at Harold Wood, Brentwood and Shenfield. Gidea Park which had been opened in 1910, had been built with four platform faces. In 1934 a single line connection was made off the local lines of the main line at Shenfield to Mountnessing siding on the Southend line. This was signalled for Down trains only. In 1961 it was signalled for bi-directional working.

At the Centenary Celebrations of the Stockton and Darlington Railway held from 1 to 3 July 1925, two former GER locomotives took part in the cavalcade. They were D15 Class 4 4 0 No 8900 *Claud Hamilton* and Y6 0 4 0 tram locomotive No 7133.

The origins of the rail ferry service from Harwich lie in the Great War 1914–18 and the need to be able to move locomotives and rolling stock from the UK into the continental rail networks. No rail ferry service had ever existed prior to the war. The need was met by the design of three train ferries on very utilitarian lines, and the commissioning of adjustable link spans able to allow the careful alignment of tracks and acceptable gradients for transferring locos and wagons between ship and shore.

From 1 to 3 July 1925 celebrations were organized by the LNER to celebrate the Centenary of the Stockton and Darlington Railway at Stockton and Darlington. Two former GER locomotives took part. D15 No 8900 *Claud Hamilton* is seen as Unit 22 of the Centenary Procession near Darlington on 2 July 1925. *Ken Nunn*

Y6 tram locomotive No 7133 is seen as Unit 35 of the Centenary Procession near Goosepool on 2 July 1925. One wonders what some of the audience thought when they saw what to all intents and purposes looked like a self-propelled goods brake van. *Ken Nunn*

The first train ferry was inaugurated on 13 November 1917 and operated from a ferry berth in Southampton, west of the Royal Pier, to Dieppe. At Richborough in Kent on the River Stour below Sandwich, adjacent to a military camp, a train ferry terminal was established and came into operation on 6 February 1918. From there, services ran to Dunkirk, Calais, Dieppe and Boulogne at various times up to 1919. On 6 November 1918, another train ferry service was started from Southampton to Cherbourg. There were four train ferries. Train Ferries Nos.1, 2 and 3 were built on the Tyne and Clyde and completed in November 1917. They were joined in 1918 by No.4, being a former train ferry operating across the St Lawrence at Quebec in Canada. In 1919, all four ferries were laid up. No.4 was sold and converted to a tanker for Anglo-Saxon Petroleum (Shell).

In 1922, the GER and the Belgian government agreed to buy the original three ferries and establish a service between the GER's home port of Harwich, and Zeebrugge. This led to Great Eastern Train Ferries Ltd being established to operate the ferries, while La Société Belgo-Anglaise des Ferry Boats S.A. would control the rolling stock. The Great Eastern Train Ferry Company was officially registered with the issue of 400,000 £1 shares. Société Belgo-Anglaise with half of its capital subscribed by the Great Eastern Train Ferry Company was founded on 16 April 1923 to run the Belgian operations. The link spans were relocated, the one for Harwich being in the town port rather than at Parkeston Quay, and the service began in 1924.

The Southampton terminal was loaded on to two barges for the journey to Harwich leaving Southampton on 1 September 1923. On 4 September 1923, when 2.5 miles from the Cork Light Vessel dock, the cargo moved resulting in both barges sinking. It was not until October the link spans were recovered and beached at Harwich, the towers and machinery could not be salvaged and were blown up so as not to be a hazard to other shipping. The Richborough towers and machinery originally intended for Zeebrugge were then delivered to Harwich as a replacement and, together with the link span from Southampton, were erected on their current site. The Dunkirk terminal was now transferred to Zeebrugge.

Whilst the new terminal was being built, at Immingham, where the three train ferries had been laid up, work commenced to dry dock and overhaul each in turn. Train Ferries Nos.1 and 2 had been designed and built by Sir W. Armstrong-Whitworth at his Wallsend yard whilst Train Ferry No.3 was built at Fairfield's yard on the River Clyde. On 8 April 1924, Train Ferry No.2 arrived at Harwich still carrying a war time ambulance train for berthing trials; she undertook similar trials later at Zeebrugge.

At 11.00 on 24 April 1924, a special train arrived at Harwich town station with Prince George, later Duke of Kent, on board. Crowds had gathered along with school parties but the Prince failed to alight for over an hour. It was later discovered that a piece of his naval uniform was missing and he was waiting for a replacement to arrive from the Royal Naval Training Establishment at Shotley. When Prince George did alight from the train, the newly formed Harwich Town Silver Band commenced playing, their first official engagement. The Prince was accompanied by Sir Cyril Butler and officially welcomed to Harwich by the mayor, Mrs Lucy Hill. The party made their way to the train ferry terminal where the Prince officially set the bridge machinery in motion. After the official opening ceremony, Captain Grigor, who had been master of Train Ferry No.2 since it was brand new, gave the party a guided tour of the new ferry before setting sail on the inaugural voyage. The following day, Train Ferry No.3 arrived at Harwich from Immingham for that day's sailing. The service was nightly in each direction but without a Sunday service. To complete the train ferry fleet, Train Ferry No.1 arrived at Harwich on 17 July 1924. During 1925, all three vessels were converted at Antwerp to coal fired boilers from oil burning.

The *Daily News* of Friday 25 April 1924 carried an article on the opening and showed Prince George turning the wheel which lowered the bridge and allowed the first train on the ferry. The *Great Eastern Railway Magazine*, in its editions for May and July 1924, carried articles on the train ferries; whilst the edition for June carried an article on the

24 April 1924 saw the inauguration of the Harwich to Zeebrugge train ferry service by Prince George, later the Duke of Kent. This photograph taken at Harwich on 29 July 1958 shows the link span. I do not know the identity of the train ferry in the background. *Frank Church*

opening of the train ferry as did the June edition of the *North Eastern Railway Magazine* for the opening. Similarly, the *Railway Magazine* for June 1924 carried an article on the train ferry including the opening.

On 9 January 1926 40 officers and men from the 17th Medium Battery together with 100 horses in trucks arrived at Harwich on Train Ferry No.2 from the Rhine via Zeebrugge. After exercising the horses that morning, they departed by special train to Bournemouth that afternoon. One of the largest shipments took place on 5 October 1930 when a Sentinel-Cammell steam rail car was shipped to Zeebrugge, an export for the Belgium Railways. On 20 March 1933, 304 tons of electrical equipment in 17 wagons was shipped via Zeebrugge for the Danish State Railways.

The new service proved to not be very financial viable and by 1932 the annual loss had reached £3,485. On 27 July 1933, the Great Eastern Train Ferry Company was officially declared bankrupt. The assets were sold, with the LNER purchasing the three train ferries, the Harwich terminal and the train ferry company's shares in Belgo-Anglaise des Ferry Boats for £150,000. On 1 August 1933, under the new ownership, the service re-commenced. On 5 November 1931, a secondary service with Calais was opened. According to the *Locomotive Magazine* for November 1931, 'Harwich–Calais Train Ferry – A new train-ferry service between Harwich and Calais commenced on Thursday, November 5. The return voyage left Calais on Sunday, November 8, with nine railway wagons laden with furniture on board. The voyages will be made twice weekly.' When the Southern Railway Company opened their train ferry link between Dover and Dunkirk on 6 October 1936, the secondary route was closed.

In 1932, when the Southern had decided to have its own train ferry service, its General Manager, Sir Herbert Walker, had had an interview with Lord Darynton, the Chairman of Great Eastern Train Ferries with a view to formulating a satisfactory arrangement. Walker wanted nothing short of the withdrawal of the Harwich to Calais service as far as the Southern was concerned. Understandably, Darynton wanted compensation for Great Eastern Train Ferries. Walker did not feel that an agreement could be reached.

Walker also had a conversation with the Chief General Manager of the London and North Eastern about a traffic pool. To be effective, this could embrace Continental traffic via Dover, Folkestone, Gravesend, Newhaven, Southampton and Harwich and would require the concurrence of the French, Italian and Swiss railways. Should it be possible to reach an agreement, the pool would be of such dimensions as to be unworkable. Walker asked the permission of his board to make public the Southern's intentions and to ask for tenders for the three ships that would be needed to operate its service. This was given. At this point, Sir Charles Barrie MP who was a member of the London and North Eastern's board and sometime Chairman of that Company's

Steamship Committee, visited Walker and advocated a service from Richborough to Calais again. At the December 1932 meeting of the Southern's Board, Barrie's idea was put on record with a note of the tidal difficulties at both ports. This made a ferry dock at Dover imperative.

According to Charles Klapper in *Sir Herbert Walker's Southern Railway* (Ian Allan 1973), prior to the opening of the Dover to Dunkirk train ferry service by the Southern, traffic from Italy to Great Britain had been conveyed with 1,300 wagons specially adapted for use in this country hired by the Societa dei Ferryboats per l'Inghilterra, which company was a subsidiary of the Italian State Railways, from its parent company. In 1935, with a view to the Southern getting a share of the traffic it was proposed to liquidate the Societa dei Ferryboats per l'Inghilterra and to form a new Societa dei Ferryboats Riuniti, having a capital of 10,000lire (£166) comprising the Southern, the London and North Eastern and the Societa dei Ferryboats per l'Inghilterra. The office of the new company would be in Milan, the expense of which would be shared. From that there should develop with the LNER an arrangement for the division of train ferry traffic between the United Kingdom and Italy, Switzerland, Spain, France and Germany. It was not until 1936 that the new scheme came into effect.

By the time that the Dover to Dunkirk train ferry came into operation, the pooling arrangement with the LNER covered Belgium, Germany, Switzerland, Italy, Austria, Hungary, Yugoslavia and Czechoslovakia, whilst the Southern was deemed to cover traffic from France, Spain and Portugal. The Netherlands are not mentioned, but given the LNER's long standing connection to the Netherlands, one must assume that that Company covered that country. The companies concerned with garnering Continental consignments for the two English companies included the Societa dei Ferryboats Riuniti with E.C. Cox and later E.F.E. Livesey as the Southern representative and A.L. Gibson, the London and North Eastern's Continental Traffic Manager, as that company's representative.

In January 1937, the largest-ever load of sprats arrived from Brightlingsea in twenty-one trucks for shipment to Belgium.

The train ferry was not the only new service from Harwich to the Continent. In 1927, the Stoomvaart Maatschappij Zeeland or Zeeland Steamship Company changed the English terminus of its route to Vlissingen from Folkestone in Kent to Harwich. The change took effect from 1 January 1927.

Cook's Continental Timetable for August 1939 shows the following places served by ship from Harwich: Antwerp, Esjberg, Vlissingen and the Hook of Holland.

The early years of the LNER were marred by two strikes. From 21 to 29 January 1924 there was a strike by the Associated Society of Locomotive Engineers and Firemen (ASLEF) which rather disrupted services. Services on the Great Eastern Section of the

LNER were particularly badly affected. Southend did not see a train by that Company during the whole of the strike.

In May 1926 there was the General Strike. The Strike lasted nine days, from 4 to 12 May and was called by the General Council of the Trades Union Congress (TUC) in an unsuccessful attempt to force the British government to act to prevent wage reductions and worsening conditions for 1.2 million locked-out coal miners. Some 1.7 million workers went out, especially in transport and heavy industry. The government was prepared, and enlisted middle-class volunteers to maintain essential services. There was little violence, and the TUC gave up in defeat.

According to Julian Symonds in *The General Strike* (Readers Union 1957), the British railway system's prestige suffered a body blow during the Strike as its dependence on skilled workers in a time of emergency was clearly shown.

During the strike, a limited train service was provided. From the evidence available by the end of the strike, trains were running from London to all of the principal main line and suburban destinations – Chingford, Enfield, Epping, Ongar, Ilford, Gidea Park, Southend, Southminster, Cambridge, Ely, Yarmouth and Norwich. Between 4 and 7 May, the Harwich to Hook of Holland service was suspended but on its resumption from Harwich on 8 May trains started running to Harwich (Parkston Quay). The return sailing from the Hook of Holland restarted on 10 May. Some cross country and local trains outside of the London area also ran. Passenger trains were run by the LNER on all days except Sunday 9 May when only goods trains were run. The independent Southwold Railway did not suffer from the strike and maintained a normal service. A problem for the railways was that some of the bus companies outside of London did not go on strike, for example the National Omnibus and Transport Company in Essex, which meant some people simply switched to road transport.

The experiences of Stanley H. Evans who was a volunteer fireman is quoted by F.A.S. Brown in *Nigel Gresley Locomotive Engineer* (Ian Allan 1961). Evans was lucky as he had a former LT&SR driver as his driver. They had a L77 0-6-2 tank locomotive and did very well working trains to and from Ongar. According to him, one of the amateur drivers managed to derail a Claud Hamilton right outside Liverpool Street station 'thoroughly boxing things up for several hours'. Evans said that he was glad not to get a Claud Hamilton class or a 1500 class locomotive as the Railway Company had to provide them with an extra fireman and they (him and his driver) could see them sweating over the fire build-up before they started. He said that those volunteers brought back some harrowing tales.

To give another example, the first train that was run from Liverpool Street to Southend on 5 May turned into something of a comedy. A telegram arrived at Southend to say that a train had left Liverpool Street at 10.45am, but that it was not known when it would arrive. The stationmaster and other officials at Southend at intervals made attempts to find out where it was. Late in the afternoon it was announced that it had passed Romford at 4 30pm. Eventually a message was received that the train had no hope of reaching Southend and that it had been abandoned at Wickford. What happened was that forty-five minutes after arriving at Wickford, the engine reversed and returned to London.

Those on strike did make attempts to stop the trains from running. According to the *Essex and Suffolk Free Press* of 13 May, strikers at Kings Lynn attempted to stop the running of a daily train from there to Ely by obstructing the working of the crossing gates at the former place.

The strike also brought tragedy. On 10 May, a stopping train from Cambridge to Liverpool Street hauled by Claud Hamilton class 4-4-0 locomotive No 8894 was standing at Bishop's Stortford station when it was run into by a following through goods train hauled by G58 class 0-6-0 locomotive No 8231. In the collision, one passenger who had alighted from the passenger train was killed by the collapse of the station roof. Another person was seriously injured and two others suffered minor injuries. The cause of the accident was as follows. Firstly, the volunteer driver of the goods train thought that he had a clear road to London and secondly he underestimated his speed and was travelling in excess of the scheduled speed of 25mph, although he did reduce speed approaching the curve at Bishop's Stortford. The three men on the footplate did all in their power to bring the train to a stand immediately the danger was realised. The fact that they were not approaching the station prepared to stop and allowing for the restricted view resulted in the accident. In the late 1960s I met a man who had been at Stansted (now Stansted Mountfichet) station, which is the first station north of Bishop's Stortford, that day in 1926. He told me that he and some other men were aware of the passenger train and signalled to the crew of the goods train to slow down, but to no avail. *The Times* of Tuesday 11 May reported:

> About 3.15 p.m. yesterday a goods train from Cambridge crashed into the rear of a stationary passenger train at Bishop's Stortford Station on the London North-Eastern Railway. The goods engine was derailed and two of the coaches of the passenger train were lifted off the line. The roofing of the platform was also brought down. One man who was leaving the passenger train had his leg broken. When the wreckage was cleared away, the body of a man named Burrell, living at Warwick Road, Bishop Stortford, was found.

The *British Gazette*, which was an official newspaper produced by the government during the Strike, in its edition of Wednesday 12 May said:

> A passenger train from Cambridge to Liverpool Street was standing at Bishop's Stortford Station on Monday afternoon when it was run into from behind by a goods train. The guard's van was telescoped into a preceding empty carriage, but the guard was on the platform. The only casualty was a Mr Martin A Bailey of Bishop's Stortford, who was slightly hurt'.

The *Essex Chronicle* of Friday, 14 May reported:

> TRAINS COLLISION BISHOP'S STORTFORD SIR WALTER GILBEY'S AGENT KILLED On Monday a goods train on the Cambridge line collided with a stationary passenger train at Bishop's Stortford Station. The goods train was derailed, and two of the passenger coaches were lifted off the line. A portion of the station roof was also brought down. At first it was thought there was only one casualty apart from cases of shock. Later, however a man's body was discovered among the debris, the deceased was Mr. Burrell, 18 Warwick Road, Bishop's Stortford - Another man fractured his leg and rib, and young lady also received injuries.

This was not the only fatal accident on the railways of the Eastern Counties during the strike. The *Diss Express* of 14 May reported that a volunteer fireman by the name of Kenneth Kevell of Thorpe, Norwich was killed at Rose Bridge near Palgrave. According to the newspaper:

> It appears that the deceased was a volunteer fireman on a cattle train proceeding from Trowse [Norwich] to Romford which passed through Diss Station at 9 am. The unfortunate man was engaged in trimming the coal on the tender of the engine when his head struck the parapet of the bridge near Palgrave level crossing and was hurled off and fell on the permanent four foot way. It appears obvious that being a volunteer and not therefore acquainted with the line he misjudged the amount of clearance under the bridge with the consequent fatal result'.

The train was immediately pulled up and help summoned, but the unfortunate man was pronounced dead. Given that the event occurred on the day that the newspaper was published it is quite clear that the newspaper that day came out later in the day.

Following the end of the General Strike, the miners remained on strike until forced by their own economic needs to return to work. By the end of November most miners were back at work. One effect of the miners remaining on strike was that because of problems in obtaining coal there was a reduction in train services. Engine performance suffered and on the Southend and Cambridge lines there was a virtual failure of some stopping services.

The *Great Eastern Railway Magazine* was not published between issue No 184 for April 1926 and issue No 185 for September 1926.

Another consequence of the General Strike was the withdrawal of the passenger train services from Fenchurch Street to Blackwall and Millwall Junction and North Greenwich. Even before the General Strike, the LNER had decided that because of competition from road services, the services were expendable and had planned to withdraw them from 30 June. Because of the Strike, the services last ran on 3 May and were not resumed afterwards. This was not the first closure as the former Colne Valley and Halstead Railway station at Haverhill had seen its passenger services withdrawn from 14 July 1924. Another service which was withdrawn was that from Tottenham (Hale) to Gospel Oak on the Tottenham and Hampstead Joint Railway. After 6 September 1926, only special trains continued to run during summer bank holidays until 6 August 1939. At Haddiscoe, the Eastern Spur ceased to be used after 8 September 1934, but was not finally lifted until January 1939. In 1931 the connection to the LMS at Romford was severed.

During the period covered by this chapter, the motor bus developed into a competitor to the railway. From the solid tyre buses of both single and double deck types and the open-top double deck buses of the immediate post war period which were not very comfortable, the motor bus became pneumatic tyred and with the top deck roofed over. The motor bus also became more comfortable. Not only did it become a competitor for short distance traffic, but in the form of the motor coach a competitor for long distance traffic.

In the period 1 January 1923 to 2 September 1939, the following lines lost their passenger services and their replacement by bus services. The first to go was the Wisbech to Upwell tramway on 2 January 1928. On 22 September 1930, it was the turn of the branch lines from Downham to Stoke Ferry and Somersham to Ramsey. Ely to St Ives via Haddenham and Mellis to Eye followed on 2 February 1931 followed on 29 February 1932 by Bentley to Hadleigh. In all instances the lines remained opened for goods traffic.

The Southwold Railway, which had remained independent, began to experience financial difficulties during the years 1926 to 1928, bus competition being the principle cause. In early 1929, an approach was made to the LNER in the hope that it might take over the smaller railway. At the beginning of April 1929, the LNER replied that it could not provide financial help to the Southwold Railway. Southwold Corporation had also been approached for financial help but declined. The Directors of the Southwold Railway decided to close it. The last passenger train ran on 11 April 1929, with the last goods train and empty stock working taking place on 20 April. The Southwold Railway, although in existence, became derelict. There were a number of unsuccessful revival proposals to revive the Railway prior to the outbreak of the Second World War.

In Essex in the mid-1930s the LNER unsuccessfully tried to withdraw the passenger service on the line from Woodham Ferrers to Maldon.

In the 1930s there were proposals for the conversion of two branch lines into motor roads. One in 1933 was for the Wivenhoe to Brightlingsea line and the other was for the Mid Suffolk Light Railway. Neither of these proposals came to fruition.

The history of bus companies is somewhat complicated. More so than that of railway companies, the easiest way is to summarise the position in 1939 at the outbreak of the Second World War. Within the London area and parts of Hertfordshire and Essex, local services were operated by London Transport. In Essex, away from the south of the county, and in the parts of Hertfordshire served by the former GER away from the areas served by London Transport, the Eastern National Omnibus Company was the principal operator. In the south of Essex, Westcliff-on-Sea Motor Services was the principal operator. The Eastern National Omnibus Company commenced operating in 1929 as a joint venture between the LNER, the LMS and the National Omnibus and Transport Company. The National Company had originated in 1909 as the National Steam Car Company, operating steam bus services in London. The London services ceased in 1919, when the company was renamed National Omnibus & Transport Company. The company expanded outside London, first in Essex (1913), where the company bought the bus operations of the GER around Chelmsford, and later in Bedfordshire, Gloucestershire, Somerset, Dorset, and Devon and Cornwall. During the years up to 1929, the National continued to expand in Essex, Hertfordshire and Bedfordshire. During the 1920s, whilst there was some expansion of railway operated bus services, the legal powers of the railway companies to run bus services were unclear and each promoted private legislation (the Road Powers Acts of 1928) to obtain clarity. One result was that the railways were in future to refrain from taking a controlling interest in bus undertakings. This led the companies to enter into partnerships with the bus companies, including the National. In 1929, the LNER, the LMS and the National formed the Eastern National Omnibus Company, to which all three companies transferred their bus operations in Essex, Hertfordshire, Buckinghamshire and Huntingdonshire. In 1931, a controlling interest in the National Omnibus Company was acquired by the Tilling Group. From then on, Eastern National was run as a Tilling company, although the railways retained their shares in the Company until 1948. In 1934, Tillings acquired control of Westcliff-on-Sea Motor Services, whose origins went back to 1914, but the aforementioned railway companies did not have any shares in the Company. The Eastern Counties Omnibus Company was formed in July 1931 and was a combination of the four existing bus companies in East Anglia: Eastern Counties Road Car Company of Ipswich; Ortona Motor Company of Cambridge; and Peterborough Electric Traction Company all owned by Tilling & British Automobile Traction and United Automobile Services. Upon completion, the major shareholders were United Automobile Services, Tilling & British Automobile Traction, London & North Eastern Railway and London Midland & Scottish Railway. Also included was the Eastern Coach Works in Lowestoft.

In 1933, the London Passenger Transport Board was created to operate local transport services within an area whose eastern boundaries in relation to the former GER were Buntingford, Braughing, Bishop's Stortford, Harlow, Ongar and Brentwood. This included not only buses, but also trams, trolley buses and trains other than those operated by the four main line railway companies. Unfortunately, the Metropolitan Railway, which regarded itself as a main line railway company but had not been included in the 1923 Grouping, despite strenuous opposition was taken over by the Board. The Metropolitan Railway had a main line stretching over 50 miles to Verney Junction in Buckinghamshire and a branch line to Brill in Oxfordshire. As well as passenger services, unlike the other railways taken over by the Board it operated goods services. Also, unlike the other underground railways in London, the Metropolitan Railway used steam locomotives for goods and also passenger services, albeit in the outer extremities of the system. They hauled goods trains north of Finchley Road and passenger trains north of Rickmansworth. The Company was quite prepared to relinquish its sections of the Inner Circle (now Circle Line) together with its running powers over the rest of the Circle, but to no avail. The principal bus operators prior to the creation of the London Passenger Transport Board were the London General Omnibus Company and London General Country Services, which latter was the country arm of the former. The National Omnibus and Transport Company was also an operator within this area. Any operators of local services wholly within the Board's area which had an approximate radius of 30 miles were taken over by the Board. Only the four main line companies were excluded, as they would not agree to their London suburban services being included in the Board, arguing that they could not be separated from their long distance networks.

Prior to the creation of the London Passenger Transport Board the Road Traffic Act 1930 had introduced a structure of licensing, which, whilst it greatly improved the standards of safety within the road transport industry, created its own problems. It introduced five types of licence of which the road service licence created the greatest problem. Without this type of licence, it was illegal to run a regular bus service or to advertise an excursion of any kind or a tour. It conferred on the holder the privileges and responsibilities of a state-controlled monopoly.

The Road Traffic Act of 1930 and the creation of the London Passenger Transport Board had an effect on the existing operators – both bus and coach. Most affected was Edward Hillman, who was something of an entrepreneur. It is necessary to understand that because of an agreement between the National Omnibus and Transport Company and the London General Omnibus Company the former would not provide a through bus service from London to Chelmsford. Hillman started operations on 7 December 1928 with a scheduled service from Stratford to Brentwood. In 1929, the route was extended to Chelmsford and Colchester, followed in 1930 by Clacton. By the end of 1930, Hillman was operating a total of fifty-seven coaches. During the summer there were six coaches a day to Ipswich and two each to Norwich and Yarmouth. Unlike other coach operators, Hillman eliminated booking agents. This lack of overheads meant that his fares were cheap enough to attract large numbers of passengers.

By the spring of 1930, Hillman had fifty-six departures a day from Stratford. Unfortunately, he began to encounter opposition from other bus and coach operators and the LNER. Unlike other long distance coach operators, Hillman's drivers would always stop to pick up a person if they hailed them and would charge a local fare for a short trip. There were bus stops and thus a Hillman coach could scoop up many people waiting for other coaches or buses. The fares charged by Hillman were 5s to Ipswich, 6s to Yarmouth and 7s 6d to Norwich. By having these cheap fares, Hillman was taking off-peak passengers away from the railway, the attraction being price and convenience. An added bonus was that the coaches looked modern compared with the majority of the trains. On a train there was no guarantee that your train would comprise the latest rolling stock hauled by the latest type of locomotive i.e. the Sandringham class. Hillman did not neglect peak hour passengers and extra coaches were put on during those hours and also Saturday afternoons, giving Romford a service of one coach every 2.5-5 minutes. Season tickets for monthly and quarterly periods were issued. This prompted a number of other companies to try an imitate Hillman's success such as Sunset Pullman and Green Line, but without success.

In 1931, Hillman opened a coach station at 133 Bow Road in London (near to Bow Church). His coaches were running every 5 to 10 minutes to Brentwood, every 15 minutes to Chelmsford and from hourly to two-hourly to Colchester. The service to Brentwood and Chelmsford was somewhat better than that provided by the railway. Then things started to conspire against him. Following appeals in the traffic courts, the Ministry of Transport imposed certain conditions on the service, including the imposition of a 1s minimum fare as from 23 January 1933. 1933 also saw Hillman suffer two strikes; one in March and one in July. During the latter strike, Hillman dismissed all of the strikers and employed new staff who were recruited from as far away as Clacton. Further problems were heaped on Hillman when under the Ministry of Transport under the Road Traffic Act 1930 ruled that a minimum 6d stage should apply instead of the previous 1d or 3d stage.

On 23 July 1930, Green Line Coaches started a service from Charing Cross (Embankment) to Brentwood. Green Line Coaches Limited had been formed on 9 July 1930 by the London General Omnibus Company which, starting in 1927, had built up a network of coach services from London to towns up to 30 miles away. As well as express services operated by the London General Omnibus Company, some were run by subsidiary companies such as East Surrey Traction & Autocar Services and some on the London General Omnibus Company's behalf by the National Omnibus & Transport Company. The Green Line livery and fleet name was rolled out across the existing express services.

What finally killed off Hillman's coach service was the formation of the London Passenger Transport Board in April 1933. This ended all private coach operation within the extensive London Transport area, but it was not until 1934.that the end came. In that year, the London General Omnibus Company acquired the Bow to Brentwood section of Hillman's route, whilst the Brentwood to Chelmsford section passed to the Eastern National Omnibus Company. The latter Company wanted the remainder of Hillman's routes into Essex, Suffolk and Norfolk, but they were thwarted by the Eastern Counties Omnibus Company and Grey Green Coaches, the latter having been formed in the early 1920s, starting a coach service from London to Ipswich in June 1928. The opposition was backed by the LNER standing counsel. The licensing authority i.e., the Ministry of Transport through the regional traffic commissioners, was utterly hostile to anything associated with Hillman and the obsession which existed to ensure that the Eastern National Omnibus Company did not obtain a London to Chelmsford fare point. The result was that the Eastern National Omnibus Company lost its application on both counts and the regional traffic commissioners declared Hillman's long distance services to be redundant, despite the high passenger numbers and they were to be purchased by the Eastern Counties Omnibus Company and Grey Green Coaches by agreement with Hillman. Following the passing of the Brentwood to Chelmsford section of Hillman's route to the Eastern National Omnibus Company, the latter extended its No 10 route from Chelmsford to Brentwood to London, but the Company was not allowed to pick up passengers for London west of Brentwood or from London set down passengers for places west of Brentwood.

On the route from London to Cambridge and beyond there had been competition from Varsity Express Motors and Westminster Coaching Services. Whilst the former served Cambridge only, the latter served the city on routes to Bury St Edmunds, Ely,

Wisbech, Yarmouth and Norwich. Although slower than the trains, their return fare was only 2s and they were both more frequent and had the advantage of being able to run from the centre of Cambridge right into the West End of London. Both companies were sold to the Eastern Counties Omnibus Company in 1933.

Returning briefly to Green Line Coaches, the Company had itself applied to run services from London Chelmsford and Cambridge, but the applications had been refused by the regional traffic commissioners in September 1930.

John Hibbs in *The History of British Bus Services* (David and Charles 2nd edition 1989), gives details of the number of daily express services from London in the summer of 1930: fifteen to Lowestoft and Yarmouth; thirteen to Clacton and Walton-on-the Naze; nine to North Essex and Suffolk; five to Norwich; four to Chelmsford; three to Southend; two to Cambridge; two to Felixstowe; one to Burnham-on-Crouch; one to Cromer and Sheringham; one to Harwich and Dovercourt; and one to Hunstanton.

The principal bus services serving Southend from London in the early 1930s were Westcliff-on-Sea Motor Services from Wood Green via Ilford, Romford, Brentwood, Billericay, Wickford and Rayleigh, and the City Coach Company, which served the same places, with a route starting in Kentish Town. The City Coach Company's origins can be traced back to the early 1920s. In 1934 the City Coach Company negotiated the purchase of the Westcliff-on-Sea Motor Services route to Southend, effective from 1 January 1935.

It should not be thought that even on local routes there was not competition. For example, between Chelmsford and Colchester, Eastern National had direct competition from Moore's bus service. Moore's origins went back to the 1850s, but started bus operation in 1914 and survived right through the period of this chapter and beyond, only being taken over by Eastern National in 1963.

Between London and the Essex coast resorts of Southend and Clacton, but also as far north as Yarmouth the railway in the summer had competition from coastal steamers, principally of the General Steam Navigation Company, which had been incorporated in 1824, and the New Medway Steam Packet Company, which the former purchased in 1936. Despite being slower than trains and only serving the coast, for someone travelling from London to the coastal resorts, they had the advantage of being more spacious, so that rather than being confined to the seat of a motor coach or at best only being able to walk along the corridor of a train, one could stroll on deck. By the outbreak of the Second World War, both paddle steamers and screw propelled motor ships were in service.

Another form of competition that emerged during the interwar period was air travel. The first passenger-carrying air services had started off in 1919 between London and

Paris and by the time the first edition of Bradshaw's International Air Guide appeared in November 1934, within Europe, including the British Isles, a large network of routes had been established. It was possible to travel throughout the year not only from London to Pars, but also, amongst other places, to Antwerp, Brussels, Amsterdam, Rotterdam and Cologne and in the summer from Liverpool to Amsterdam and London to Copenhagen. All of these, apart from the Paris service, were in competition with the services of the Great Eastern section of the LNER. The ABC Railway Guide for April 1939 shows a similar pattern of air services.

There were a number of different airlines of which the most famous during this period was Imperial Airways. Of the others one was Hillman Airways. Even before Edward Hillman had been driven off the road, he was becoming tired of road transport and in 1931 he bought a two-passenger De Havilland Puss aircraft and on 26 November that year took a lease on Maylands Aerodrome, Maylands Farm, Harold Wood. His first flights were for charter or taxi-work.

In April 1932, Hillman Airways established a service to Clacton using two or more Puss Moths and some Fox Moths, which seated three or four passengers. The journey took 30 minutes each way compared with the three hours for a coach journey or just over 2 hours for a train journey at a fare of 12s 6d single or £1 return. This new service proved to be very popular and during the next year, services were extended to Manston for the Thanet towns. Hillman publicised his new venture with the 'Essex Air Pageant' at Maylands on 24 September 1932 which was attended by 20,000 people. Financial success did not come easily, though. In the first year there was a trading loss of £670 and a total debt of £1603.

The popularity of this venture encouraged Hillman, who maintained that the customer was always right. His ultimate aim was to provide a cheap and regular flight to Paris. But he realised that this could only be accomplished with a suitable plane. He went see Geoffrey De Havilland about the design of a new aircraft. According to one account, which may or may not be true, the result was the De Havilland Dragon, which had a passenger capacity of eight. The prototype first flew from De Havilland's airfield at Stag Lane, Hatfield on 12 December 1932. Eight days later it flew into Maylands where it was named – *Maylands* – at a brief ceremony by Amy Mollinson (nee Johnson).

Within a few months, the design of the Dragon was improved by the implementation of six-cylinder engines, this revised version being known as the DH89 Dragon Rapide of which 727 were built.

Edward Hillman commenced a twice-daily air service to Paris on 1 April 1933. The journey took 2 hours and cost £3 single or £5 10s return, compared to Imperial Airways £5 single and £8 10s return. There was also a weekend return for £4 15s.

Bradshaw's International Air Guide shows Hillman Airways operating the following services: from London to Paris and in the summer from London via Liverpool and the Isle of Man to Belfast. On 31 December 1934, Edward Hillman suffered a fatal blood clot at the age of 45. It robbed the transport scene locally of one of its most flamboyant characters.

It is possible that Hillman's death hastened the subsequent amalgamation with Spartan and United Airways later in 1935. With the loss of the coach revenue, the financial state of the old company sank and it was only the merger and the opening of new services from Heston that saved it. The new airline was registered under the name of Allied British Airways on 29 September 1935 but one month later it had dropped the 'Allied' to become 'British Airways'; not be confused with the present British Airways. Soon the airline was flying from Croydon and Gatwick.

If one talks about competition, one must not forget the rise of private motoring, be it the motor car or the motor bike or for that matter the motor van and motor lorry. It is difficult to judge their impact. The railway companies used motor vehicles for delivery services. Some companies used goods vehicles rather than use the railway. Some upper- and middle-class people used cars rather than the train. Equally some people of all classes had motor bikes.

The other competitor to the Great Eastern section of the LNER was other railways including the LMS to Southend and the Great Northern section to Cambridge, as well as the latter and the Midland and Great Northern Joint Railway to Cromer even after the LNER took over the local administration of the Joint Railway in 1936.

The service from King's Cross to Cromer via the Midland and Great Northern Joint Railway survived until the outbreak of the Second World War brought its curtailment and it was not restored after the end of the war.

Of the two routes between London and Cambridge, at the time of the Grouping the former GER route was very much the dominant route compared with the former Great Northern route, being both shorter in length and having more services. Liverpool Street was better situated for the City of London as opposed to King's Cross. For a time after the Grouping, the LNER ran in the summer a through express from King's Cross to Hunstanton. This was in replacement of a similar service which in the summer of 1922 and 1923 was running from St Pancras. The LNER also used King's Cross as the London terminus for Newmarket race specials. It was not until 1932 that the situation regarding the service between London and Cambridge saw some change. The reason for the change was that the exit from Liverpool Street had rather severe speed restrictions and north of Tottenham there was congestion due to the heavy goods traffic from the north. That year saw the introduction of five new trains a day each way between King's

Cross and Cambridge. The trains included third class carriages with arm rests dividing the seats into three, which was a novelty for the time, and a buffet car. The trains proved a great success and soon the original three coach formation was increased in length and at times reached nine or ten carriages. For a time, trains on the new service were faster than those by the former Great Eastern route despite the latter being shorter than the former – 55¾ miles as opposed to 58½ miles – however, by the time of the outbreak of the Second World War, the Great Eastern section discovered that it could run much faster trains than previously between Liverpool Street and Cambridge.

Southend enjoyed the benefit of being served by two different railway companies – the former LT&SR section of the LMS and the former Great Eastern section of the LNER. Passenger services on the former LT&SR route were in the hands of a variety of 4-4-2 side tanks, of which the earliest dated from 1880 and which had all gone by the early 1930s and the latest were built between 1923 and 1930 to a design dating from 1909. The LT&SR had introduced a class of 4-6-4 side tanks in 1912 just after that Company's takeover by the Midland Railway and the GER promptly banned them from working over its section of line between Gas Factory Junction and Fenchurch Street. The Midland Railway had intended to electrify the direct line from Fenchurch Street to Southend and Shoeburyness via Upminster but the First World War had intervened and subsequently nothing was done. Throughout the period of the life of the LMS, the former LT&SR remained steam worked, although in 1932 the Metropolitan District Railway was extended over newly built lines from Barking to Upminster. On the former GER route to Southend passenger services were in the hands of a variety of locomotives – principally tender locomotives such as the Claud Hamilton Class 4-4-0s and the 1500 Class 4-6-0s. In 1927 when additional motive power was required for the service a 2-6-4 side tank locomotive of a power approximately equal to that of a 1500 Class was designed. According to F.A.S. Brown in *Nigel Gresley – Locomotive Engineer* (Ian Allan 1961), unfortunately the derailment of a River Class 2-6-4 side tank locomotive on the Southern Railway at Sevenoaks which resulted in the deaths of thirteen passengers threw doubts on the wisdom of using such engines on fast passenger trains. Although the press criticism was unjustified, as the track bed of the former GER was somewhat better than that of the former South Eastern Railway, the design was abandoned and in its place ten new 1500 Class locomotives were built. On the LMS, a new class of 2-6-4 side tanks was put into service in 1927, following reassurance from the Ministry of Transport that they were perfectly alright provided that they were not used on fast services! In 1935, the LMS put into service on the former LT&SR line a new class of three cylinder 2-6-4 side tanks. Large tank locomotives did appear on the GE Southend services starting in 1938 in the form of Class V1 2-6-2 side tanks. Later members of

Class V3 side tanks followed and in post-war years L1 2-6-4 side tanks and for a short time in 1951, when the turntable at Liverpool Street was undergoing modifications to take the new Britannia Class locomotives, A5 4-6-2 side tanks.

According to Alan A Jackson in *London's Termini* (David and Charles 1969), by the late 1920s, when there were some 50,000 passengers on 300 trains handled daily at Fenchurch Street station, the LMS's presence was overshadowing that of the station's rightful owners – the LNER. *Bradshaw's Railway Guide* for October 1931 shows LNER trains running to destinations on the Loughton, Epping and Ongar line, the Chigwell loop line, the Colchester main line west of Shenfield and to North Woolwich. The LMS ran trains to destinations on the former LT&SR. Of the five platforms at Fenchurch Street station only one – Platform 4 – was used exclusively by LT&SR line trains. Platform 3 was occasionally by that line's trains. The LMS did use other London termini for its LT&SR line trains. Principally there was St Pancras, reached via the Tottenham and Forest Gate and Tottenham and Hampstead line, but there was also Broad Street, which had first been used in 1923 following an agreement in 1922 between the Midland Railway and the London and North Western Railway. There was also the Ealing to Southend through trains operated jointly with the Metropolitan District Railway. It was because of the growth of the LMS's Southend line traffic that something had to be done and in 1932 a scheme costing £250,000 was started to increase the capacity of the station. To put things simply, the number of platforms was reduced from five to four of which two – numbers 3 and 4 – were sufficiently long to accommodate the Southend trains being 750 long; the other two – numbers 1 and 2 – were shorter at 550 feet. There was also some remodelling of the exits/entrances of the stations as well as track work including signalling and a new overall roof. The work was completed in April 1935, which was when the new three cylinder 2-6-4 side tanks started appearing on the line. The *Railway Magazine* for that month recorded that these locomotives were now working into the station. The service from Broad Street to Southend ceased on Saturday, 27 April 1935. The Ealing to Southend through trains lasted longer and gradually declined but were not withdrawn until at the start of the Second World War. The exact date is not known but probably at the end of the first week of the war. The *Railway Magazine* for July 1935 carried an illustrated article titled 'Remodelling Fenchurch Street Station LNER'. The *LNER Magazine* of September 1935 carried an illustrated article on the rebuilt station, including photographs, both exterior and interior, of the new signal box which had been built, typical daily scenes at the station, views of parts of the reconstructed station and views of the reconstruction underway.

In regard to traffic in general, it would be fair to say that, like the rest of the LNER, the Great Eastern section suffered as a result of the Great Depression which lasted from

1929 to 1939. Not only was industry affected, but also agriculture. Agriculture, which provided a substantial portion of the Great Eastern section's traffic, had seen a boost in the early 1920s with the introduction of sugar beet and the establishment of sugar beet factories which by 1925 had expanded by 25 per cent over the pre-1914 figure. The number of acres growing sugar beet rose from 230,000 in 1927 to 347,000 acres in 1930. Unfortunately, agriculture in general went into decline during the period between the two world wars. Land which had been used for growing crops during the First World War once again ceased to be used for such. The main event regarding goods traffic was the establishment of Whitemoor Marshalling Yard at March in Cambridgeshire, which was completed between 1929 and 1933 and was the first such marshalling yard in Great Britain to be completely mechanised and equipped with electrically operated rail-brakes or retarders. It comprised two yards – the Up Yard completed in 1929 and the Down Yard completed in 1933. According to the *Locomotive Magazine* of February 1927:

> In order to cope with the increasing goods and coal traffic passing from the North and the Midlands to the Eastern Counties and the South, the London and North-Eastern Ry. Company have sanctioned a scheme to cost £300,000 for providing a new marshalling yard, including a new tranship shed, immediately north of March, adjacent to their marshalling yard at Whitemoor. It is anticipated that when this additional accommodation is available, it will have the two-fold benefit of effecting economies and expediting the working of traffic to and from the districts mentioned.

Even before the Up Yard had been completed, the *LNER Magazine* of February 1928 had an article on it titled 'Rail Brakes for New Up Marshalling Yard, March'. The *Railway Magazine* for April 1928 reported that the work on the marshalling yard was now more than half finished and that, when it was completed, the sidings would be the largest and most up to date sorting sidings in Great Britain. The *LNER Magazine* for February 1929 reported that 'Two T.I class 4-8-0 large type shunting engines have already been transferred from the N.E. area for special work in the new Whitemoor Yard.' The same magazine for April 1933 carried an article titled 'Whitemoor Marshalling Yards: Further Developments.' Later ex GCR design class S1 worked the yards.

One should not try to look at another period of history from the perspective of the time that one is writing in, but one does get the impression that the LNER was only really interested in the East Coast Main Line from London to Edinburgh and Aberdeen and its offshoot to the West Riding of Yorkshire. The Company was quite happy to let the former Great Central Railway main line from London to Manchester via Sheffield carry on its merry way without introducing new classes of locomotive until the LMS put its new Jubilee Class locomotives on the rival former Midland Railway line in 1935. On the former GER lines, the new B17 Sandringham Class were put into service in 1928. In 1924 some five coach articulated suburban carriages were built for the Great Eastern section inner suburban services. On the Southend service, new high roofed non-corridor stock appeared.

The lines of the former GER abounded in bridges of moderate weight-carrying capacity, whilst the locomotive turntables were somewhat short, mostly being only 50ft long. With the increasing train weights, something more powerful than the existing locomotives of the D14, D15 and D16 classes of 4-4-0 and the B12 class of 4-6-0 was needed. Because of the aforementioned, anything such as a 4-6-2 was prohibited. According to F.A.S. Brown in *Nigel Gresley Locomotive Engineer*, there are circumstantial reports that Gresley prepared a design in 1925 for a 3-cylinder 4-6-0 with a boiler pressure of 180lb psi, but no record exists of such a design. According to Geoffrey Hughes in *Sir Nigel Gresley, The Engineer and his Family,* there was an unacceptably high loading on the centre coupled axle and that alone ruled out the possibility of a heavy 3-cylinder 4-6-0 as far as the Liverpool Street services were concerned. Hughes says that Doncaster works produced two designs of 4-6-0s, of which one was too heavy for the bridges and the other too long for the engine lay-bys at Liverpool Street and the turntables in the GE Section. What was wanted was a 3-cylinder 4-6-0 with an axle loading restricted to 17 tons. He says that the Board of the LNER appeared to have lost patience and the Deputy Chairman, Lord Farringdon, opened direct negotiations with Sir Hugh Reid, the Chief Managing Director of the North British Locomotive Company (NBL). One wonders what Gresley thought of this.

Hughes says that it is not entirely clear how the design work for the new class was shared between the LNER and the NBL Company. It seems that the latter was responsible for the general layout of the locomotives. In its design, the latter company moved the inside cylinder further forward than in the original proposals and in doing so transferred the weight to the four wheel bogie. According to the website LNER Encyclopedia, on 14 February 1928 the NBL Company presented two designs with 18 ton and 19 ton axle loadings. Although neither design met the initial requirement of a 17 ton axle loading, the 18 ton design was chosen. Hughes says that that was a 12½ per cent increase over the axle loading of the B12s but was more acceptable due to the improved balancing of the 3-cylinder locomotive. The LNER accepted that this axle loading would restrict the B17's route availability to 'certain GER main lines' and not the full range which was originally intended. On 17 February, an initial order for ten locomotives was placed. The first B17 No 2802 was delivered on 30 November 1928

– thirteen weeks late. According to the *Locomotive Magazine* for January 1929, the new locomotives were run in on slow trains between Edinburgh and Glasgow. The Magazine said that they were numbered and named as follows:

2800 *Sandringham*
2801 *Holkham*
2802 *Walsingham*
2803 *Framlingham*
2804 *Elveden*
2805 *Burnham Thorpe*
2806 *Audley End*
2807 *Blickling*
2808 *Gunton*
2809 *Quidenham.*

The *LNER Magazine* for February 1929 said that the engines were named after notable Country Homes in the Eastern Counties, and, by special permission of His Majesty the King, the first locomotive was named *Sandringham.*

Class B17 first appeared in 1928 and were originally specifically designed for the Great Eastern Section. No 2806 *Audley End* is somewhat away from its namesake house and is passing through Westerfield with an East Suffolk line express about 1930. *Photomatic*

Other new classes introduced by the LNER were: J39 0-6-0 in 1926, Y1 0-4-0 and Y3 0-4-0 Sentinel tank locomotives in 1925 and 1927, Y10 0-4-0 Sentinel tram locomotives in 1930 and V1 and V3 2-6-2 side tanks in 1938/9, V1 first having been built in 1930. Sentinel railcars first built in 1925 and Clayton railcars railcars first built in 1927.

Class V1 first appeared in 1930 and were followed in 1939 by class V3 with a higher boiler pressure. In 1938 some fifteen of the locomotives were sent to the Great Eastern section. In this photograph we see No 67673 of Norwich shed running light near Shenfield on 26 June 1948. *Photomatic.*

The two class Y10 Sentinel tram locomotives were the last steam tram locomotives built for use in Great Britain. They were built for the Wisbech and Upwell tramway where they were not altogether successful and gravitated to the Great Yarmouth quay lines where No 8404 is seen in 1939. *Author's collection*

The first new class of pure London and North Eastern Railway design to appear on the Great Eastern section was class J39 which first came out in 1926. No 2712 is seen on a Southend train at Bow Junction in about 1930. The use of the class on Southend trains was common. *Photomatic*

The following classes of locomotives either built by or to designs that originated with other constituent companies were put into service on the GE Section in the period 1923 to the 1939. From the GNR:

C12, D1, D3, J50, K1, K2, K3, N2 and O2

Prior to the Second World War only two former Great Northern Railway class C12 4 4 2 side tanks worked on the GE section. Nos 4016 and 4509. Here we see the latter at Saffron Walden on 11 June 1938. *Ken Nunn*

A number of the locomotives of the other constituents of the LNER were built by the Company. Class O2 No 2435 is seen on a goods train near Bishop's Stortford on 19 March 1938. The class originated on the Great Northern Railway and was built between 1921 and 1943. *Photomatic*

From the GCR:

C4, D9, F2, J10, J11, L1, N5, O4 and S1

From 1934 some members of former Great Central Railway class C14 were allocated to Great Eastern Section depots; initially Bury St Edmunds and later Ipswich, Kings Lynn, Cambridge and Norwich. In 1938, No 6128 is seen near Ipswich on a semi-fast train. *Photomatic*

From the NER:

G5, J21, J26, J27 and T1

Between 1935 and 1937, five ex North Eastern Railway class J21 locomotives were loaned to the Great Eastern section. No 300 is seen at Dereham on 29 June 1936. The locomotives were designed by T.W. Worsdell who joined the North Eastern Railway from the GER. *Photomatic*

From the NBR:

J37 and Y11

From the C&HR:

N18

The LNER, as well as completing orders at Stratford for members of classes D16, J68 and N7 in 1923–4 also built further examples of classes B12 and N7.

Some members of class B12 were fitted with ACFI (*Societe l'Auxiliaire des Chemins de Fer et de l'Industrie*) feedwater heating apparatus. As they looked as if they were carrying rucksacks they were given the nickname 'Hikers' Many locomotives of classes B12, D16, J19, J20 and N7 were rebuilt or in the case of N7, built with round topped fireboxes.

The LNER was very impressed with class N7 and following the last ten built at Stratford 112 new locomotives were built by or for the Company between 1925 and 1928. No 918 is seen near Stratford in the mid-1930s on a train bound for Fenchurch Street. *Photomatic*

In 1928 the LNER had ten new B12 locomotives built for it by Beyer Peacock and Company. About 1930, No 8573 is at Bow Junction on a Liverpool Street to Southend train. *Photomatic*

The LNER made a number of modifications to former GER locomotives. A number of the B12s were fitted with ACFI feed water apparatus and No 8508 is seen at Bury St Edmunds on 1 August 1933. Because of the resemblance of the apparatus to rucksacks, the engines so fitted were nicknamed 'Hikers'. *Photomatic*

The principal change that the LNER made to GER designed locomotives was to replace their Belpaire firebox boilers with round topped firebox boilers. Classes B12, D16, J19, J20 and N7 were the classes in question. B12 No 8575 is seen on an up express near Ipswich in the mid-1930s. *Author's collection*

A number of former GE locomotives were sent to other sections. These were B12s to the GNOS and GN Sections. F4s to the NB Section, F7s to the GC and NB Sections E4s to the GN and NE Sections. Some N7s worked on the GC and GN Sections.

J15s and J65s worked over the former C,V&H and J65s over the former MSL

Following the LNER taking over the working of the Midland and Great Northern Joint Railway, the following ex GER classes are known to have worked on the Railway:

B12 4-6-0s
D15 and D16 4-4-0s
F4 and F6 2-4-2 side tanks
J15 and J17 0-6-0s
J65, J68 and J69 0-6-0 side tanks.

Further details on locomotives will be found in the Appendix.

Great Eastern section passenger trains tended to be something of a mixture during the period covered by this chapter. Apart from new carriages built by the LNER, there were a variety of carriages built not only by the GER, but also by the LNER's other constituent companies. Whilst some were lit by electricity, some were lit by gas. Both eight wheeled bogie carriages and six wheeled carriages survived throughout the period of this chapter, but the last four wheeled carriages went in 1936. Branch line trains tended not to have the most modern rolling stock. The more important the line, the more up to date the rolling stock.

The crack trains of the Great Eastern section were the Continentals serving Harwich Parkeston Quay. These were 'The Hook Continental' connecting with the service from Harwich to the Hook of Holland, 'The Flushing Continental' which connected with the service from Harwich to Flushing (Vlissingen), 'The Antwerp Continental' which connected with the service from Harwich to Antwerp and 'The Scandinavian' which connected with the service from Harwich to Esjberg. There was also the unofficially named 'North Country Continental' which connected Harwich with Liverpool and Manchester. All of the trains from London conveyed Pullman cars. The only other train to have Pullman Cars was 'The Eastern Belle'. This was a summer excursion train starting in 1929 which ran to various places on the East Coast. According to John Watling writing in *Great Eastern Journal* No 69, these were in 1933; Felixstowe, Aldeburgh, Lowestoft, Yarmouth, Cromer, Sheringham, Hunstanton, Skegness and Clacton. Clacton was a special case. In 1922, a summer Sundays only Clacton Belle train from London to Clacton had been started. From 1929 this went under the name 'The Eastern Belle'.

The only other named train to appear on the GER section during the period of this chapter was 'The East Anglian'. Following the success of 'The Silver Jubilee' streamlined train introduced in 1935 between London King's Cross and Newcastle, the LNER rather got the streamlined train bug. In 1937, three new streamliners were introduced. These were 'The Coronation' between London King's Cross and Edinburgh, 'The West Riding Limited' between London King's Cross and Bradford and 'The East Anglian' between London Liverpool Street and Norwich, Whilst the first three trains were hauled by Nigel Gresley's A4 Class streamlined 4-6-2 locomotives and for which it was necessary to pay a supplement to travel on, in the case of 'The East Anglian', as A4 Class locomotives were not permitted to run on the GER main lines out of London, two B17 Class 4-6-0s were streamlined. They were No 2859 *East Anglian* formerly *Norwich City* and No 2870 *City of London,* formerly *Tottenham Hotspur* and previously *Manchester City.* As the speed of 'The East Anglian' was not up to that of the other three streamliners, no supplementary fare was required to travel on it. The new train went into service on Monday 27 September 1937 and the *LNER Magazine* for November of that year carried an article on it in which it said that the introduction of 'The East Anglian' marked a distinct advance in the service between Norwich, Ipswich and London. The *Railway Magazine* in writing about the train said that a schedule of two and a quarter hours in each direction with a six carriage train hardly called for enthusiastic comment. An average speed of less than 55mph between London and Norwich was not the same as the rather faster speeds on the East Coast Main Line! According to The *Railway Observer* for January 1939 at the end of November/beginning of December 1938 whilst No 2859 was undergoing overhaul and the train was being worked solely by No 2870 on 29 November B12 No 8516 (one of Stratford's crack B12s) worked the Down train. The *Railway Observer* for February 1939 reported that B12 No 8517 worked the Down train on 29 December. Streamlined B17 No 2859 did a return working to Colchester on 17 January and to Cambridge on 18 January. According to the *Railway Observer* for May 1939, whilst No 2870 was away at Doncaster at the end of March/beginning of April, the working of 'The East Anglian' was shared by non-streamlined B17s No 2840 *Somerleyton Hall* and 2872 *West Ham United.*

In complete contrast to 'The East Anglian', according to the *Railway Observer* for November 1938, on Wednesday, 26 October 1938 preserved GNR Stirling 8ft 4-2-2 single No 1 built in 1870 which was exhibited at Norwich Civic Week (24-29 October) worked a public excursion train of vintage six wheeled carriages from Norwich to Ipswich and return. The first time that a single driving wheeled locomotive had worked

In 1937, two B17 locomotives were renamed and streamlined for 'The East Anglian' express. No 2859 *East Anglian* formerly *Norwich City* is seen passing Goodmayes with the up East Anglian on 29 September 1937 shortly after the train's introduction. *Ken Nunn*

over the GE Ipswich to Norwich main line since the early part of the century. The train arrived at Ipswich at 2.9 pm one minute ahead of schedule and after turning at the station departed at 3.35 pm. According to the *Scotsman* of 21 October there would be an excursion from Norwich to Yarmouth on 28 October. According to Norman Groves in *Great Northern Locomotive History Vol 2 1867-1895 The Stirling Era* (RCTS 1991) the excursion from Norwich to Yarmouth did take place.

The Great Eastern section gained an additional source of traffic with the opening of holiday camps at Dovercourt in 1937 and Clacton in 1938.

In 1927, the LNER sold the farm at Dodnash Priory in Bentley in Suffolk, which the GER had purchased in 1916. The reason for the sale was that the farmer had reached 70 and had retired. The siding serving the farm had been removed in May 1925.

The 1930s saw the end of slip carriage working on the Great Eastern section, the last ones being at Waltham Cross on the Cambridge line on 25 September 1936 and at Marks Tey on the Colchester line on 30 June 1939. Other than on the Great Western Railway, this latter was the end of slip carriage working in Britain.

During the period of this chapter a London–Norwich Travelling Post Office and a Norwich–London Travelling Post Office were started on 3 May 1931 and continued running until 22 September 1939. They had originally been the London–Ipswich and Ipswich–London Travelling Post Offices which had been renamed from the Ipswich sorting tender on 3 March 1929 and which was extended to Norwich in May 1931.On 3 March 1939, an East Anglian Travelling Post Office was started running via Ipswich and having portions for Norwich and Kings Lynn, which latter was detached at Haughley Junction and worked to Kings Lynn via Ely.

The LNER was a great user of steam railcars. Although only six were inherited from a constituent company, the Company acquired ninety-one steam railcars, of which eighty came from Sentinel and eleven from Clayton. Two of the former and four of the latter saw service on the Great Eastern section in the Cambridge, Norwich, Yarmouth and Lowestoft areas. They were not a success.

It was during the period of this chapter that the first steps were taken that would ultimately see the electrification of the former GER suburban and main line routes. The initial routes to be electrified were not as one would expect the lines to Chingford and Enfield, but rather to Shenfield, Chigwell, Loughton, Epping and Ongar.

By the end of the 1920s, overcrowding on the services between London and stations to Ilford on the line to Shenfield had become a real problem. The reason for the problem

Between 1928 and 1937 some Clayton steam railcars worked out of Lowestoft. They were not particularly successful. They were numbered in the carriage series as opposed to the locomotive series. No 43302 *Chevy Chase* is seen approaching Norwich on 2 May 1931 on the 4 26 Lowestoft to Norwich service. *Ken Nunn*

was the thousands of central London workers who had been enticed to purchase low-cost new houses on either side Eastern Avenue between Newbury Park and Wanstead. Eastern Avenue was built as a bypass of the A12 (now A118) which went through Romford, Chadwell Heath, Goodmayes and Ilford before meeting the A11 at Stratford and was originally designated the A106. The origins for this go back to 1919 when under the City of London Corporation Act of that year the Ilford suburb of Gants Hill was created. In 1921, the government cut off subsidies when only 220 houses had been built and the remaining land which already been covered with the footings for houses reverted to farming land. In 1922, following the building of the first part of Eastern Avenue, bus services brought the district to life.

According to Geoffrey Hughes in *LNER* (Ian Allan 1996), in 1927 outline plans were considered for a £7.5 million scheme returning 5.1 per cent for the electrification between Liverpool Street and Shenfield with a new station at Crowlands between Chadwell Heath and Romford and the Ongar branch. The report was compiled by Fred V. Russell, who had devised the 'Jazz Service' of 1920. In 1929, a scaled down version was produced which gave a better return on the investment amounting to 11.9 per cent after 10 years in which allowance appears to have been made for increased traffic. Savings were made by cutting the Shenfield line electrification back to Gidea Park and reassessing the need for new rolling stock. Both of these projects included the need for major civil engineering works including widening and a flyover at Ilford. Because of the economic situation, neither of these plans came to fruition. In 1930 the LNER announced that Messrs Mott, Hay and Anderson had been engaged to prepare plans and estimates for a tube railway between Liverpool Street and Ilford. The scheme and its variations were examined, but the cost at £7 million was reputedly too much for the Company to raise and the combined effects of the 1931 financial crisis and uncertainty about the forthcoming London Passenger Transport Bill killed the proposal. Meanwhile, the Ilford and District Railway Users Association were campaigning for better railway facilities for Ilford and these included an extension of the Central London Railway from Liverpool Street to Redbridge Lane/Eastern Avenue and thence via Eastern Avenue to Romford with a branch line to Barkingside and Claybury. In March 1933, it petitioned Parliament and in December 1933 it sent a deputation to Lord Ashfield, who was the Chairman of the London Passenger Transport Board and who pointed out that electrification by the LNER or an extension of the Central London Line, as the Central London Railway had now become, could not possibly be self-supporting.

At the same time as this was going on, the London County Council was in the process of building the huge Becontree estate which stretched between the former GER Shenfield main line and the former LT&SR lines via Upminster and Purfleet. As mentioned, the Metropolitan District Railway was extended from Barking to Upminster in 1932. The nearness of the new Metropolitan District Railway electric trains to stations on the line parallel to the Great Eastern section between Forest Gate and Gidea Park would no doubt have attracted passengers away from the latter to the former.

In 1933, the LNER had prepared a report into electrifying the lines from Liverpool Street to Shenfield, Stratford to Ongar, Woodford to Ilford Carriage Sidings, Fenchurch Street to Stratford and for additional running lines between Liverpool Street and Stratford. The report was dated 15 May 1933. The report proposed the electrification of approximately 50 route miles, or 170 single track miles which included 152 running lines and approximately 17 siding miles. Regarding new works, it proposed to construct two additional lines between Liverpool Street and Bow Junction to join up with the existing up and down lines of the Fenchurch Street to Stratford branch and the construction of a new single line signalled for two way working between Bow Junction and Stratford. It was proposed that rather than having through working from Fenchurch Street to the Shenfield and Ongar lines as existed at that time, there would be only a shuttle service from Fenchurch Street to Stratford with passengers from and to those lines having to change for Fenchurch Street at Stratford. To avoid interference between fast and slow traffic, it was proposed that the local lines become the through lines and vice versa between Stratford and a point just short of Ilford and that a flyover be constructed to carry the local lines over the through lines to join their then existing course. In order to avoid interference with electric trains running in the direction of Shenfield on the local lines, it was proposed to construct a single line flyover from the Up branch line from Woodford over the down local lines at Ilford Carriage Sidings Junction. A new station was proposed near Crowlands Signal box about 1 mile and 25 chains from Chadwell Heath and 1 mile and 5 chains from Romford. The electrical system to be used was 1,500 volts direct current using overhead current collection with uninsulated return by the running rails. Rolling stock for the electrification was to consist of 66 trains. 33 were to be converted from existing 325 existing 54ft bogie carriages. The remaining 33 would be new built trains. The latter would have compartments appreciably wider than hitherto used on Great Eastern London Suburban trains. The standard formation was to be a nine coach train composed of three train units composed of 3-carriages which would consist of one motor coach, one trailer coach and one driving trailer coach. This would enable trains of three, six and nine carriages to be used, with off peak trains being composed of three or six carriages as required. For working the Fenchurch Street to Stratford service there would be four trains comprising seven carriages. One must assume that some units would have been composed of four carriages, in order for these trains to have seven carriages. As regards services, it was proposed to run twenty-four trains per hour in the peak hours to Ilford of which the report seems to imply twelve would go to Grange Hill and Woodford on the Chigwell loop and twelve to Shenfield. On the Ongar line, the service would be twelve trains per hour to Woodford. Details of the service to Loughton, Epping and Ongar are not given. There would be six trains per hour between Fenchurch Street and Stratford. Off peak the services would be six trains per hour suggesting three going round the Chigwell loop and three going to Shenfield. On the Ongar line, the service would be four per hour to Woodford with no details of the service to Loughton, Epping and Ongar. There would be three trains per hour between Fenchurch Street and Stratford. For signalling it was proposed to adopt automatic and non-automatic electric colour light signalling. To feed the electricity to the system there would be sub-stations at Bishopsgate, Stratford, Ilford, Romford, Brentwood, Shadwell Woodford and North Weald. The report goes into exceedingly long details of the costs and benefits of the proposed electrification scheme. The total gross capital costs were £7,101,322. According to the report, it was considered that sixty-three steam locomotives and twenty coaches would be released from working the existing steam services on the lines to be electrified. The estimated replacement value of the steam locomotives was £214,000 and the coaches £19,226. The total credit to the electrification scheme was £233,226. Taking the saving from the capital costs gave a total net capital cost of £6,868,096. All of the LNER's proposal for electrification would have involved the construction of new platforms on the existing through lines at Stratford and Maryland Point, Forest Gate and Manor Park.

From information in *The Twopenny Tube* by J. Graeme Bruce and Desmond Croome (Capital Transport 1996), it is clear that the LNER's scheme was considered by the joint main line companies/London Transport Joint Committee in conjunction with a proposal to extend the Central London Line from Liverpool Street to Goodmayes (Little Heath) via Mile End and North Ilford. The large proportion of peak traffic and the high cost of construction indicated that both schemes would be permanent loss makers. The government would not agree a subsidy and the LNER stuck to its scheme. Adjudication resolved the impasse by diverting the Central London extension through Newbury Park and then grafting on the Chigwell Loop and the Loughton, Epping and Ongar Line. This left the LNER only with the electrification of the lines from Liverpool Street to Shenfield and Fenchurch Street to Stratford.

On 5 June 1935 the Chancellor of the Exchequer, Neville Chamberlain, announced in the House of Commons a £35 million plan for the improvement of London Transport. The plan included not only the extension of the Central London Line from Liverpool Street in a tunnel via Mile End to Stratford, Leyton, Loughton, Epping and Ongar as well as the line from Woodford to Newbury Park including the electrification of the

LNER lines from Leyton eastward and those from Liverpool Street to Shenfield and Fenchurch Street to Stratford, but also an extension of the Central London Line in tunnel from Leytonstone to Newbury Park. In the west, the line was to be extended from North Acton to Denham via Greenford and West Ruislip alongside the GWR/LNER (former Great Central Railway) Joint Line. There were also other extensions of underground railways of which from the point of view of this chapter the most important was that on the Great Northern Section from Finsbury Park to Highgate, Alexandra Palace, High Barnet and Edgware, with an extension from the latter to Bushey Heath. The name by which the new works were known was the 1935-40 New Works Plan.

The *Chelmsford Chronicle* of 7 June 1935 reported:

> At last railway electrification from Liverpool Street to Shenfield and Liverpool Street to Loughton. And a tube as well. Chamberlain, the Chancellor of the Exchequer, announced in the House Commons a £35,000,000 plan for the improvement of London transport. The programme covers electrification of the. suburban line from Liverpool Street to Shenfield, together with the Loughton and Grange Hill branches. Extension the Central London underground line to connect with the Loughton and Grange Hill lines, to permit the running of through trains to stations in the West End and beyond. Extension of tube railways to give new connections with the City and the West End. The Central London Tube will be extended as far as Newbury Park.

The *News Chronicle* 6 June 1935 reported:

> The vast growth of population in East London is one of the main causes of the traffic problem. An official outline of the proposals shows that on the L.N.E.R. suburban lines it is proposed to electrify the line from Liverpool Street to Shenfield, also the Loughton and Grange branches. The Tube railway will be built in continuation of the Central London line from Liverpool Street eastwards to a point where it will connect with the Loughton and Grange Hill lines to give through trains to stations in the West End and beyond.

I will now mention the three underground lines which either did or would or could affect the Great Eastern Lines. There was the Piccadilly Line running from Cockfosters to Hounslow and Uxbridge via Finsbury Park, King's Cross, Holborn, Piccadilly Circus, Hammersmith and Acton. The Edgware, Highgate and Morden Line, connecting the afore-mentioned places via Camden Town, Euston and Kennington and which in Central London served the West End via Tottenham Court Road, Leicester Square and Waterloo and the City via Moorgate, the Bank and London Bridge. The Central London Line ran from Liverpool Street to Ealing. via Oxford Circus and Shepherd's Bush.

First of all, the Piccadilly Line. The line had been extended from its original northern terminus at Finsbury Park to Cockfosters on 31 July 1933 and took passengers off the Enfield Town line from the district between Stamford Hill and White Hart Lane. Some using buses, others, trams and other walking to get to the new line.

The Edgware, Highgate and Morden Line will only become relevant a bit later other than to say that on 28 August 1937 it was renamed the Northern Line.

On 28 August 1937, the Central London Line was renamed the Central Line. Its extensions involved more than just extending the line. It was necessary to change its current collection system in use on the Line from a three-rail centre rail system to the standard London Transport third and fourth rail system. In the former, the current returned to earth via the running rails and in the later current was collected from an outside live rail and returned to earth via an inner liver rail.

On the line from Liverpool Street to Shenfield and Fenchurch Street to Stratford, the works proposed were similar to those proposed in the 1933, other than there would not be a flyover from the Chigwell Loop at Ilford.

According to George Dow in *By Electric Train from Liverpool Street to Shenfield* (British Railways 1949), work on the electrification scheme started in 1937 but because of the outbreak of the Second World War in September 1939 work was halted in the summer of 1940 when some of the bridge reconstructions and station and signalling alterations were advanced, and the Ilford flyover completed. Six miles of overhead gantries had been erected between Harold Wood and Brentwood and the emplacements for them had been prepared from Brentwood to Shenfield. The *Locomotive Magazine* of April 1939 reported that the LNER had 'placed contracts for the passenger stock to be used on the lines being electrified between Liverpool Street and Fenchurch Street and Shenfield' and that the new coaches were of all-steel construction and of the open saloon type and fitted with electro-pneumatic doors which may be opened by the passenger pressing a button, or may be controlled by the train staff The trains comprised a third class motor coach, a first class and third class composite trailer coach and a third class driving trailer coach. The body shells of six of trains had been completed prior to work ceasing for the duration of the war. Ilford locomotive depot had closed in May 1939 in preparation for the site to be used for the new electric train carriage depot.

On the extension of the Central Line, the first contract had been let in October 1936 and work on it had begun in the same month. This was for the Mile End to Leyton section. When work was halted in the summer of 1940, the tunnels east of Liverpool Street including those under Eastern Avenue had been completed as well as the new interchange platforms at Stratford. According to Keith Shirland in *Drapers' Field Depot and the Central Line Works at Leyton* (London Railway Record July 2022), the rails had highly likely been laid in the eastbound tunnel from Liverpool Street to Drapers' Field, Leyton, by 1940. A photograph of Stratford station taken in 1940 reproduced in *Great Eastern Journal* No 70 shows sleepers and what looks line running rails but not current rails having been laid. As to whether any London Transport works trains operated through from Liverpool Street to Leyton hauled by battery locomotives before work ceased in 1940 is not known. Many miles of the Loughton branch and the Hainault Loop had been laid with conductor rails. At Loughton a new station had opened on 28 April 1940 built by the LNER. The new station had two island platforms on the embankment serving three tracks. The station was designed for the LNER by the architects J. Murray Easton and Robertson Fellows who were instructed to deliberately avoid any undue similarity with London Transport stations. The roadbed of the western extension had been finished as far as Greenford and laid with double track. Some work on station reconstruction had been done, as had some civil engineering work beyond Greenford. Both the new rolling stock depots at Hainault and Ruislip were complete. Rolling stock for the extended Central Line was what was known as Standard Tube Stock, which dated from the 1920s and early 1930s and which was used on the Bakerloo, Northern and Piccadilly lines. The Central Line at that time was using a mixture of rolling dating from the early 1900s and early 1920s. These and Standard Tube Stock had a large equipment compartment behind the driver in the motor coaches. The stock was being transferred from the Northern Line, which along with the Bakerloo Line was receiving new 1938 Tube Stock in which the motors were under the carriages. The only exceptions to this were some trains of flat fronted 1935 Tube Stock to be used on shuttle services. 1935 Tube Stock was the first tube stock to have the motors underneath the carriages. Three out of the four trains of this were streamlined but were not very successful. All of 1935 Tube Stock was originally used on the Piccadilly Line. Trains on the Metropolitan and (Metropolitan) District Lines were called Surface Stock on account of them being built to the dimensions of the main line railway companies, their lines having been built before the tube lines.

The *LNER Magazine* for May 1939 had an article on the electrification titled 'Equipment of the "Shenfield Lines" for Electric Working' which included photographs of the work under construction and a plan of the lines being electrified.

Regarding the opening dates, these changed somewhat, but all one can say is that all would have been completed by early 1941. In November 1939 the London Transport Board agreed to try and complete the extensions of the Central Line to Loughton and Greenford before all work on the Central Line was stopped for the duration of the war. In early May 1940 it was intended to begin trial running eastward of Liverpool Street on 1 October with a view to opening the section to Loughton and Grange Hill via Woodford in November. On the Loughton line, as I shall call it, under the powers obtained for the electrification, the House of Commons Select Committee had imposed obligations for six level crossings to be replaced by underpasses or overbridges before electric trains could run and for the existing antiquated footbridge at Snaresbrook to be replaced by a more modern structure. According to *Rails Through The Clay* by Desmond F. Croome and Alan A. Jackson (2nd edition Capital Transport 1993), it might have been possible to open the Loughton line before the shutdown of July 1940, but an ill-conceived comment by Frank Pick, the Vice Chairman and Chief Executive of London Transport, in September 1939 suggesting that the wartime extension of electric working be confined to Woodford via Hainault caused the closing of level crossings on the Loughton line to be further delayed.

What of the proposed services for the Central Line and the Shenfield electrification? Below is a table of the proposed services. I wish to acknowledge the help of the London Underground Railway Society in compiling this:

To and From	Peak Mon to Sat	Off Peak Mon to Sat	All day Sun
Ongar and Loughton	2S**	1⅓S**	1⅓S**
Epping and Loughton	6S+	4S+	3S+
Loughton through City	8	4	4
Woodford through City	8	4	4
Woodford and Hainault	8S++	4S++	4S++
Hainault through City	8	4	4
Leytonstone through City	16	8	8
Greenford through City	11	8	4-6
West Ruislip through City	6	4	2-3
Denham through City	6	4	2-3

S** Shuttle to and from Loughton.

S+ Shuttle to and from Loughton. Some originating from and terminating at Ongar.

S++ Shuttle as indicated.

To and From	Peak Mon to Sat	Off Peak Mon to Sat	All day Sun
Liverpool Street and all stations to Gidea Park	6	6	6
Liverpool Street, Ilford, Romford and all stations to Shenfield	3	3	3
Fenchurch Street and Stratford	6	6	6

Even before the work was finished there were proposals for further new works, the 1940–1950 New Works Plan.

At this point, it is necessary to explain about the Northern Line and the 1935–1940 New Works Plan. At the time of the creation of London Transport, the Edgware, Highgate and Morden Line extended from starting in the south at Morden via Tooting Broadway and Clapham Common to Kennington where the line divided. One branch went via Waterloo, Tottenham Court Road, Euston and Mornington Crescent to Camden Town. The other branch went via London Bridge, Moorgate and Euston to Camden Town, but not serving Mornington Crescent. At Camden Town the lines branches joined and then immediately split into two branches. one going via Kentish Town to what was then named Highgate, but is now named Archway, while the other went via Golders Green and Hendon to Edgware. Under the plans for the Northern Line, the Highgate branch was to be extended north under the Highgate station of the former Great Northern Railway Edgware, High Barnet and Alexandra Palace branches to join the High Barnet and Edgware branches at East Finchley. The lines from East Finchley to High Barnet and Edgware via Finchley Church End (later Finchley Central) would be electrified on the London Transport third and fourth rail electrification system. At Edgware, the line would not use the former Great Northern station but would use a new connection to the existing Northern Line Edgware station. From there, a new line would be built via Brockley Hill and Elstree to Bushey Heath. East of East Finchley the Northern Line would take over and electrify the former Great Northern Line to a new high-level station at Finsbury Park where a new connection would be made with the Great Northern and City section of the Metropolitan Line. This latter was opened in 1904 as the Great Northern and City Railway with the purpose of enabling Great Northern Railway trains to run to the terminus at Moorgate. For various reasons this did not happen and in 1913 the Railway was acquired by the Metropolitan Railway. Apart from a siding connection to the former Great Northern Railway, the Railway had no connection to the main lines. Its terminus at Finsbury Park was a low level one. The

Railway was unusual as a tube railway in being built to the same dimension as a main line railway. Under the plans, trains from Moorgate would run to Alexandra Palace and East Finchley via Finsbury Park and Highgate and some in the peak hours to High Barnet. All this was intended to be completed by the spring of 1941.

The 1940–1950 New Works Plan proposed duplicating the Northern Line from Morden to Clapham Common but on a shorter alignment and calling only at Tooting Broadway. From Clapham Common, a new tube line would be built to Finsbury Park via Victoria, Green Park, Bond Street, Great Portland Street and Camden Town.

North of Finsbury Park there would be a junction similar to that at Camden Town. One branch would merge with an extension from the low level former Great Northern and City Railway line and continue in tube to surface at Bowes Road and run along electrified LNER lines to Cuffley replacing the former Great Northern Line stations at Harringay, Hornsey and Wood Green (now Alexandra Palace), whilst the other would run in tube to Seven Sisters and thence to Enfield Town. According to *The Victoria Line – A Short History* by M.A.C. Horne (Douglas Rose 1998), with the Northern Line trains running express through the new tube from Morden to Clapham Common calling only at Tooting Broadway and the existing 'all stations' diverging from the old road at Clapham Common and running express to Victoria, passengers could change as necessary at Clapham Common. Looking at the plans, two things spring to mind. Firstly, presumably a new line would have had to be built between beside the Great Northern Line between Bowes Park and Cuffley, otherwise there would have been electric London Transport trains and steam London and North Eastern trains running along the same lines. Secondly, as the Northern Line would have taken over the Enfield Town branch of the former GER Line, presumably all trains from Liverpool Street that formerly ran to Enfield would now run to Palace Gates, as that was the other branch from Seven Sisters. One might even speculate that following the completion of the Shenfield electrification, the lines from Liverpool Street to Chingford and Palace Gates would be electrified. In the 1938 timetable, whilst Chingford was served by direct trains from Liverpool Street, Palace Gates was mostly, but not exclusively, served by a shuttle service from Seven Sisters. All this became irrelevant as the report proposing this was signed on Thursday, 31 August 1939. The following day, Germany invaded Poland and on 3 September 1939 Great Britain and France declared war on Germany.

These were not the only new works proposed. Amongst them were from North Walsham to Cromer, Thorpe-le-Soken to Clacton, Westerfield to Felixstowe. Of these the LNER obtained powers to double the line from Thorpe-le-Soken in 1936 with the work being completed in 1941. On the Felixstowe branch, powers were obtained in 1938 to double the line and enlarge Felixstowe (Town) station. In 1939, an additional platform was provided at the station, but because of the Second World War the plans for doubling the line did not materialise. There were other proposals of which some were carried out during the period of this chapter. The section of line from Soham to Snailwell was doubled in June 1939. At Colchester, the straightening of the main line through the station although authorised was not carried out as was the rebuilding and enlargement of Southend station, nor was the authorised doubling of the line from North Walsham and Cromer.

The period covered by this chapter saw the first use of colour light signalling and track circuits on the former GER lines. The first uses were between Gidea Park and Shenfield when that section of the main line was quadrupled in 1934. This was followed in the same year by the sections from Bethnal Green to Hackney Downs and Clapton Junction and Enfield Town, the only exception being at Seven Sisters, the junction for Palace Gates and the Tottenham and Hampstead Junction Line which retained its signal box and semaphore signals. In 1937 the section of main line from Shenfield to New Hall signal box just east of Chelmsford was so equipped. 1938 saw the sections from Clapton Junction to Chingford and Shenfield to Southend so equipped. On the latter, the signal box at Wickford the junction for the line to Southminster was retained. On the sections being electrified at the beginning of the Second World War, colour light signalling and track circuits were being installed, that on the extension of the Central Line to be London Transport's own system. Prior to this, all-electric signalling had been introduced at Cambridge in 1926. Although not electrically controlled, the three signal boxes controlling the triangular junctions at respectively Manningtree and at East Gate, Colchester had at each location been brought under the control of a single signal box instead of three boxes in 1925.

The period of this chapter saw the GER Lines carry the bodies of two members of the Royal family to their last resting place. On 20 November 1925, Queen Alexandra, the widow of King Edward VII died of heart attack at Sandringham and on 26 November, King George V and Queen Mary quickly arranged for her body to be taken back to London and ultimately Windsor for burial. Class D15 4-4-0 No 8794 hauled the funeral train from Wolferton to Kings Lynn and locomotive No 8848 of the same class hauled the funeral train from Kings Lynn to King's Cross.

On 20 January 1936 King George V died at Sandringham. On 23 January, the special train carrying the king's body left Wolferton for Kings Lynn hauled by B12 4-6-0 No 8520 from where B17 4-6-0 No 2847 *Helmingham Hall* worked the train to King's Cross. After a lying in state in Central Hall, Westminster the king's body was taken for burial at Windsor on a train hauled by Great Western Railway Castle Class 4-6-0 No 4082 *Windsor Castle.*

With the approach of the Second World War efforts were made to rescue Jewish children from Nazi-controlled territory. During the nine months prior to the outbreak of the Second World War the United Kingdom took in nearly 10,000 children. The first party of 196 children arrived at Harwich, Parkeston Quay on the TSS *Prague* on 2 December 1938. The *News Chronicle* of 3 December 1938 reported:

> Two hundred German Jewish refugee children, each with a baggage label tied round the neck for identification, arrived by bus here [at Dovercourt Bay] early today from Parkeston Quay, Harwich, where they had landed. Dark circles under their eyes are the only sign of the horrors they have left behind them. They laugh, shout and play like other children. Mercifully, the novelty of the journey seems to have blurred their worst memories. Among them are children from the Konigsberg orphanage. They were driven from their beds into the fields, wearing only their nightgowns.

The *LNER Magazine* of January 1939 carried a photograph of the arrival of the children at Harwich and a short article on them. The article read:

> Refugees Arriving at Harwich.—This is a photograph of some of the 200 Jewish child refugees from Germany who arrived in this country by the L.N.E.R. steamer *Prague* from Hook of Holland on December 2. After disembarking at Harwich, the children were taken to a holiday camp at the adjacent seaside resort of Dovercourt, where they were to remain pending dispersal to homes throughout the country. It is probable that further parties will follow at intervals.

There are a number of sculptures on the route of the Kindertransport including one at Liverpool Street station, the London terminus at which they arrived. Where I live in Stock there was a lady, by the name of Ruth Sellers, nee Hirsch, who came to this country as part of the Kindertransport. Ruth told me that her suitcase was used as the model for the suitcase in the sculpture at Liverpool Street station.

The winter of 1938-9 saw heavy snow just before Christmas which disrupted road and railway travel. *The Times* of 22 December reported, 'Suburban trains were between 10 and 20 minutes late at Liverpool Street in the morning, and the disorganization of the Continental trains made the boat trains late, the Antwerp train being an hour behind time.' The *Herts and Essex Observer* of 24 December 1938 reported that one of the engines on the Saffron Walden to Audley End branch line had frozen up and had to be thawed before it could be put to use. Because of the treacherous conditions on the roads, the railway had benefitted as most people fell back on it for safety. The *Lynn News* of 27 December reported that whilst ice and snow had interfered with the operation of points and signals, the railways had benefitted from the diversion of parcels and goods traffic from road to rail. Ironically the only problems the railways encountered were in their road deliveries. According to the *Railway Observer* of February 1939, in the week preceding Christmas 1938 the severe weather conditions made the operation of trains in the London area very difficult. On the Monday, owing to frozen points, there was an average delay of 30 minutes in the morning and 20 minutes in the evening. On the following day, a fog service was introduced and as the week progressed matters improved until frozen points on Christmas Eve caused sufficient delay for it to be mentioned on the BBC news. (Fog service was that normally introduced when there was severe fog). Although the weather conditions returned to normal on 27 December, it was not until 31 December that the full service was restored on the Enfield and Chingford lines.

18 June 1939 was the centenary of the formal opening of the first section of the Eastern Counties Railway. Neither the *LNER Magazine* or the *Railway Magazine* carried an article on the centenary – only the *Locomotive Magazine* did.

Chapter 2

The Second World War

On Friday, 1 September 1939 Germany invaded Poland and at 11am on Sunday, 3 September, Great Britain declared war on Germany. They were followed in this by France and the rest of the British Empire. Since the Munich Crisis of the previous year Britain, along with France, aware of Germany's territorial ambitions, had been making preparations for war including the evacuation of children and expectant mothers from major cities including London. The evacuation began on 1 September 1939. The Great Eastern Section of the LNER was involved in this. According to Norman Crump in *By Rail To Victory – The Story of the LNER in Wartime* (LNER 1947), during the days preceding the outbreak of the war, Stratford District alone ran specials from twelve stations, including Liverpool Street and Stratford. The procedure was that London Transport carried expectant mothers and children in buses to the station where they were to entrain. The LNER officers responsible for planning the evacuation knew approximately the size of the party coming from each particular district of London, and also the number of evacuees which each country town or village was prepared to absorb. Those officers had the duty of deciding the destination of each detachment so that a village that was prepared to receive 100 evacuees received that number. They also did their best to avoid cross-country journeys. Thus, a Hackney detachment would be sent to a village on the Cambridge line rather than one on the Ipswich line. Originally 203 trains carrying 203,484 passengers were scheduled to run from Liverpool Street and the suburban stations in the Stratford area, but as many of those on the list preferred to stay at home in town it was only necessary to run 82 trains from that district carrying 101,540 passengers. According to *Locomotives of the LNER,* most of the trains were hauled by class N7 locomotives, but a few were hauled by classes B12 and V1 locomotives.

Because of the evacuation, the LNER's streamliners including the East Anglian were cancelled on 1 September. They briefly resumed but were then cancelled indefinitely from 11 September.

The evacuation of children and expectant mothers were not the only movements of people resulting from the outbreak of war. The army again went to France and, according to Crump, units of the British Expeditionary Force were moved down to

Southampton for embarkation to France. Because of the fear of bombing, no troops were to be taken through the London area. One result of this was that the Guards units stationed at Brentwood were taken first to Cambridge and from there by the LMS cross-country line to Oxford and thence by the GWR to Reading and to Basingstoke and thence by the Southern Railway to Southampton.

These were not the only evacuations. Government offices had to be moved from London. The London docks were an obvious target for the German air force and so had to be cleared. For three days on end, a procession of trains proceeded north with butter, bacon, cheese, meat and tobacco. Crump mentions one of the movements to an emergency food depot that had been established at Ely in early 1939.

Even the LNER's offices, along with those of the other major railway companies, were moved away from the major centres of population. The Eastern Control headquarters moved to Shenfield.

In the summer of 1939 prior to the outbreak of the war, but with war on the Continent imminent, the Government had embarked on a programme of ambulance train construction. There were three types of Ambulance Train., Overseas, Home and Casualty Evacuation, the last named being built to the orders of the Ministry of Health for air raid casualties. The trains were built in the carriage shops of the four main line railways by converting existing vehicles, whilst Home and Casualty Evacuation were vacuumed braked, Overseas were Westinghouse air braked.

With the outbreak of the war, a number of changes came into effect. Immediately there was the blackout which prohibited the showing of lights that would be visible to enemy aircraft.

Initially, lighting was very restricted. According to a comment in the *News Chronicle* of 19 September, certain trains travelled without any light whatsoever during the blackout hours. The *Chronicle* said that standardised lighting for all railway carriages during black-out hours would be adopted as soon as possible, according to a Railway Executive Committee official. By the beginning of October, blue electric light bulbs began to be installed, but improvements were on the way.

The *News Chronicle* of 26 October reported:

> Night travellers on all express trains will shortly find their carriages well enough lighted for reading and writing letters. The four railway companies are now experimenting with a new type of window blind. Special lampshades will also be used so that doors can be opened at stations during the black-out. An attendant will turn off the lights by a special switch in case of an air raid warning. This improved lighting scheme will apply only to corridor trains. On suburban lines the 'blue bulbs' will have to suffice, say the railway companies.

Bernard Darwin in *War on the Line* (Southern Railway 1946) says that the white lights were extinguished by a master switch in the case of air raids, which was the duty of a new official, the train-lighting attendant, who turned on the blue lamps when the white ones were extinguished, shut the windows and pulled down the blinds 15 minutes before black-out time and patrolled the train to see that the rules were observed. In carriages, a notice appeared which said 'During Black-out hours – for your own safety keep all blinds down'.

This was all very well for express trains with corridors, but not non-corridor trains. By early December, experiments were being made with white reading lights in non-corridor trains

According to *The Locomotive* of December 1939:

> WAR TIME LIGHTING. The aim of railway engineers has been to restore white lighting of an intensity sufficient to afford a reasonably good reading light. This they have succeeded in doing by installing shades specially designed to throw the light below the level of the carriage windows. To prevent the emission of any light it is necessary for the blinds of all carriage windows to be kept drawn throughout black-out times and a border of black paint has to be applied to the windows to prevent light showing behind the blinds. What this involves can best be appreciated when it is remembered that the British railways have some 40 ,000 carriages with about 250,000 compartments. The total number of windows to be painted with a black band is about 1,500,000 and many of these have to be fitted with blinds or curtains. In each compartment at least two of the special shades have to be fitted to the lights, and it is estimated that at least 500,000 shades will have to be fitted.

And that was just passengers. On locomotives, stuffy anti-glare sheets had to be wrapped round the cab to prevent the glare from the firebox revealing it to enemy aircraft. Stations were a problem. In order for trains to stop at the right point a little light was placed near the end of the platform. Marshalling yards were a problem. The shunters working there had to know each inch of the yard. Very difficult with no light.

When the restricted services came in in September, restaurant cars, which included buffet cars, were withdrawn. However, some were reinstated in October, but in 1941 and 1942 they gradually disappeared 'for the duration.'

On 2 September, Parkeston Quay was requisitioned by the Admiralty for naval purposes and all of the services operating from there ceased to operate, with the masters of the vessels in Continental ports being ordered to return home as quickly as possible.

On 4 September it was closed to civilian traffic on the orders of the Admiralty. Many of the LNER ships based there were soon transferred to Southampton where they were first employed in transporting the British Expeditionary Force to France. These were, according to the website 'LNER Encyclopedia' the *Amsterdam*, the *Antwerp*, the *Prague*, the *Bruges*, the *Vienna*, the *Archangel* and Train Ferries Nos 1, 2 and 3 and as is implied in *By Rail to Victory*, the *St Denis*. All services from Harwich to the Continent ceased.

According to Cecil J. Allen writing in the *LNER Magazine* in late 1939, passenger services continued as normal for the first week of the war, but on Monday, 11 September the full emergency service came into effect. Before the week was out, additional trains were announced. On 25 September, a considerably less spartan train service was announced. In early October still more trains were announced. By 16 October it was possible to reinstate the restaurant cars which had been withdrawn on all principal long-distance trains on 11 September. Michel Bonavia in Volume 3 of his history of the LNER covering the years 1939 to 1948 (George Allen and Unwin 1983) says that it was 4 December when new timetables were introduced. Bonavia also says that when the new timetables were introduced on 11 September, the overall average speeds did not exceed 45mph with the maximum everywhere limited to 60mph. The reason for the emergency service was that the government had expected intensive bombing to start immediately and so decided that only a skeleton service could be maintained. He also says that the Great Eastern Section did not fare so badly as the other sections of the LNER as prewar its speeds had been somewhat lower than the other sections and so the 60mph maximum did not make so much difference as on, for example, the East Coast Main Line.

Travel under the restricted services could only be described as hell! Utter hell in the case of compartment carriages which predominated on the suburban lines. Not only were there the seated passengers, but also the number of standing passengers, which were greater than in normal circumstances in peace time. According to *The Times* of 12 September, trains entering Liverpool Street were crowded and late with those from the outer suburbs having 20 to 22 people in a compartment.

According to the *News Chronicle* of 13 September, crowds had stood many deep on the platforms at Liverpool Street and that passengers had rushed for seats before the incoming train had come to a standstill. When a compartment was apparently full and even all the standing room had been taken, there were others who had opened the doors and by sheer force pushed their way in. In view of this, the LNER had decided at once to strengthen their suburban services with an additional 18 rush hour trains which would run until further notice.

Shortly after the start of the war, a number of lines lost their passenger service. On the Great Eastern Section these were Woodham Ferrers to Maldon, Wymondham to Forncett and Angel Road to Lower Edmonton. In the case of the first two, although both lines officially closed to passengers on 10 September, in practice it was 9 September as neither line had a Sunday service. In the case of the third, the last service ran on Friday 8 September as it only ran on Mondays to Fridays and consisted of only one train a day. Certainly in the case of the Woodham Ferrers to Maldon line, the closure to passengers caused some hardship, particularly at Purleigh which was served by Barons Lane Halt and had a service of six trains a day on Monday to Saturday and was now reduced to one bus a day in each direction on Monday to Saturday and a couple of other buses during the week which did not run daily. The situation was not resolved until January 1941. After the end of the war, parish councils served by the line pressed for the passenger service to be restored, but it was not. Instead, the bus service between Maldon and Woodham Ferrers via Purleigh, Cold Norton and Stow Maries was improved and timed to connect with trains on the Southminster line at Woodham Ferrers. The Forncett to Wymondham line on at least one occasion was used as an alternative route to Norwich when the line into Norwich became impassable due to bomb damage. The only mention that I have ever found in the press or railway magazines is in the first edition of *Railways*

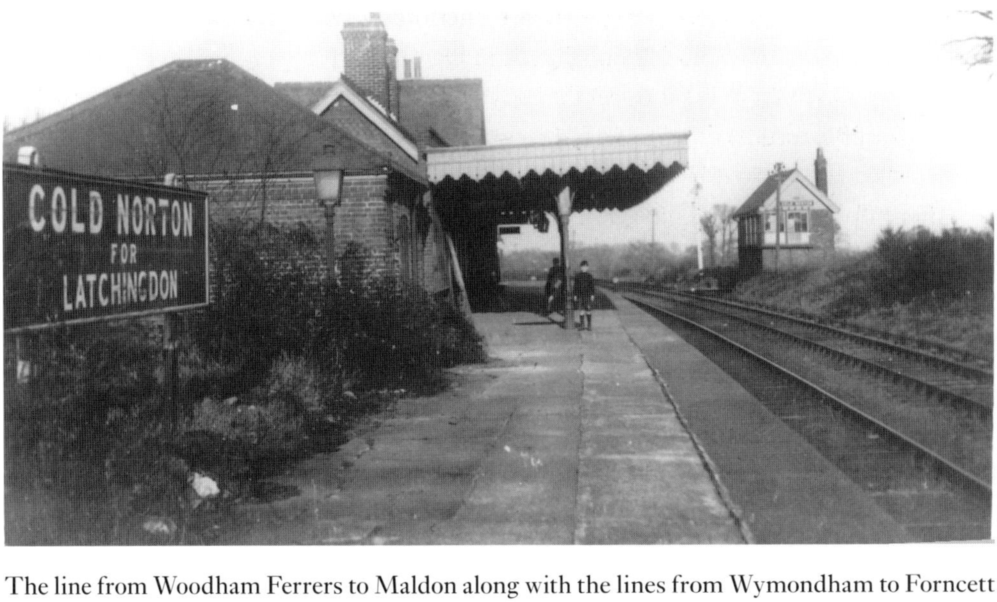

The line from Woodham Ferrers to Maldon along with the lines from Wymondham to Forncett and Angel Road to Lower Edmonton lost their passenger services at the start of the Second World War. Cold Norton station on the first mentioned line is seen at some time during the war. *Author's collection*

for December 1939 which lists all 'Passenger Train Services withdrawn or suspended since the Commencement of the War.'

The Second World War also saw the destruction of the derelict Southwold Railway as part of the national drive for scrap metal. Work commenced at the Halesworth end in July 1941 and was completed by January 1942.

To assist with the movement of traffic should the normal route be put out of action, a number of new connections were put in during the course of the war. At the west end of Gospel Oak station on the Tottenham and Hampstead Junction Joint Line a connection was put in between that line and the North London Line of the LMS on 11 March 1940. At Wood Green a few yards of line were laid to provide a through connection from the Palace Gates branch to Bounds Green on the Great Northern section Hertford Loop on 9 July 1944. At Romford, a short connection was put in to connect the Ipswich main line to the LMS LT&SR section Romford to Upminster Branch on either 21 July or 4 August 1940.

There was one other piece of new work that was completed during the Second World War and that was the doubling of the Clacton branch from Thorpe-le-Soken, which was completed in January 1941.

Petrol was an important fuel during the war, particularly for aircraft, and even before the start of the war a number of petrol depots had been opened by the Air Ministry. These were on the Great Eastern Section at Thetford in June 1939, Claydon and Saffron Walden in August 1939 and Mountnessing in October 1939.

The winter of 1939–40 was particularly harsh. There was thick snow. The *Essex Chronicle* of 9 February 1940 reported:

> After Fifty Years: For the first time in the history of the Southminster branch railway line laid fifty years ago, a snow plough was seen passing Woodham Ferrers station to clear the track of snow drifts 6ft deep. In the evening the elements became worse, and a train leaving Woodham Ferrers was snowbound a mile outside, and the engine had its fires extinguished. In an attempt to assist this train another engine became snowbound, thereby completely blocking the line. The staff at Woodham Ferrers under the direction of the Stationmaster, Mr. T.W. Armer. worked unceasingly for over 24 hours, and with the assistance of the snow plough were able to resume a normal service by 5.45am next day. The public will bow to the men who under terrible conditions maintained the indispensable service of the 'iron road'.

According to the *Biggleswade Chronicle* of 16 February 1940, on the Buntingford branch a train got to within 800 yards of Buntingford station and ran into a snow drift which the engine could not shift. The passengers were detrained and the train had to be dug out. According to *The Times* of 31 January 1940 some of the branch lines in East Anglia were blocked and the *Railway Magazine* for March reported that there were snow drifts 10 to 15ft deep in such places as Buntingford and Fakenham.

After the battering of Britain and the continent by the weather, the spring of 1940 saw the war heating up. By the end of June, Germany had control of Denmark, Norway, Belgium, the Netherlands and France.

To rescue the British troops on the Continent, the British launched 'Operation Dynamo' or as it is commonly known 'the Dunkirk Evacuation'. Operation Dynamo lasted from 26 May to 4 June 1940. Of all the four major railway companies in Britain, the LNER was less concerned than the other three companies. Of the 576 trains run to carry troops returning from Dunkirk 15 trains went from Harwich, the other 561 went from ports served by the Southern of which Dover saw the largest number with 326.

Operation Dynamo was followed by Operation Aerial which lasted from 15 to 25 June and was the evacuation of Allied forces and civilians from ports in western France. In addition to invading the Low Countries and France in the spring and early summer of 1940, the Germans also invaded the Channel Islands, which required an evacuation of civilians.

In May 1940, the *St Denis* was sent to Rotterdam to pick up British civilians, but after receiving bomb damage from the advancing German forces the ship was scuttled and abandoned to the advancing German forces. The *Malines* was also sent to Rotterdam to evacuate British civilians, under heavy bombing attacks by the advancing German forces. The ship also collected the crew from the scuttled *St. Denis* and sailed unlit at night. Crump contradicts this saying that the crew of the *St Denis* got away from the Hook of Holland on the last British destroyer to leave the port.

The *Malines* along with the *Prague* took part in the Dunkirk evacuation. The former made two trips back to Dover and Folkestone with a total of 1469 troops, some rescued from the sinking destroyer HMS *Grafton*. The *Prague* made two trips back to Folkestone on 29 and 31 May 1940 with a total of 2,911 troops, but while returning on a third passage with over 3,000 French troops, the ship was damaged by bombs landing close to its stern. The troops aboard were transferred to other vessels and the *Prague* under tow was beached at Deal before being taken to the Thames for repairs, which were effected in 1941.

The *Malines* along with the *Antwerp*, the *Vienna* and the *Archangel* took part in the evacuation of British troops from western France.

As the German army advanced through France some British troops were moved from Le Havre to Cherbourg. The *Bruges* was allocated to this duty and whilst anchored off Le Havre on the morning of June 11, received a direct hit from a bomb and was beached as a total loss.

The *Antwerp*, the *Malines* and the *Archangel* took part in the evacuation of civilians from the Channel Islands as did the *Sheringham*, which, having in December 1939 been operating from Ipswich to Antwerp and Zeebrugge, by June 1940 had been transferred to the GWR service from Weymouth to the Channel Islands.

Train Ferry No 1 had been requisitioned in September 1939 for military movements between Harwich and Calais, comprising ambulance trains and road vehicles. In June 1940, the ship took part in evacuations from the Channel Islands.

Train Ferry No 2 had been requisitioned in September 1939 to carry military traffic to and from Calais, then in June 1940 to assist the evacuation of troops from St. Valery-en-Caux. On 13 June, she was damaged by shore batteries and beached and abandoned off Le Havre.

Train Ferry No 3 in September 1939 had been requisitioned to carry military cargo to and from Calais, and in June 1940 assisted in the evacuations from the Channel Islands.

Returning to the Dunkirk evacuation, Crump says that some of the ships from Dunkirk unexpectedly arrived at Harwich. To cope with the troops which they carried, eight special trains were put on at short notice to carry them from Parkeston Quay to the Midlands. Harwich also witnessed a tragedy when a ship carrying refugees was bombed and sank just outside the harbour. The refugees were rescued and brought ashore covered in oil, where they were put straight on a train and taken up to Liverpool Street. The condition of the train after that journey had to be seen to be believed!

With the fall of France and the Low Countries, there was now a real threat of the Germans invading Great Britain and those parts of the country bordering the Channel and the North Sea became restricted areas to which only residents, those on official business and those engaged in military activity were permitted to enter. These areas included parts of Essex, Suffolk, Norfolk, Cambridgeshire and the Isle of Ely. These restrictions were sometimes eased, but then later reinstated during the war until after D Day in 1944. At the same time, all evacuees in those areas were evacuated from those areas as were 40,000 children from eighteen East and South East coast towns and another 8,000 from areas within ten miles of the coast of Kent, Essex, Suffolk and part of Norfolk. Further evacuations took place in the middle of September. These were for civilians. In the case of the eastern counties 101 trains were scheduled to carry 80,000 of the civilian population from Ipswich and Colchester to the Midlands. However, most of the people refused to leave their homes and only 23 trains ran carrying 11,636 people.

With the threat of invasion, measures were taken to ensure that if the Germans landed they would not be able operate the railways. The easiest way to prevent this was to remove all locomotives from depots in coastal towns. For example, according to Crump, Harwich locomotives were moved to Manningtree. According to the RCTS History of Locomotives of the LNER Part 3C, Southend locomotives were moved to Stratford. Plans were drawn up to sabotage every locomotive depot in the event of the Germans landing.

In the event of an invasion, plans were drawn up to amongst other things to carry 237,900 people away from all the East Anglian coastal towns from Southend to Great Yarmouth as well as Colchester and Ipswich. Fortunately, this plan was never needed. It was also recognised that heavy bombing might drive people away from the towns before they could be taken away by train and to meet this possibility the Refugee Emergency Scheme was prepared. This was given the sub-title Crash Evacuation. Under this, four trains were to pick up Chelmsford people at Shenfield, six trains were to pick up Colchester people at Chappel, whilst Norwich and Kings Lynn were each given twelve trains to call at Wymondham and Magdalen Road respectively.

Aware of the increasing threat of a German invasion, a whole series of measures were taken. There was the Home Guard or Local Defence Volunteers as it was originally called. This came into being even before Dunkirk following a broadcast on the BBC by the Secretary of State for War, Anthony Eden. Railwaymen, like scores of others who joined the new organisation to act as a secondary defence force in case of an invasion, were formed into units of it.

Then there was the danger of enemy parachutists. To make life hard for them station name boards amongst other things that would indicate where a place was were removed or covered over . Whilst this would serve its intended purpose it also made life very hard for anyone who did not know where they were, but had a legitimate excuse to be there. The innocent stranger could be mistaken for any enemy spy! A solution was found by putting station name boards at right angles to the line, but under cover. That way by leaning out of the window except perhaps those passengers at the end of a very long train and those in the carriage exactly opposite could read it. As the war drew to a close station name boards and other indications of the name of a place were put back in their correct place or uncovered.

At the meeting of the Ambulance Train Committee of the Wartime Railway Executive Committee on 28 May 1940, just after the start of the Dunkirk evacuation, discussion took place on ambulance train requirements in the event of an invasion. Of the fifty-nine trains that had been ordered, four Overseas had been completed, thirteen Home had been completed and eighteen Casualty Evacuation plus a further eight as a temporary measure. Whilst Home trains comprised nine vehicles, Overseas trains comprised sixteen vehicles and it was proposed to split each of them in to two trains of eight vehicles to which would be added a Westinghouse fitted LNER brake third and two piped open third forming eight 11-coach trains. To work the trains, eight locomotives of either class B12 or B17 would be allocated to them, each provided with two crews. As it is not known which specific locomotives and men were detailed for the eventuality, as the invasion did not occur, the four trains remained in store until 1944, when they were used for the role for which they had been originally constructed.

A whole series of other anti-invasion measures were taken. In August 1939, orders had been given for the preparation of rail-blocks to add as obstacles to German tanks at vital points. Other plans included the placing of explosives to blow up bridges and tunnels. Throughout the country, a whole series of defence lines were constructed. Pill boxes were built at strategic places, for example Chapel Viaduct. Even the never completed Mistley, Thorpe and Walton Railway saw use when four miles of the abandoned railway were used in the construction of an anti-tank ditch.

Armoured trains were formed. There were twelve of these, using eleven armoured plated F4 and one F5 2-4-2 side tanks. The trains were lettered A to M, excluding I. The trains were initially equipped with two QF 6 pounder Hotchkiss guns and six Bren Guns by the Royal Engineers and were manned by Royal Armoured Corps troops. The LMS supplied armoured tenders to increase their radius of operation. Of the trains, A, D, G and M were based in the eastern counties in LNER territory at respectively Hitchin, Mistley, Heacham and Spalding. Train C at one time stationed at Canterbury on the Southern was later moved to Westerfield on the East Suffolk line. Train F was based at Tilbury in LMS territory. The locomotives involved were: 7071, 7072, 7077, 7172, 7173, 7178, 7180, 7189, 7244 and 7573, which were all class F4, whilst 7784 was class F5. Additionally, F4s Nos 7111, 7174, 7177 and 7586 were also armoured.

The F4 and F5 locomotives were not the only former GER locomotives taken over by the government. In 1939, the War Department took over fourteen J69 and one J68 0-6-0 side tanks. The numbers of the J69s were: 7054, 7056, 7058, 7081, 7168, 7197, 7271, 7272, 7274, 7344, 7362 and 7388, whilst that of the J68 was 7041.

There was also a proposed use of some F4 and F5 locomotives that did not take place. According to *Locomotives of the LNER Part 7* published by the Railway, Correspondence and Travel Society, during the Second World War thirty-six locomotives of classes F4 and F5 were prepared to suit the restrictions of the underground railways sub-surface lines loading gauge by decapitating their chimneys to form short stovepipes. They were to have been used on the Metropolitan and District lines in the event of damage to key power stations and some older ex GER suburban train sets were earmarked for this purpose. None was called upon to perform these emergency duties. The engines earmarked were F4s 7075, 7076, 7078, 7147, 7171, 7179, 7184-7, 7219, 7232, 7233, 7573,

7574, 7578, 7584, 7588 and F5s 7095, 7096, 7100, 7103, 7141-4, 7188, 7589, 7590, 7782, 7783, 7785, 7787, and 7788. Several J15s were fitted with short cast iron chimneys to permit working over London Transport lines to the Southern in a case of war emergency. From 1941 onwards all locomotives were painted black as an economy measure.

During the war the following new classes were put into service on the GE Section:

V4 2-6-2 in 1941, which only lasted a short time on the GE Section
B1 4-6-0 in 1942 which became the mainstay of the GE Section to the end of steam.
J45 0-6-0 diesel electric shunters in 1944 - the LNERs first diesel shunters and used at Whitemoor Marshalling Yard. These had been ordered shortly before the death of Gresley in April 1941. Their electrical equipment was supplied by English Electric.
O1 2-8-0 in 1944 a rebuild of O4 2-8-0s.
Q1 0-8-0 side tanks in 1942 – a rebuild of Q4 0-8-0s

Additionally:

British War Department 2-8-0s and 2-10-0s in 1943
U S Army Transportation Corps 2-8-0s of Class S160 in 1943
O6 2-8-0s which were LMS 8F built for the LNER starting in 1944 and returned to the LMS in 1946-8

The Fall of France was followed by the Battle of Britain which lasted from 10 July to 31 October and has been described as the first major military campaign fought entirely by air forces.

The following Royal Air Force fighter stations were served by the Great Eastern Section at the time of the Battle:

For 11 Group covering the South East of England the critical approaches to London these were Debden, North Weald, Martlesham Heath, Rochford and Stapleford Tawny. Hornchurch was partially served by the section but principally the LMS LT&SR Section and the District Line of London Transport.

For 12 Group covering the Midlands and East Anglia these were Duxford and Coltishall.

With the entry of the Americans into the war a number of the US Army Transportation Corps class S160 2-8-0s were loaned to the British railway companies. Here is No 1703 of March shed. In the background is No 2634 of Stratford shed. *Author's collection*

Class J45 diesel shunters although ordered in February 1941 did not enter service until 1944. The class consisted of four members Nos 8000-3. They were based at March for the Whitemoor marshalling yards. Nos 8000-2 are seen here. Post war the LNER intended to build 176 diesel shunters. *Photomatic*

At least on one occasion during enemy action to an airfield disrupted rail traffic. On 28 August, Rochford airfield was heavily bombed with buildings damaged. About thirty craters were left behind and the adjacent railway line was blocked. Train services were terminated at Rayleigh and a replacement bus service was put on between Rayleigh and Southend until the line was repaired. During that time, passengers for Southend from Liverpool Street were told to go to Fenchurch Street and use the LMS to Southend.

During the latter stages of the Battle of Britain, the Blitz began, starting on 7 September 1940 and lasting until 11 May 1941. The term 'blitz' was first used by British press and originated from the German word 'blitzkrieg' meaning lightning war. Of the cities bombed during the Blitz, London suffered the worst, with daylight and night air raids beginning on 7 September. Liverpool, Hull, Bristol, Cardiff, Portsmouth, Plymouth, Southampton, Swansea, Belfast, Glasgow, Birmingham, Manchester, Sheffield and Coventry were also bombed. London was bombed on all but one of the 57 following days and nights after 7 September. The worst time was the first night; during the afternoon of 7 September, Channelsea carriage sidings were set on fire. In the terrible holocaust, shunters got to work. Locomotives were coupled up and carriages rescued from no less than ten roads. Only fourteen carriages were lost. During the same afternoon the Cambridge line was blocked at London Fields. Shadwell and Bow Road, Fenchurch Street and Gas Factory Junction were bombed. On the North Woolwich line, Custom House and Canning Town signal boxes were destroyed and the line blocked elsewhere. At Stratford, all the lighting failed and at Spitalfields Goods Station the electricity failed. On the main line at Bethnal Green, a bridge was damaged. There then followed a night of intensive bombing. At about 1am things eased off a bit and Mr Chilvers, the Assistant District Superintendent at Stratford, went outside to have a look. He found that all the lines through Stratford were intact, but that the signalling had failed and all the trains were standing still. The drivers and the firemen had stuck to their locomotives though the bombs were falling all around them. One must not forget any passengers on the trains. In the case of non-corridor trains, they would have been stuck without the guard being able to give them any information. Chilvers took an inspector was with him and they both had torches. They told the driver of the first train to follow them and by the light of their torches they guided the train at walking pace down the line. When they had seen it through, they went back for the next train. So, one by one the standing trains were helped on their way. This was going on during the middle of London's worst air raids. When daylight came and the bombing ceased, the damaged done was assessed and was described as terrific.

24 September was another bad night. Bow Junction was hit and all the lines into Liverpool Street were blocked. The next day, Up main line trains from the Colchester

line were reversed at Stratford and sent up via Lea Bridge to Tottenham. There they reversed again and went into Liverpool Street via Hackney Downs. Local trains were dealt with in the same way, except that, to save congestion, the second reversal was made at Wood Street, Walthamstow. In all cases, passengers were given the chance to alight at Stratford, but were warned that that if they wanted to get to town, they would have to walk, as the roads were blocked as badly as the railways. One must quite reasonably assume that trains from Liverpool Street were worked in the opposite way to those going in. The engineers then got to work and by 3.30pm, two lines were repaired through to Liverpool Street. By 7pm all four lines were clear.

After October 1940, the Blitz became a night campaign. According to Michael Bonavia in Volume 3 of his history of the LNER, Liverpool Street Station, Stratford and Temple Mills Yard were all bombed. At Liverpool Street, the big block of offices over the west side of the station was burned out on 11 May 1941, whilst on 11 January 1941, Hamilton House, the big block bridging the east side, lost one of its two wings. Bombs fell on Platforms 1, 4 and 18. A delayed action bomb in the engine sidings at the country end of platform 10 later exploded and killed two railway men who were carrying on with their work after four wagons loaded with ballast had been place in position to act as a screen. Shadwell, Fenchurch Street, Gas Factory Junction, Custom House, Canning Town and Bethnal Green were all bombed. That at Custom House on 7 September 1940 was so great that all trains on the North Woolwich branch terminated there and did not reach North Woolwich again until 7 January 1941. Carriages and wagons were destroyed. Because sections of lines were sometimes put out of action, trains had to be diverted by different routes. Both the Cambridge and Ipswich main lines were at some time blocked. The staff had to work under the most horrendous conditions in danger of being killed or injured from the bombs. Jim Hill, who was a Stratford driver at the beginning of the war, in 1941 decided to move to Enfield, where he originally lived. In *Buckjumpers, Gobblers and Clauds* (Bradford Barton 1981), he recorded that during an air raid on London, a bomb fell on Liverpool Street station and the shrapnel killed the driver of F6 class locomotive No 7008. As Hill was the senior applicant for the job, he replaced the unfortunate man and also took over his locomotive which still had the holes in the roof. The large marshalling yards at Temple Mills were a pretty hazardous place during air raids and incendiary bombs caused quite a few fires, once to a whole string of wagons. The local fire brigade was called to Ruckholt Road Bridge, which crossed over the lines at the south end of the yard. The firemen climbed on the parapet of the bridge and sat there with their legs dangling over and their hoses between their knees. A pilot engine was got and backed on to the far end of the burning train. Slowly it propelled the train under the bridge. As the first wagon emerged under the firemen, the train stopped for a minute or two whilst the firemen hosed the wagon. When this wagon's fire was put out, the engine moved on a few yards and pushed the next wagon into place until eventually all the fires were put out. Petrol trains were a great source of anxiety for those working there; fortunately, none were hit otherwise there would have been a catastrophe. Once two wagons of petrol were punctured by red hot bomb splinters. Fortunately, they were hit underneath so that the splinters were quenched in the liquid spirit. As it was, 7,500 gallons of aviation spirit were spilt all over the yard and for five hours before it soaked into the ground or evaporated all work stopped on the windward side. All engines had to shut off steam. Everyone gave the lake of petrol a wide berth and treated it with the utmost respect, except for one man who came along and splashed through it smoking with no obvious effect. Once or twice there were experimental wagons loaded with poison gas standing in the yard. The yard master, a Mr Rose, decided wisely to keep quiet about this. He decided though that if on one of the nights of the bombing he had an uncontrollable fire, the only thing to have been done would have been to ask the Civil Defence to clear everyone out of the adjacent town of Leyton. Mercifully, it never happened.

Temple Mills' worst night was the last of the heavy raids on 10 May 1941. On that night, 71 out of the 158 sidings in the yard had been knocked out of use. The end of the Blitz did not mean the end of the bombing. Indeed, bombing in some form or other continued until the spring of 1945. After the Blitz, the most famous German air raids were the Baedeker raids of April and May 1942. The name is derived from the Baedeker travel guides. They were attacks on cultural centres such as Norwich, which took place on the nights of 25/6 and 26/7 April causing 67 deaths. Only one locomotive was lost during the raids – former Midland and Great Northern Joint Railway 4 4 0 No 047.

The worst incident involving a train and a bomb did not occur in the London area, but between Shenfield and Ingatestone on the Ipswich main line. In the late evening of Wednesday 4 March 1943 at 9.45pm, a bomb was dropped on the main line blowing out part of the embankment half a mile north of the bridge over the single-track loop of the Southend line. The signalman at Shenfield heard the explosion and lost contact with Ingatestone signal box. A ganger was sent to investigate, but before he could report back, the 8.45pm; Liverpool Street to Harwich train hauled by B12/3 class locomotive No 8580 (which had been held at Shenfield) was ordered to proceed at caution thus avoiding any further delay. In the pitch dark, hampered by the blackout, the locomotive and tender fell into the crater killing the driver and fireman. The only other casualties were injuries to a passenger and the guard. For three days, whilst the line was being repaired, the Eastern National Omnibus Company and also – according to one source – the City Coach Company, ran a shuttle service between Shenfield and Ingatestone.

The incident was not reported at the time, but according to the *Essex Chronicle* of 4 June 1943, notices were posted at Liverpool Street Station early the next morning that read 'Because of a failure at Ingatestone, the mainline service to Colchester and onwards is subject to delay'. During the period that the line was out of action, goods services were diverted by a number of different routes. One route, though, that was not used was via Wickford, Woodham Ferrers, Maldon and Witham. The limited route availability of the locomotives that could have used the two Maldon branches, combined with the restrictive single line Train Staff and ticket working, would have hampered the number of trains that could have used the lines. Additionally, at that time the section of the Woodham Ferrers to Maldon line between Woodham Ferrers and Cold Norton was used only for wagon storage and civil defence exercises making that diversion impractical. Apparently, according to Peter Paye in *Branch Lines to Maldon* (Lightmoor 2016), the idea of using the route was briefly considered but was speedily rejected.

It was not only bombers that railwaymen had to contend with. Crump records how a Stratford locomotive inspector told him that when he was driving a slow goods train up Brentwood bank, he was chased by a Messerchmitt. He said that he was only too thankful when a Spitfire joined in the hunt.

The period also saw more withdrawals of passenger services. The service from Fenchurch Street to North Woolwich, or rather the North Woolwich branch, was withdrawn on 27 October 1940. The Beckton branch was closed after suffering severe bomb damage in September 1940, but was briefly reopened and then closed on 28 December 1940. Passenger services on the Gallions branch ceased after German bombs put the line out of action on 7 September. Although the line was repaired, it was only used for wagon and van storage. The other wartime closure that took place was the service from Victoria Park on the North London line of the LMS to Canning Town which was suspended on Sundays from 31 March 1940 and weekdays from 1 November 1942. Victoria Park station itself was closed by the LMS on 8 November 1943. The service from Broad Street to Poplar was suspended on 15 April 1944 and was officially withdrawn on 14 May 1944. A substitute replacement bus service then operated until 23 April 1945.

As mentioned in the previous chapter, work on the extension of the London Transport Central Line to Stratford, Leyton, Leytonstone, Loughton, Epping, Ongar, Newbury Park, West Ruislip and Denham was halted in the summer of 1940 for the duration of the war, by which time the tunnels east of Liverpool Street including those under Eastern Avenue from Leytonstone to Newbury Park had been completed as well as the new interchange platforms at Stratford. In the eastbound tunnel from Liverpool

Street to Drapers' Field, Leyton, it is highly likely that the running rails had been laid and that many miles of the Loughton branch and the Hainault Loop had been laid with conductor rails. At Loughton a new station had opened on 28 April 1940 built by the LNER. The road-bed of the western extension had been finished as far as Greenford and laid with double track. Some work on station reconstruction had been done, as had some civil engineering work beyond Greenford. Both the new rolling stock depots at Hainault and Ruislip were complete. In regard to the tunnels under Eastern Avenue, Canon Charles Bayes writing in *Great Eastern Journal* No 18 recalled that on 11 February 1940 'train services were suspended between Leyton and Snaresbrook to allow tunnelling operations to take place. A bus service provided by London Transport "Q" and "T" single-deckers linked the two stations and bore the notice "On hire to the LNER".'

During the war some use was made of the uncompleted works. The section of new line in the tunnel between Leytonstone and Newbury Park was turned into a factory producing aircraft components. Access to the factory was via the three unopened stations at Wanstead, Redbridge and Gants Hill and at two other intermediate points at Cambridge Park and Danehurst Gardens. A miniature railway had to be built to convey the material used in the manufacture of aircraft components. Special air conditioning had to be installed. Cloakrooms had to be warmed and temperatures thermostatically controlled. First aid rooms had to be provided with mechanical ventilation. A subterranean canteen for 600 people and four mess rooms capable of seating 1,600 people were necessary. Following the entry of the United States into the war in December 1941, Hainault depot was used by the US Army Transportation Corps for railway rolling stock assembly between June 1943 and January 1945.

Some parts of the proposed extension were used as air raid shelters. The westbound tunnel east of Liverpool Street as far as and including Bethnal Green station, as well as, further east, the tunnels at Gainsborough Road, Leytonstone, Westdown Road, Leyton and Queen Street, Stratford. The trouble with air raid shelters was that they were not always the safest places to be. The most notorious accident occurred on 3 March 1943 at Bethnal Green station on the unopened section of the Central Line. At 8.17pm, the air raid sirens went off over London. Hundreds of people started to head towards the station and down the staircase to take shelter. Although people were used to the crowds on the stairs and were careful if it was dark, a middle-aged woman and a child fell over, three steps up from the bottom and others fell around them, tangled in an immovable mass which grew, as they struggled, to nearly 300 people. Some got free but 173, most of them women and children, were crushed and asphyxiated and about 60 others were taken to hospital. News of the disaster was withheld for 36 hours and reporting of what had happened was censored, giving rise to allegations of a cover-up, although it was in line with existing wartime reporting restrictions. Sadly, it later turned out that the air-raid warning had simply been a test – there was no bombing raid. There is evidence that the disaster could have been prevented. Apparently, Bethnal Green Council had told the London Civil Defence authority that the stairs on the station needed crush barriers to avoid such an accident as early as 1941. These were installed the day after the disaster.

On the electrification of the Ipswich main line from Liverpool Street to Shenfield and Fenchurch Street to Stratford, some of the bridge reconstructions and station and signalling alterations were advanced, and the Ilford flyover had been completed but not brought into use. Six miles of overhead gantries had been erected between Harold Wood and Brentwood and the emplacements for them prepared from Brentwood to Shenfield. The body shells of six of the new trains had been completed. Ilford locomotive depot had closed in May 1939 in preparation for the site to be used for the new electric train carriage depot.

The war saw a number of changes in the work place. Women were again employed as in the First World War, but some remained in railway service after the end of the war, unlike the previous war. The only jobs that they were not employed in were engine crew and goods shunters, the former because engine crews took a long time to train and shunters because the job was regarded as a very dangerous one.

The war years saw two serious accidents on the Great Eastern section. On 10 February 1941, there was a collision between two passenger trains between Harold Wood and Brentwood at 10.46am. The 10am Liverpool Street to Norwich train hauled by B17 class locomotive No 2828 *Harewood House* had come to a stand on the Down Through lines some two miles beyond Harold Wood station owing to a shortage of steam when ascending Brentwood bank. It had been standing for about eight minutes when it was run into from the rear by the 10.04am stopping train from Liverpool Street to Southend hauled by B12 class locomotive No 8556, which had passed the preceding automatic colour-light signal at danger. The collision, which occurred at about 30mph, was violent and five passengers were killed outright and two others, including a railwayman, died later. Seventeen passengers and the two enginemen of the Southend train were taken to hospital with serious injuries. A further thirty subsequently complained of minor injuries or shock. The primary cause of the accident was driver error by the driver of the Southend train. A secondary cause was the failure of the guard of the Norwich train to properly protect the train and fatigue on the part of the driver of the Southend train.

On 16 January 1944, there was a collision between two express trains in the fog at Ilford. At 7.20pm on the day in question in darkness and dense fog the 2.40pm express passenger train from Norwich to Liverpool Street hauled by B12 class locomotive

No 8564 passed a succession of signals at danger and collided at a speed of 20–25mph with the rear of the 2.38pm express passenger train from Yarmouth hauled B17 class locomotive No 2868 *Bradford City* which was about to restart on instructions from the signalman after a stop at the box. The fog signalmen had been called out but had not arrived at the Up line signal posts. In the collision, nine passengers lost their lives, twenty-eight passengers had to be detained in hospital and ten other passengers complained of shock or minor injuries. The primary causes of the accident were driver error on the part of the driver of Norwich train, coupled with the fog and excess speed. A secondary cause was an error on the part of the fireman of that train.

The American Class S160 locomotives had from the point of view of British enginemen a design fault. The water gauge instead of the glass tube used on British locomotives consisted of a thick sheet of glass serrated on the water side, and built into a metal frame. The water level showed black by refraction and the steam space above showed silver by reflection. The top and bottom shut off cocks and drain cock were not of the plug variety used on British locomotives, which turned through ninety degrees between open and shut, but instead consisted of screw valves. Their disadvantage was that the open and shut positions were not apparent by sight, but only by feel. These disadvantages resulted in three accidents. That at Thurston on the GE Section 12 January 1944 involving locomotive No 2363; both enginemen survived. The driver sustained a broken thigh and burns on his left side, whilst the fireman was blown off the footplate, sustained severe bruising, burns and shock and could remember nothing of the accident. In the other two accidents there were fatalities.

Like so many other railway works, during the war, Stratford manufactured components for the military. These included parts for tanks, landing craft, coastal defence guns, Hotchkiss Machine Guns, forgings for mortar bombs, valves for oil tankers and parts for road vehicles, according to John Watling in *Great Eastern Journal* No 62.

A lesser-known aspect of the war is that sometimes railways caused problems for bus operation. The aspect in question was when some buses were converted to run on producer gas to save fuel. This involved towing a trailer burning anthracite. Buses running on this fuel had a range of 80 miles. The bus engine had to be kept running on full power all the time – even when stationary – to maintain the flow of gas into the engine. If not, the fire in the trailer would go out. Both Eastern National and Eastern Counties converted some buses to run on producer gas. Eastern Counties were centred at Cromer depot and Eastern National at Maldon depot. Maldon had a level crossing and the bus company made complaints to the railway company about the delays the level crossing was causing.

At the start of the war, the Sandringham Hotel at Hunstanton was first used by the LNER's Accounts department, but in 1940 it was requisitioned by the War Department and used by various British and Canadian regiments for the rest of the war, before being returned to the railway company after 1945.

Following the bombing of Pearl Harbor by the Japanese on 7 December 1941, America and Great Britain declared war on Japan the next day. As Japan had an alliance with Germany and Italy (which had joined Germany in the war on 10 June 1940) both nations declared war on America on 11 December 1941. America had been providing significant military supplies to Great Britain and her Allies since 1940, despite remaining neutral. With the entry of the America into the war, British Empire and Allied forces stationed in Britain were supplemented by American forces.

The RAF had begun bombing military targets in Germany such as docks and shipyards in March 1940; the first raid though was on the air base at Hörnum on the island of Sylt, on the night of 19-20 March 1940. The RAF began targeting Berlin in August 1940. From February 1942 onward the bombing campaign against Germany became less restrictive and increasingly targeted industrial and civilian areas.

The Americans first bombed Germany on 27 January 1943 when the USAAF 8th Air Force sent 64 planes from their base in England to the port of Wilhelmshaven. Beginning on 10 June 1943 and lasting until 12 April 1945, the British and the Americans carried out the Combined Bomber Offensive firstly against Luftwaffe targets which were the highest priority from June 1943 to 1 April 1944. From June 1944 they were against V-weapon installations and from September 1944 against petroleum, oil, and lubrication plants. Additional targets included railway yards and other transport targets, along with, in the final stages of the war in Europe, army equipment.

The British bombing campaign was chiefly waged by night by large numbers of heavy bombers until the latter stages of the war when German fighter defences were so reduced that daylight bombing was possible without risking large losses. The American effort was by day – massed formations of bombers with escorting fighters. Together they made up a round-the-clock bombing effort except where weather conditions prevented operations.

This period saw the building of more airfields. In *By Rail to Victory* there is a map showing airfields in East Anglia. I have to say, though, that from local knowledge it is not totally accurate as at least two in Essex were never constructed, one near Ingatestone and one near Maldon at the former Royal Flying corps airfield at Stow Maries, which was to be known as RAF Cold Norton. *By Rail to Victory* gives a list of stations to which bombs for American airfields were dispatched between D Day 6 June 1944 and early September 1944: Brandon, Two Mile Bottom, Haughley,

Drayton, Norwich, Earsham, Ellingham, Tivetshall, White Colne, Earls Colne, Felstead, Stansted, Bishop's Stortford, Clare and Rayne.

To build the airfields, rubble, bricks, tarmac and cement were required. *By Rail to Victory* mentions bricks being delivered to such places as Fakenham, Attleborough, Sudbury, Bures and Colchester. For tarmac, the book says that Air Ministry sidings were available at such places as Attleborough, Dereham, Saxham, Haughley and Tivetshall. For cement, fifteen railheads were originally intended, but only nine actually functioned, the most active being Parkeston, Lowestoft, South Lynn, Roundham, Crown Point, Norwich City and Downham. Dereham also handled a heavy tonnage. To cope with the increased use of aviation fuel, there were more Air Ministry petrol depots established: at Hethersett in July 1943 and at Ellingham and at Chapel, both in March 1944. Additionally, there were Petroleum Board depots to which train loads were run at: Histon, Kings Lynn, Norwich Victoria, Ipswich, Barnwell Junction, Bury St Edmunds, Sudbury and Ely; it was not just for fuelling the aircraft and associated ground vehicles that petroleum was needed. *By Rail to Victory* says that train loads were delivered to the following places: for fog dispersal – Saxham, Foulsham, Downham, Southminster and Melton; for smoke screen – Yarmouth Vauxhall; for transport overseas – Foulsham and Drayton.

Originally in the war petrol wagons were conveyed by normal goods service, but later special trains were arranged. In July 1940, because of air raids it was decided to keep oil tank wagons out of marshalling yards and so schedules were set up under which by combining destination stations block train loads were made to the farthest possible point. Some eight or ten composite trains were arranged for a time, but as the quantities increased, through loads to go to each destination became possible. The War Office had a term for an area of the country that was vulnerable in the event of invasion. It was called the 'Pink' Belt Area. In the east of England, it ran from the coast to a line through Retford, Newark, Stamford, Bedford and Luton and across to Epping, thence bypassing London on the east to a point in Kent. In August 1941 it was decided that during the hours of darkness no petrol train could move within the 'Pink Belt'; arrivals at destination stations were to be given early in the day, unloading finished and the empty wagons removed before blackout. The main sources of supply at the time were the oil refineries at Avonmouth and Stanlow, with the latter being the heavier. Because no nearby suitable stabling facilities on the LMS could be found and because Peterborough was in the 'Pink Belt' and considered too vitally important from a railway point of to view to risk damage, a concession was granted authorising petrol trains to be brought through to Whittlesea for stabling. The prohibitions lapsed when the menace of enemy bombing diminished and the demand for petrol became more insistent.

Other fuel had to be supplied to the airfields in the form of coke for stoves to heat the buildings. In the winter of 1943-4, the demand became acute and following meetings between officials of the Air Ministry and the Ministry of Fuel and Power (Coke Controller) it was arranged that heavy supplies should be drawn from Becton Gas Works.

With bombs and other ammunition being transported around, the chances of an accident occurring involving a train carrying the dangerous material was something that must have worried the railway authorities. Unfortunately, an accident did happen – early in the morning of 2 June 1944, at Soham in Cambridgeshire. Benjamin Gimbert was the driver of British War Department 2 8 0 locomotive No 7337. His fireman was James Nighthall. According to Gimbert's account reproduced in *By Rail to Victory*, he had signed on 10.10pm on 1 June to work the 11.40pm goods from Whitemoor Yard to Goodmayes, but the starting point of the train was diverted to March to start at 12.10am on 2 June for White Colne. The train started at 12.15am and consisted of fifty-one wagons and the guard said that they would be going via Marks Tey and Ipswich to the destination. According to Gimbert, at no part of the journey was there any jerking of the train or application of the brake. Gimbert said in his driver's report that he did not notice anything wrong with any of the wagons until after passing the Soham distant signal, which was off. He thought that he noticed steam coming from the locomotive's injector and looking out he saw that the wagon next to the locomotive was on fire. The flames appeared to be getting all over the bottom of the wagon and seemed to be spreading very rapidly, which seemed to suggest to him that something very inflammable was alight. Gimbert sounded the engine's whistle to notify the guard and immediately took steps to stop the train carefully, knowing what the wagon contained and stopped the train by the station end of the goods shed where Nighthall, under Gimbert's instructions, uncoupled the wagon from the rest of the train. He told him to take the coal hammer with him in case the coupling was too hot to handle. On Nighthall having done this and having rejoined the engine, Gimbert proceeded with the wagon which was on fire, with the intention of getting well clear of the station .and surrounding buildings and to leave it there and to proceed to Fordham. The Soham signalman came from his box on to the platform and Gimbert said, "Sailor, have you anything between here and Fordham? Where is the mail?" He did not get a reply from him as the explosion occurred at that moment. The engine and the wagon were moving slowly at the time and the regulator was shut. Gimbert did not notice if the signalman had a bucket which he understood was found outside the signal box. According to Gimbert, about six or seven minutes elapsed from the time that he first saw the fire on the wagon to the time of the explosion. In the explosion, James Nighthall was killed immediately and the Soham signalman Frank

Bridges died the next day. Miraculously, Benjamin Gimbert survived, whilst Herbert Clarke the guard, although stunned by the blast and suffering from shock, managed to walk to the next signal box to warn the signalman there what had happened. Five others received severe injuries and another twenty-two minor injuries. The explosion created a crater 66ft in diameter and 15ft deep. The station building was almost demolished and there was severe or moderate damage to over 700 properties within 900 yards. Emergency repairs by American troops in the neighbourhood meant that the line was opened for goods traffic within eighteen hours and passenger traffic resumed the next day.

The newspapers reported the accident as follows. The *Daily Herald* of 3 June carried the headline 'Railmen died to save a town. Drove a blazing bomb truck'. The newspaper said that Gimbert was blown over the station and was calling 'Look after the train, the train. Look after my mate.' The *News Chronicle* of the same date reported, 'Signalman gave his life to save a town from destruction. Race to halt bomb train.' According to that newspaper, Gimbert on being found said, 'Look after my mate; save my train – bomb.' Gimbert was thrown over 300 yards. For their bravery both Gimbert and Nighthall were awarded the George Cross; the latter, sadly, posthumously.

The cause of the fire was never fully explained. The wagon in question had previously been used to carry a load of bulk sulphur powder. Although the wagon would have been cleaned in between loads, the possibility remained that some of the sulphur powder was still present. Although the wagon was sheeted, the theory advanced was that a cinder from the engine had landed in the wagon and had ignited some sulphur. This in turn set alight the wooden body of the wagon.

The American service personnel stationed in Britain could be very helpful as seen in clearing up after the Soham explosion, but they could also sometimes cause problems. Norman Crump mentions the case at Finningham when an American bulldozer came down the road on its carrier and got jammed under the arch of the railway bridge there. The driver tried to shift it and shifted the bridge instead – 2ft 6in out of line. This meant a rush engineering job to repair the bridge!

On 6 June 1944, British, Canadian and American troops took part in Operation Overlord, which was the beginning of the liberation of the Continent. In the build up to the operation, a lot of preparations had to be undertaken. It involved the movement of men and materials to sealed off assembly camps in the south of England and later to the ports. During this time, certain passenger and goods trains were withdrawn without explanation. Any complaints were met with 'an impenetrable veil of apparent ignorance and stupidity'. The planning involved the movement of stores. At the same time as stores were moving to the embarkation ports for shipment, munitions were coming into the ports from America. To handle this, two 'double transit sheds' were built. One was at

Micheldever on the Southern Railway between Basingstoke and Winchester and the other was at High Meads, Stratford, near the London docks. At each shed, wagons were unloaded and their contents transferred across the benches to empty wagons waiting to take them to their final destination. Of the embarkation ports, the LNER served only Hull, Grimsby and the Royal and West India docks in London. The latter two were the Company's main focal point. The principle marshalling yard was Temple Mills. Leading to the two docks were the GER main line, the North London line via Dalston and Victoria Park, the Tottenham and Hampstead line via Willesden and Kentish Town round the back of North London to Tottenham and the newly installed connecting line from the Great Northern line at Bounds Green to Palace Gates. The North London and the Tottenham and Hampstead lines were the principle feeders. A lot of things had to be done. Drivers from Stratford and Hornsey locomotive sheds and from the LMS had to learn the route down to the docks. There was the wholesale cancellation of passenger trains on the North Woolwich and Palace Gates lines. Traffic from Messrs Cory's coal wharf and the large coal dump at Becton was 'equally slaughtered'. Crump also gives some examples of train movements. The following involved on the Great Eastern section three trains a day from Clumber Park (Worksop) to Tilbury and the Victoria and Albert docks either via Forest Gate Junction for the LT&SR line or via the Great Northern line and Canonbury and Victoria Docks or by the LNER throughout for the Victoria and Albert Docks.

In the plans for the invasion of the Continent, the British undertook to provide all the ambulance trains for the allied armies. Construction of the additional trains that would be required began in 1942. The plan was that the trains would be shipped to France when the front had advanced far enough to require evacuation of the fighting area by railway to base hospitals and to ports. In the first weeks of the invasion, all of the casualties would have to be shipped back to England for hospital treatment. The planners calculated that during that period, seven Home Ambulance Trains would suffice for the British Army, including Canadians and other Allied formations. For the Americans, five Home Ambulance Trains would be sufficient. To supplement these if needed, twenty-one Casualty Evacuation Trains would be made available. The Americans had other ideas and in December 1943 the American authorities informed the Railway Executive Committee that they calculated that their daily requirement would be fifteen trains. They did not favour the Casualty Evacuation Trains as they were not suited to their mode of operation and instead requested that during the first ninety days of Operation Overlord, they be allowed to use seven of the Overseas Ambulance Trains that had been allotted to them. When the Ambulance Train Committee met on 10 January 1944, the Americans had increased the number to ten. Understandably, the railways were most reluctant to grant the Americans their request and pointed out to them the operating difficulties that would arise from having to handle Westinghouse air brake fitted trains in Britain. However, the need to preserve inter-Allied harmony prevailed and on 14 January 1944, the Committee produced detailed proposals to meet the Americans wishes. From D Day minus 15, ten Overseas Ambulance Trains would be made available to the Americans. To haul the trains, ten suitably equipped locomotives would be provided, accompanied by two drivers, two passed firemen and a fitter. The Class B12/3 with their wide route availably and their ability to haul trains at express speeds probably made them an automatic choice. The men would be housed on the train and fed by the Americans. Initially, guards would be provided by the companies over whose lines the trains ran. Given that rationing was in force at that time, the prospect of receiving the somewhat better food provided by the Americans than that available to the British must have seemed quite attractive to the railwaymen. Furthermore, their pay rates were rather attractive by the standards of the day; £12 per week for drivers and £10 10s for other grades. Understandably, the proposal that other companies should provide the guards brought a justifiable protest from the men's union, on the grounds that it would be unsafe to make them responsible for a braking system with which they were unfamiliar. The LNER was then called upon to second two guards for each train. The prospect of losing seventy experienced men for up to three months probably posed more problems for the GE section than the loss of ten main line locomotives. The problem was only slightly eased by the Southern Railway offering to make at least six guards available with experience of steam hauled Westinghouse braked trains to share the ambulance train duties. Those manning the trains were given 48 hours leave once a month and worked under the orders of the Americans. The trains went to various depots on the Great Western and Southern railways. According to Geoff Balfour writing in *GE Journal* No 61 there were eleven trains. Nos 11-15, 17, 27, 31, 33, 36 and 37. Of these No 11-15 and 17 were built by the LMSR, 27 and 31 by the LNER, 33 by the GWR and 36 and 37 by the SR. No 11 was stabled at Old Oak Common, 12 and 13 at Newbury, 14 and 33 at Westbury, 15 and 17 at Dubridge, 27 and 31 at Bournemouth, No 36 at Templecombe. Additionally, there was an eleventh train – No 37 – which was the reserve train and was stabled at Wem. Nos 15 and 17 were intended for Westbury, but siding accommodation was not yet ready.

The locomotives equipped to work the trains were 7449(8535)/8509/10/16/19/25/30/42/47/49/54/55/57/67. There is a little bit of confusion as to which locomotives were permanently attached to the trains. Balfour says Nos 8509/10/16/19/25/54/55/57/7449(8535) but mentions 8516 twice. He says that Nos 8530/42/47/49/67 were kept in reserve. The RCTS *History of the Locomotives of the LNER* says that a number of the locomotives were used on the trains including Nos 7449 (8535)/8509/10/16/19/25/30/47/49//55/57. From a perusal of the *Railway Observer* for the period June to December 1944, the following locomotives are known to have worked ambulance trains: Nos 7449 (8535), 7479 (8565), 8509, 8510, 8516, 8518, 8519, 8525, 8530, 8547, 8548, 8549, 8551, 8554 8555 8557. Just to make matters more interesting, according to a report in the *Observer* for August 1944, class B1 No 8305 *Oryx* was also on similar duties. Given that B1s were not fitted with Westinghouse air brakes, one can assume that the locomotive was only used on domestic vacuum braked ambulance trains. It was known that assisting engines would be needed over heavier gradients. In order for them to control the brakes on the ambulance train, a specially designed proportional valve was fitted to the B12s. These were known as vacuum control valves. Some of the locomotives were not permanently attached a train but were kept in reserve. Assisting locomotives were known to have been: on the GWR 4300 class Moguls, Bulldog 4 4 0s, Grange and Manor 4 6 0s; on the SR, S11 and T9 4 4 0s; on the LMS 2 P 4 4 0 or 4F 0 6 0, but a Class 5 4 6 0 had also been seen; on the LNER a K3 2 6 0 had been seen. Many trains were worked unaided, but No 8554 hauling an empty train from a loaded run into LMS territory stalled on the eastbound climb from the Severn Tunnel on 29 July. Setting back on restarting the train weighting 428 tons caused a carriage to be derailed on the Patchway Tunnel catch points. The damage blocked the Up main line for five hours to the GWR's displeasure. Balfour says that lines regularly traversed included Bournemouth–Bath, Cheltenham–Birmingham, Swindon Town–Cheltenham and Southampton–Newbury–Didcot. The B12 hauled trains were also to seen on the Great Western and Southern main lines to Bournemouth and the west, whist there were isolated observations as far afield as Bedford, Northampton, Nottingham and Harrogate. By 1 June 1944, all the trains were at their stabling bases. The aforementioned vacuum control valves caused problems if the train was piloted by a locomotive other than a GWR one as on 16 June instructions were issued that if a vacuumed braked locomotive of the SR, LMSR or LNER was attached in front the vacuum pipes between the two locomotives were not to be coupled leaving the driver of the train engine in sole control of the brakes. According to RCT's *History of the Locomotives of the LNER*, the vacuum control valves were not too reliable and some very jerky stops were made much to the discomfort of the occupants of the ambulance trains. An alternative proposal to replace the B12 with Austerity 2 8 0s was not accepted by the Ambulance Train Committee Beginning in August, the ambulance trains were steadily withdrawn from home service and by the middle of December 1944 all of the ambulance trains, but not the locomotives, had departed for the continent, the last one embarking on 7 December. Balfour says that all of the B12s should have been released by then, but one was observed on a non-Westinghouse braked ambulance train in the Eastleigh district on 30 December 1944, having worked it from Netley into Southampton and then on to the Up main line. Peter Smith, who was a fireman in the latter days of the Somerset and Dorset line, said in *Mendips Engineman* (OPC 1972) that a driver of that line surprised him by claiming to have piloted 'an LNER locomotive to Blandford on an ambulance train during the last war'. He adds that it was a B12. Peter Smith said that the railway photographer Ivo Peters saw a similar train passing over a road bridge near Bitton just after dawn on its way to Bath.

In *Footplate over the Mendips* (OPC 1978), Smith expands a bit more. He said that the pilot engines of such trains, where they were necessary, being vacuum brake fitted were coupled up to the B12 but left the actual braking of the train to the crew of the train engine. This bears out the instruction of 16 June 1944. Smith mentions that the train crew consisted of two drivers, two firemen, one fitter and two guards. He said that one of the ambulance trains (No 36) was berthed at Templecombe and consisted of 14 carriages weighing 435 tons. It had the capacity for 252 patients in a lying position and 64 in a sitting position. The engine that was coupled to it was No 8549, which was shedded at Templecombe. Trains No 27 and 31 were berthed at Bournemouth West carriage sidings and the B12 belonging to them was shedded at Bournemouth. On the Southern Railway on 19 August 1944, No 8549, piloted by former London and South Western T9 No 714, worked a Red Cross ambulance train from Exeter to Clapham Junction, according D L Bradley in the second volume of the *Locomotives of the London and Western Railway* (RCTS 1967).

A week after D Day, the first V (*vergeltungswaffen* – 'retaliation weapons') bombs hit Britain. The first were the V1 flying bombs commencing 13 June 1944 and the second were the V2 rockets commencing on 8 September. The first V1 scored a direct hit on Grove Road railway bridge near Coborn Road station between Bethnal Green and Stratford. Permanent Way Inspector Manning who saw it early that morning of 13 June mistook it for an enemy aircraft approaching at a low altitude. The V1 took out the main lines to Chelmsford, Colchester, Ipswich, Norwich and Yarmouth and local lines to Stratford, Loughton, Epping, Ongar, Ilford Gidea Park Shenfield and Southend along with some surrounding houses. Whilst the damage was being repaired, some trains ran from Fenchurch Street via Bow Road. In repairing the damage, firstly the damaged girders of the bridge were taken away and then temporary timber trestles were erected in front of the existing abutments of the bridge to shorten the span and so enable lighter girders to be used to form a temporary new bridge. The girders were then put in place to carry the two local lines, which were then reopened. This was done within the space of 36 hours. The work to open through lines then followed, taking several days. V1 attacks continued until 27 March 1945 when one hit Orpington. On the same day, the last V2 to hit Britain landed in Vallance Road, East London. The V weapons caused an awful lot of damage both in the London area and outside the capital. One V2 in November 1944 hit Stratford depot and destroyed J17 locomotive No 8200. This was the only former GER locomotive to be destroyed during the Second World War.

With the V weapons there was another evacuation children and mothers from London and Kent. Whilst some went north other went to the south west. By the end of the year the evacuees were starting to return to their homes.

In addition to those ships lost during the evacuation of France, the following other ships were lost during the war. The *Archangel* was bombed on 16 May 1941 whilst on a trooping voyage from Kirkwall to Aberdeen and beached and broke up 5 miles south of Newburgh. The *Amsterdam,* built in 1928, was sunk off Juno Beach on 7 August 1944 whilst serving as a Hospital Carrier. Train ferry No 3 was damaged by a mine off Dieppe on 17 March 1945 and sank the next day.

During the latter stages of the war the Great Eastern section got involved in the supply of food to the Dutch following the Germans cutting off the transport of food and fuel in the part of the Netherlands that they still occupied. The reason for the Germans action was that the Dutch railway workers had gone on strike on 17 September when the Allied offensive towards Arnhem began. Unfortunately, the offensive got bogged down before it reached Arnhem. Eventually the Germans did allow some food and fuel supplies through. These were flown from airfields in the eastern counties and the food was sent to the railheads near them in trains of forty or fifty wagons at a time.

According to Crump, following the liberation of Antwerp on 4 September 1944, sailings from Harwich to Antwerp resumed in 1945 when two leave boats used to arrive and leave Harwich every day. In *Parkeston – A Century of Service* the date is given as 5 November 1945, after the end of the war.

The war in Europe ended on 8 May 1945, VE Day, following the surrender of the German forces. This was followed on 2 September by VJ Day, following the surrender of the Japanese forces.

The Second World War saw the first edition of C.F. Langley Aldrich's *The Locomotives of the Great Eastern Railway*, published in 1944. The *Locomotive Magazine* for April 1944 said of it, 'A well-illustrated book in which is gathered together interesting details of all the locomotive types that existed on the old GER when that company lost its separate identity in 1923, together with particulars of changes that have taken place since then.'

After the war the LNER, along with many other organisations, published the story of it during the war. The book *By Rail To Victory* by Norman Crump came out in 1947.

Chapter 3

From the End of the Second World War to the End of the LNER

This chapter covers the period from the end of the Second World War in 1945 until the winding up of the LNER as a company on 23 December 1949. The period saw the nationalisation of the main railways of Great Britain and the completion of the Central Line electrification from West Ruislip to Epping including the opening of the tunnel under Eastern Avenue and the electrification of the Colchester main line from Liverpool Street to Shenfield.

The General Election of 1945 saw the election of a Labour government who had pledged to nationalise a number of the major industries including the coal mines and the railways. The railways of Britain were nationalised on 1 January 1948, but as mentioned above, the LNER was not wound up until 23 December 1949. Under the railway nationalisation, the LNER was divided into three regions. These were the Eastern Region comprising the lines of the former Great Central, GER and Great Northern railways, the North Eastern Region comprising the lines of the former North Eastern Railway and the Scottish Region comprising the lines of all the lines of the London and North Eastern and LMS railways in Scotland. Initially as part of the LMS, the lines of the former LT&SR were included in the London Midland Region which comprised of the lines of the London Midland and Scottish Railway in England and Wales, but on 20 February 1949 the line was transferred to the Eastern Region.

Following the end of the war things started slowly to return to peacetime conditions. According to the *LNER Magazine* for December 1945, the Harwich to Hook of Holland service resumed on 14 November 1945, the inaugural sailing being undertaken by the *Prague* which had returned from war service. According to the *Magazine* the Chairman, the Directors and the Chief General Manager of the Railway along with the Netherlands Ambassador and his staff arrived at Liverpool Street station at 7.30 pm to witness the departure of the first postwar Hook Continental at 8pm. To celebrate the occasion, the station was bedecked with flags and bunting. The *Magazine* carried an account of the inaugural trip and the return trip. According to Cecil J. Allen in *Titled Trains of Great Britain* (Ian Allan 1967), initially the service was only three time a week but became daily a year later. The following year the *Prague* was joined on the service by the Zeeland

Line's *Oranje Nassau* and in 1947 by the new *Arnhem*. 1946 also saw the resumption of the civilian service to Antwerp as well as the Zeebrugge train ferry service using the surviving train ferry ship (No 1 now named *Essex Ferry*) and the Rotterdam cargo service. On 27 May 1946, the service between Harwich and Denmark was resumed with the arrival of the *Konprins Frederick* from Esjberg.

Following the end of the war, it was decided that all LNER locomotives except for the A4 4-6-2s and the W1 4-6-4 would be painted apple green. The A4s and the W1 were painted garter blue.

In 1946, the LNER introduced a comprehensive re-numbering scheme designed to place all engines of one type in numerical groups so that engine types could be readily identified by the locomotive number, for example all 4-6-0 and the V4 2-6-2 locomotives were numbered in the block 1000 to 1999.

The following classes of locomotive were put into service between the end of the Second World War and the end of the LNER.

Class B2 4-6-0 in 1945 – rebuilds of Class B17, K1 2-6-0 in 1945 a rebuild of Class K4 2-6-0 with new builds in 1949, Class K5 2-6-0 a rebuild of Class K3 2-6-0 in 1945, Class L1 2-6-4 side tank in 1945. Some WD 2-8-0s were purchased by the LNER in 1946 and classed O7.

Class L1 was the first new LNER class to appear after the end of the Second World War. Only the prototype No 9000 was built before nationalisation, after which a further 99 were built. No 67710 originally 9009E is seen leaving Gidea Park for Liverpool Street on 5 October 1949. *Ken Nunn*

Class K1 originated in 1945 as a rebuild of a class K4. In 1949 70 locomotives to a slightly different design appeared. No 62015 is seen near Bishop's Stortford on the 10.20am Temple Mills to Whitemoor goods on 31 August 1951. *Ken Nunn*

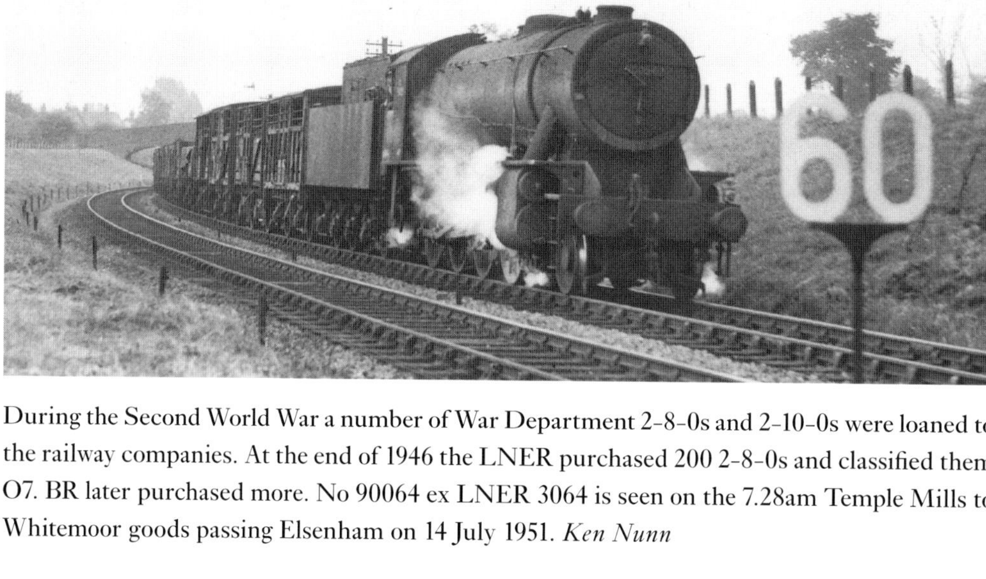

During the Second World War a number of War Department 2-8-0s and 2-10-0s were loaned to the railway companies. At the end of 1946 the LNER purchased 200 2-8-0s and classified them O7. BR later purchased more. No 90064 ex LNER 3064 is seen on the 7.28am Temple Mills to Whitemoor goods passing Elsenham on 14 July 1951. *Ken Nunn*

A 0-6-0 diesel electric shunter whose electric equipment was supplied by Brush was built in 1947 and entered service in 1949.

A 0-6-0 diesel mechanical shunter built by the Vulcan Foundry on behalf of the Drewry Car Company in 1947 ran trials on the GE Section between May and September 1948.

From 14 to 16 June 1946 there was an exhibition in the goods yard at Ipswich to celebrate the centenary of the opening of the Eastern Union Railway from Colchester to Ipswich on 15 June 1846. On display were Class B1 No 1003 Gazelle, L1 No 9000 and diesel electric shunter No 8000.

On 31 December 1947, the last day of the LNER, there was a total of 1,037 locomotives in service on the GE Section plus one waiting to go into service.

Under BR all locomotives originally were given a suffix W for ex-GWR, S for ex-SR, M for ex-LMSR and E for ex-LNER. Later this was changed to ex-GWR retaining their numbers, ex-SR locomotives had 30000 added to their number, ex-LMSR had 40000 and 50000 added to their numbers, ex-LNER had 60000 added to their numbers. Diesel and gas turbine locomotives were given numbers in the series 10000 to 19999, whilst electric locomotives were given numbers in the series 20000 to 299999. BR Standard steam locomotives and ex WD 2-8-0s and 2-10-0s were given numbers in the series 70000 to 99999. BR introduced a classification based on that used by the LMSR.

Class B1 first went into service in 1942 and became the backbone of steam traction on the Great Eastern section until its final demise at the end of 1963. No 1048 is seen at Liverpool Street on 26 April 1947 with the 6 40 pm the down East Anglian for Norwich. *Ken Nunn*

0 to 9F, 0 to 8P and 0 to 7MT. Later new diesel locomotives had the suffix D to their number and new electric locomotives the suffix E to their number. Later still, a class number was used to suffix the numbers of diesel and electric locomotives.

On 7 October 1946, the East Anglian train was restored. The *LNER Magazine* for November 1946 carried an article on both that train and the Yorkshire Pullman, which was restored on 4 November. The *Magazine* included a photograph of the East Anglian passing Stratford behind a B1 class locomotive and not one of the B17 locomotives that had been streamlined for the service in 1937. In April 1951 their streamline cladding was removed.

Following the creation of British Railways two new named trains were introduced. The first was the Norfolkman, introduced in October 1948 and running between London and Norwich. The train departed London in the morning and returned in the evening as opposed to the East Anglian which left Norwich in the morning and returned in the evening. The second was the Fenman, running between London and Hunstanton with a portion for Bury St Edmunds detached or joined at Cambridge. The train left Hunstanton and Bury St Edmunds in the morning and London in the evening. This service introduced a named train to the Cambridge line.

The *LNER Magazine* for December 1946 reported that work had resumed on the London to Shenfield electrification scheme. In connection with the scheme, the flyover at Ilford came into use on 6 October 1947. On 3 December 1946, the London Transport Central Line was extended east from Liverpool Street to Stratford and the Colchester line platforms at Bethnal Green were closed along with Coborn Road station. On 5 May 1947, the Central Line was extended to Leytonstone and westward to Greenford on 30 June. The *LNER Magazine* for July 1947 carried a photograph of the last steam train to leave Liverpool Street for Epping behind a N7 class locomotive, No.9713. The train in question was the 11.29pm train arriving at Epping at 12.25am, according to my 1946-47 suburban timetable. On 30 November, passenger trains were replaced by buses between Ilford and Woodford via Newbury Park. On 14 December, the Central Line was further extended from Leytonstone to Woodford and through the tunnels under Eastern Avenue to Newbury Park. The line from Newbury Park to Hainault depot was electrified to allow ten empty stock trains a day to run to and from the depot. Passenger trains began running from Newbury Park to Hainault on 31 May 1948. On 21 November 1948, the electrification was extended west from Greenford to West Ruislip, east from Woodford to Loughton and from Woodford to Hainault. Briefly before and just after the war there was a possibility that the Hainault line might have provided access to a second London airport. In the late 1930s there was a proposal for an airfield on Fairlop Plain. After the end of the war the proposal was to develop RAF Fairlop, which had been built in late 1940, into a civilian airfield. Neither of the proposals came to anything. On 25 September 1949, electric trains reached Epping. In *The Twopenny Tube*, by J. Graeme Bruce and Desmond F. Croombe (Capital Transport 1996), considerable high level discussions were devoted to the merits of the further extension of the electrification from Loughton to Epping, but the presence of the large London County Council housing estate at Debden and the partially completed electrification swung the decision in favour of completing the electrification to Epping, The extension from West Ruislip to Denham was abandoned and for the time being the section from Epping to Ongar remained steam worked. This date also saw the transfer of the section from Loughton Branch Junction to Ongar from British Railways to London Transport. This piecemeal opening contrasted with the prewar proposals which envisaged extending the Central Line from Liverpool Street to Loughton and Woodford to Grange Hill in one fell swoop. Certainly, one cannot imagine, particularly between 5 May and 14 December 1947 when the Central Line only extended as far east as Leytonstone, that travel from places east or from other places to places east was particularly easy. Despite the extension of the electrification, there were still a few trains for staff and on Sundays the public worked by the LNER and later British Railways until 1970. The Underground timetables for the spring of 1958 show two

London Transport Central Line electric trains reached Epping on 25 September 1949, but the section from there to Ongar still remained operated by BR for London Transport. An F5 is seen at Epping with an LT train of Standard Tube Stock some time in the early to mid-1950s. *Author's collection*

trains on Sunday mornings from Liverpool Street to Epping and return. Motive power for the main service was provided by LT Standard Tube Stock dating from 1923 to 1934 and for the shuttles 1935 Tube Stock dating from 1936.

On the electrification to Shenfield, when work had ceased for the duration of the war. some of the bridge reconstructions and station and signalling alterations were advanced, and the Ilford flyover had been completed but not brought into use. Six miles of overhead gantries had been erected between Harold Wood and Brentwood and the emplacements for them prepared from Brentwood to Shenfield. The body shells of the first six electric trains had been completed and Ilford locomotive depot had closed in May 1939 in preparation for the site to be used for the new electric train carriage depot. The new electric depot was completed by the end of February 1949. Work now started on building the remaining eighty-six units. The re-signalling between Gidea Park and Liverpool Street was restarted. On restarting of the electrification, a number of changes were made to the original scheme. The proposed station at Crowlands was abandoned and both the slow and fast lines between Gidea Park and Shenfield were to be electrified, and not just the slow lines as originally proposed. By 23 March 1949, work had progressed such that the electric power was switched on between Ilford and Chadwell Heath and trial running began. By the middle of September, sufficient progress had been made that it was possible to commence carrying fare-paying passengers. The full resignalling with colour light signals from Gidea Park to Liverpool Street was completed in stages from Gidea Park to Liverpool Street, with Liverpool Street station being the last one. The service was inaugurated on Monday 26 September by the Minister of Transport, Alfred Barnes MP, who drove an electric train from Liverpool Street to Stratford. The *Daily Herald* of 27 September carried a photograph of him in the driver's cab of the first electric train to leave Liverpool Street station with the driver A.G. Turner. The *Essex Newsman* of 27 September, reporting the inauguration of the electric service, said that Chelmsford was high on the priority list for an extension of the electric railway from Shenfield. A high-ranking member of British Railways engineering executive had said in answer to a question, 'We have a whole system of electrification extensions under review. Chelmsford is high on the list.' The newspaper also said that 200 workmen had worked against time throughout the weekend including Sunday to get everything ready for the opening. Unfortunately, the day was marred by the steam locomotive of a Southend train developing some trouble which caused the train to be forty minutes late into Liverpool Street with the result that many trains lost their paths and this caused more congestion. It was not until 7 November that the full electric service came into operation. The day before, there had been a dress rehearsal held in which the public were allowed to travel on the trains. Unfortunately, the first day of the full service did not go well as the overhead line came down at Seven Kings. During the interim, the service had been operated by a mixture of electric and steam trains. One part of the original proposed electric service that was not proceeded with was the electrification from Bow Junction to Fenchurch Street. The last train from Fenchurch Street via Bow Road and Bow Junction running on 5 November as there was no Sunday service on the line. Bow Road station was closed. The reason given being to give more capacity to the LT&SR line services over the two-track section of line from Stepney East to Gas Factory Junction. However, although the shuttle service from Fenchurch Street to Stratford was abandoned, the line from Platforms 1 and 2 at Fenchurch Street to Bow Junction was electrified, primarily for diversion and emergency use. To ensure that the system worked, empty electric trains ran to and from Fenchurch Street. According to Peter Kay in Volume 4 of his *History of the LT&SR*, the Southend-on-Sea Railway Travellers Association regarded the Fenchurch Street to Stratford electrification as a 'wicked waste of money'. The last GE train into Fenchurch Street was the 12.12pm from Ilford hauled by Class L1 No 67727, whilst fellow class member No 67726 worked the last GE train out of Fenchurch Street – 12.53pm to Gidea Park. The last steam train on the Liverpool Street to Shenfield service was the 5.15pm to Gidea Park on the same day worked by L1 No 67718 decorated with a Union Jack and a laurel wreath.

The Liverpool Street to Shenfield electrification proved to be a great success. In the first nine months after the opening, passenger numbers were up 49.5 per cent compared with the corresponding period of the previous year. Prior to the nationalisation of railways, the LNER had developed plans for the postwar years. The Company intended to electrify from King's Cross to Hitchin and Liverpool Street to Chingford, Palace Gates, Enfield and Hertford East.

Motive power consisted of ninety-two 3-car emus of which the first six body shells had been built in 1940 and rest after 1945. They became BR Class 306. There was a BoBo electric locomotive used at Ilford carriage sidings and which had originally been built in 1914 for the NER's Newport to Shildon electrification, but was stored following the cessation of the electrification in 1935 and it was converted for use as a banker on the Manchester to Sheffield electrification. This use never materialised.

The use of diesel railcars in the post war period was looked at. According to the Summer 1947 edition of *Railway Pictorial*, 'a considerable number of diesel railcars are proposed for secondary services, running singly or in pairs. These would be diesel-mechanical, each of 105 bhp', but nothing further came of it due to the nationalisation of the railways. According to *Railways* for January 1948, the LNER Board had approved a proposal for the purchase of 176 350hp diesel electric shunters. Again, nothing further came of it due to nationalisation. There was also the proposal for the construction

The first three car emus entered service between Liverpool Street and Shenfield on 26 September 1949 and on 7 November the full service came into operation. The 12.38pm Liverpool Street to Gidea Park comprised of three units is seen arriving at Gidea Park on 5 October 1949. *Ken Nunn*

of twenty-five diesel-electric locomotive units designed for working that Company's heaviest main line passenger trains on the East Coast route between London and Scotland in replacement of thirty-two express steam locomotives. 'The Diesel units, each of 1,600bhp at the generator couplings, would have been used in pairs to form 3,200hp locomotives.'

April and May 1949 saw one of the first fruits of nationalisation when a former Southern Railway Battle of Britain class 4-6-2 or Pacific type ran trials on the Great Eastern Section. This was not the only former Southern Railway designed equipment to appear on the Section. Tavern Cars which had been designed by the Southern Railway's last Chief Mechanical Engineer, Oliver Bullied, could be described as a pub on wheels in a mock-Tudor appearance inside. They had rather small windows, with fake brick walls on the outside, and even a pub sign on the door. They each even had a traditional pub name. Three were allocated to the Great Eastern Section on the Norfolkman and North Country Continental, which latter required 2-cars. They had a mixed reception. The exterior brickwork was seemingly removed in early 1950, and by the middle of 1951 they had been remodelled into a slightly more conventional layout and more windows installed. In 1959, some £22,900 was spent refurbishing them into conventional dining cars.

The first 4-6-2 or Pacific type locomotive to work on the GE section was ex Southern No 34059 *Sir Archibald Sinclair* in April and May 1949. The locomotive is seen leaving Norwich for Liverpool Street with 5 pm Norfolkman on 18 May 1949. *Ken Nunn*

During the period of this chapter, a number of passenger services were withdrawn, principally on 6 October 1947 the former Ramsey Railway from Home to Ramsey North which prior to 1923 had been owned by the GER but was worked by the Great Northern Railway. The other was as mentioned the line from Fenchurch Street to Stratford.

The winter of 1946–47 was not a good one for the Great Eastern section. There was a ban on overtime and Sunday working by fitters at Stratford locomotive depot, an accident at Gidea Park on 2 January 1947, a collision between two Central Line trains at Drapers' Field just east of Stratford on 5 December 1946 and the harsh winter of 1946–47.

The ban on overtime and Sunday working by 290 fitters and mechanics at Stratford began on 25 November 1946. The cause was a demand for a wage bonus to bring their pay more in line with piece work rates. On 26 November, the LNER wrote to the men's union, the Amalgamated Engineering Union, that it was examining the fitters' claim and asking the Union to ensure normal working at Stratford. The result of the dispute was the cancellation of a number of trains. To give one example, on 31 December, sixty-nine suburban trains and one main line train had to be cancelled. According to the *News Chronicle* of 13 January 1947, on the LNER, fifty-five trains using Liverpool Street and Fenchurch Street stations had been cancelled on Mondays to Fridays and others had been retimed because of the dispute. The *Daily Herald* of the same day said that by withdrawing a number of trains and retiming a number of others, it was hoped to lessen the inconvenience to passengers. The dispute was ended when it was agreed to pay several thousand locomotive repair men throughout the country an allowance equal to a one third increase of their basic wage. The allowance came into effect on 27 January 1947 and as a result ended the dispute at Stratford, which at one time had put 200 out of the 520 locomotives used on the section out of service.

Following the opening of the Central Line from Liverpool Street to Stratford on 3 December 1946, as there was insufficient room at Stratford for the trains to reverse it was necessary for them to run through the tunnels as far as Drapers' Field to reverse. On 5 December, a fatal accident occurred. At 10.38am, following a signal failure, trains were moving under the 'stop and proceed rule' when a rear end collision occurred because the colliding train was driven too fast. In the accident, the driver of the offending train was injured as were two of the three Signal Engineer's staff travelling with him in the driver's cab to investigate the signal failure. Sadly, the third member of the Signal Engineer's staff was killed. Less than a month after this accident, another accident occurred. On 2 January 1947 in fog at about 11.17pm, the 10.23pm train from Liverpool Street to Southend hauled by Class B12/3 locomotive No 1565 was run into at Gidea Park by the 10.25pm train from Liverpool Street to Peterborough hauled by Class B17 locomotive No 1602 *Walsingham*. In the collision, seven passengers lost their lives and forty-five people were detained in hospital for injuries. All four lines through the station were blocked, but two were cleared within a couple of hours and the rest by noon the following day. The cause of the accident was the mistake by the driver of the Peterborough train to continue running at a fairly high speed in the fog on the section of line between Romford and Gidea Park whilst uncertain of his location.

December 1946 to March 1947 were particularly harsh months. 21 January to 15 March were particularly snowy .and were followed by prolonged rain for the rest of the month. The *Lynn Advertiser* of 14 February reported that passenger trains on the Wells branch from Heacham were unable to run because of snow drifts and goods trains could only get as far as Docking. Special bus services were put on to take passengers from Heacham to Wells. Train services to Norwich were considerably affected by drifts at Dereham. The *LNER Magazine* of March 1947 reported that during the weekend of 8-9 February 'acute difficulties developed in East Anglia, and nearly all the branches in North Norfolk became snowbound'. *The Times* of 29 January 1947 and the *LNER Magazine* of March 1947 recorded snow drifts 5ft deep between Burnham-on-Crouch and Southminster. *The Times* said that the drifts had been cleared by snow ploughs. The thaw brought its own problems on 17 March. After an engineer's occupation of the line between Rayleigh and Hockley on the Southend line, the locomotive of a Southend to London train somersaulted down an embankment and landed upside down. The fireman of the locomotive sustained some slight injuries, but the driver and the passengers were uninjured. The cause of the accident was subsidence trouble with that section of the embankment.

Chapter 4

From the End of the LNER to the Beeching Report

The period from the final dissolution of the LNER under British Railways in 1949 to the publication of the notorious Beeching Report in 1963 was a period of great change. It saw the former GER lines reach their peak compared to the rest of Britain's railways – a peak in relative terms that would never be reached again. It saw modernisation with further electrifications to Chelmsford, Southend, Bishop's Stortford, Chingford and Enfield, Colchester, Clacton and Walton-on-the-Naze as well as Ongar and the majority of the former LT&SR. Whilst it saw the introduction of more steam motive power, principally in the form of British Railways' Britannia Class 4-6-2 locomotives, it also saw the further introduction of diesel traction and ultimately the virtual elimination of steam power from the east of England. Although the period saw the reopening to passenger traffic of one line – the Churchbury loop in North East Middlesex – it also saw the withdrawal of a number of passenger services and some goods services and one sea route. There was one major strike during this period – that by the footplatemen's union ASLEF in 1955. Finally, the period also saw the notorious East Coast floods of 1953.

Modernisation when it came was first in the form of new steam locomotives. Under Robert Riddles, the Chief Mechanical Engineer of British Railways, a series of Standard steam locomotives were designed and built capable of being operated on any of the six Regions of British Railways. The building of some pre-nationalisation locomotive also continued.

Gerard Fiennes, who was the Assistant Superintendent of the Eastern Region at Liverpool Street, wrote in his autobiography *I Tried to Run a Railway*, that he and Stuart Ward, the head of the Passenger Section at Liverpool Street, decided to speed up the Norwich service. Thompson's B1 4-6-0s dating from 1942 which were the principal locomotives in use on the service, were not much of an improvement on Holden's B12 4-6-0s dating from 1911 which had a tractive effort of over 20,000lb. Geoffrey Hughes in *The Gresley Influence* says the same thing. According to Fiennes, the B1s would want water on the way and need coal at each end of the journeys. Fiennes had heard that the first of the new Standard locomotives was to be a 4-6-2 with a tractive effort of over

30,000lb. According to him, at that time, the engine building programmes were in the hands of a committee chaired by the Assistant Superintendents – in the Great Eastern section's case, him. Twenty-five of the new 4-6-2s were substituted for twenty-five B1s. Fiennes' account is contradictory to that of D.L. Bradley in *Locomotives of the Southern Railway Part 2* (RCTS 1976), who mentions the proposal in early 1949 to transfer fifteen ex Southern Railway West Country/Battle of Britain 4-6-2s to the Great Eastern section to replace a similar number of B1, B2 and B17 4-6-0s on express trains on the section and which saw the trial on the Great Eastern Section in April and May 1949 of Battle of Britain Class 4 6 2 No 34059 *Sir Archibald Sinclair.* According to Fiennes, to minimise the amount of faith about the new engines known as the Britannias (as the class was commonly known from the name of the first member of the class No 70000) two Battle of Britain locomotives were borrowed from the Southern Region for trials. Bradley makes no mention of this, saying instead that in April 1951 thoughts turned to replacing B1s on many of the secondary services in East Anglia. In May 1951 three Southern 4-6-2s – Nos 34039 *Boscastle*, No 34057 *Biggin Hill* and No 34065 *Hurricane* – were sent to the Great Eastern section. According to Fiennes, when Sir Michael Barrington-Ward, the Operating Member of the Railway Executive and the Chairman of its most influential committee, found out what was happening, he was initially against it, regarding the Great Eastern section as a 'tramline' and wanted the section to have the originally intended B1s instead. Fiennes said that he told Barrington-Ward that that was not possible as the new timetable based around the Britannias had already been printed. Barrington-Ward relented, save for reducing the number of Britannias allocated to the section to twenty-three. Fiennes says that with the introduction of the Britannias for a brief period of six months 'until the North Eastern caught up with us the Great Eastern tram line could have the fastest train in Britain', which with the 3.30pm from Liverpool Street to Norwich. According to the *Railway Magazine* for March 1951, the naming of the first of the Britannias had taken place at Marylebone station on 30 January and had entered service on the Eastern Region two days later. The second member of the class, No 70001 *Lord Hurcomb,* was named by its namesake, the Chairman of the British Transport Commission, at Liverpool Street station on 6 March 1951. The *Saffron Walden Weekly News* of Friday, 23 February 1951 reported that Mr C.K. Bird, the Chief Regional Officer of British Railways, in a speech at the Cambridge District station masters' annual luncheon on the previous Saturday, had said that that year the Eastern Region would be getting fifteen of the new locomotives, which had high steaming capacity and great acceleration and would be allocated mainly to the Colchester line and would mean sharp timing to Ipswich and Norwich. The locomotives did have their teething problems and when on 22 October 1951 No 70004 *William*

Shakespeare broke a connecting rod at Headcorn on the Southern Region whilst working the prestigious Golden Arrow express, all of the Britannia class were withdrawn from service for modification. On the Great Eastern section, until the modifications were complete, a further two Battle of Britain class locomotives were borrowed from the Southern Region, No 34076 *41 Squadron* and No 34089 *602 Squadron*. The section also borrowed two new British Railways Standard Class 5 4 6 0s from the London Midland Region – Nos 73000 and 73002.

The following other classes of steam locomotive worked for a time on the GE Section:

BR Standard 2 2-6-0 in 1962 and Standard 4 2 6 4 side tank in the same year.
Standard 4 2-6-0 in 1951. Five were allocated to the GE Section until the end of 1962.
Standard 9F 2-10-0 in 1954. A number were for a time allocated to the Section. Mostly at March, but in 1955 one was allocated to Stratford.
Briefly in 1958 Standard Class 6 4-6-2. The idea behind it was to allocate some members of the Class to the Section and release some Britannias for service elsewhere on British Railways. The trial was not a success. The Clans, as the Class was known, looked like a Britannia, but with a slightly smaller boiler and not much more tractive effort than a B1.

British Railways Standard 7MT 4-6-2s or Britannias were the locomotives that transformed the GE section giving it for a short time the fastest train in Great Britain. No 70006 *Robert Burns* is seen entering Liverpool Street with the 11 49 Up East Anglian on 6 May 1951. Note the dynamometer car in the formation. *Ken Nunn*

A somewhat rarer Standard class was the 9F 2-10-0s. No 92014 was allocated to Stratford shed in 1955 and is seen passing Cheshunt on 25 April 1955 with a Whitemoor to Temple Mills coal train. 9Fs could not work beyond Stratford because of their weight. *Ken Nunn*

Ex LMS classes 3P 4-4-2 side tank dating from 1923 based on the LTSR 79 class,
2 MT 2-6-0s, 4 MT 2 6 0s
Fowler Class 4 MT 2-6-4 side tank
Fairburn Class 4 MT 2-6-4 side tank,
4F 0-6-0 and 3F 0 6 0 side tanks and briefly a 2MT 2-6-2 side tank.
Twice a Stanier 3 cylinder 4 MT 2-6-4 side tanks visited Southend GE.

Ex GCR design class A5, both in Norfolk and on the Liverpool Street to Southend service when the turntable at Liverpool Street was being enlarged in 1951 to take the Britannia class. A Class N5 was used on the Wickford to Southminster branch during the time push-pull working was in use on the branch, whilst the line from Shenfield to Southend was being electrified. Previously one had spent three months working from Stratford in 1935. In 1938 one had been tried on the Felixstowe branch. In BR days, the locomotive used on the Southminster branch also worked on the Epping–Ongar line

Ex NER design J72.

Two briefly at Ipswich from May 1950 to February 1952

Only one former GWR design locomotive was ever allocated to the GE Section – 9400 Class 0-6-0 pannier tank No 9401 from January to June 1957 at Stratford.

In the 1950s, a number of former LMS version of the LTSR class 79 4-4-2 tank locomotives worked on the GE section. In this photograph we see No 41949 at Wivenhoe on the Tendring Hundred lines on 7 July 1956. *Photomatic*

A number of former London, Midland and Scottish Railway designed locomotives appeared on the GE section after nationalisation. Five class 2MT 2 6 0s were split between Cambridge and Colchester. No 46465 is seen leaving Colchester with the 5 30 pm Clacton to Cambridge via the Colne Valley and Halstead line on 5 August 1951. *Ken Nunn*

In Cambridgeshire, the Wisbech and Upwell tramway in 1952 became the first railway in Britain to be totally operated by diesel traction, when following successful trials two 0-6-0 Drewry diesel mechanical shunters took over the working of the line on 5 July 1952. Until March 1953, class J70 0-6-0 tram locomotive No 68222 stayed on the line as a backup. Like their steam predecessors, the diesels had their wheels covered by side plates and had cowcatchers at each end. The *Lynn Advertiser* of 13 June 1952 reported that the old steam locomotives on the Upwell tramway were being replaced by modern diesel locomotives.

British Railways was looking into the use diesel multiple units (dmus) and a report in 1952 recommended the trialling of lightweight dmus. A memo to the British Railways' Board that year suggested that they could replace steam operated push-pull trains on 168 routes. That year, fuel rationing, which had been in force since the early days of the Second World War, ended and an order was placed in November for twenty-one 2-car units built at Derby Works and which became known the Derby Lightweights. The new diesel units were delivered in 1954 and 1955. The first ones in the Eastern Counties went into service on the lines from Norwich to Dereham and Wells-on-Sea and Dereham and Kings Lynn on 19 September 1955 following trial running in late April 1955. The diesel trains also took over the Norwich–Cromer–Sheringham-Holt service on Sundays, according to the *Lynn Advertiser* of 2 September that year.

The AVC/BUT demonstrator 3-car rail bus was built in 1952 and was tried out on the Epping to Ongar line in the summer of 1952 and on the Wickford to Southminster line in 1953. The train is seen here at Southminster in September 1953. *Frank Church*

Even before then, dmus had appeared in the Eastern Counties, when the AVC/BUT demonstrator 3-car rail bus built in 1952 was tried out on the Epping to Ongar in the summer of 1952 and the Wickford to Southminster line in 1953.

They were not the only rail buses to see service on the GE Section. In 1958, British Railways took delivery of five *Waggon und Maschinenbau* four-wheel rail buses. They went into traffic on 7 July that year. They worked on a number of lines including the branches to Braintree, Maldon, Saffron Walden, Mildenhall and the former Colne Valley and Halstead Railway. The *Saffron Walden Weekly News* of Friday 4 July carried an article on the new raibuses accompanied by a photograph of one on the occasion of a demonstration run on the Saffron Walden branch that had taken place that week. Whilst the new railbus had accommodation for 56 seated passengers and 40 standing passengers, there was no provision for large parcels, which in future would have to be carried by lorry.

On the electrified section of line between Ilford and Shenfield in November 1950, four of the Class EM1 Bo-Bo electric locomotives destined for the Manchester to Sheffield electrification underwent running trials with passenger and goods stock.

There was an extension of the London to Shenfield electrification beyond Shenfield to Chelmsford on the main line and to Southend. The *News Chronicle* of Monday 28 September 1953 carried an article which was headed 'All electric to Southend – by 1957'. According to the article, British Railways were to extend the Liverpool Street–Shenfield

In 1958 the German company of *Waggon und Maschinenbau* of Donauworth supplied five railbuses. They were used on the Maldon, Braintree, Saffron Walden, Colne Valley and Mildenhall lines, but were not a great success. No E79963 is seen arriving at Audley End with the 11.55am from Bartlow on 19 July 1958. *Ken Nunn*

Prior to their entering service on the Manchester to Sheffield and Wath line, some EM1 electric locomotives undertook running in trials between Ilford and Shenfield. No 26002 is seen passing Chadwell Heath on 11.55am Ilford to Shenfield test train on 5 November 1950. *Ken Nunn*

electric line to Chelmsford and Southend (Victoria) – i.e., the Great Eastern section station in Southend. The work should be completed by January 1957, when the time for the journey from Liverpool Street to Southend would be one hour. There would be even faster trains in the mornings and evenings. The cost of the scheme would be about £2.5 million. The extension formed part of a bigger electrification scheme from Fenchurch Street to Tilbury and Southend (Central) – i.e., the LT&SR section. According to the *Daily Herald* of the same day, Chelmsford would be served by the extension of twenty-two of the existing trains from Liverpool Street to Shenfield to that town, whilst specially designed all-steel trains to suit daily travellers and holiday makers would be built for the Southend service. The *Daily Herald* makes the same point about the electrification in connection with the LT&SR section electrification scheme. From the papers in the National Archive, originally the electrification was to go further along the main line to Colchester and to Ipswich.

The electrification work involved quite a bit of disruption. On the main line, some services beyond Witham were diverted via Bishop's Stortford and Braintree. On the Southend line, some single line working was introduced and during the peak hours, buses replaced trains that ran contrary to the peak flow. Off peak, some trains were doubled headed to compensate for unbalanced engine workings. On the Southminster line, push-pull workings were introduced to ease operations at Wickford.

On Thursday, 7 June 1956 the Mayor of Chelmsford, Alderman Fred Woods drove the train for part of the journey of the first official electric train from Liverpool Street to Chelmsford. The electric service to Chelmsford commenced on Monday 11 June 1956.

On 28 December, the formal opening of the electrification to Southend took place when a party of invited guests travelled to Southend, where after formalities had been completed the party travelled to London in one of the new electric trains, which the Mayor of Southend, Alderman Herbert Smith, drove part of the way. On 30 December, in preparation for the commencement of full electric services the following day, apart from one train just after midnight all of the Down trains from Liverpool Street to Southend and a few of the Up trains were worked by the new electric trains whilst most of the up trains were worked by steam. Railway enthusiasts had a field day travelling over the Southend line behind steam for the last time. The new electric trains for the Southend service had a mixture of compartment and open carriages in their four-carriage formation. The last steam train into Southend was on 30 December as the 12.15am from Liverpool Street was hauled by B12 No 61553. The last steam train from Southend on 30 December was the 8.50pm to Liverpool Street hauled by B1 No 61335. The first public electric train to Southend on 30 December was the 8.4am from Shenfield worked by unit 31s. The first public electric train from Liverpool Street to Southend was the 11.15am worked by units 02s and 04s.

In September 1953, British Railways announced the extension of the electrification from Shenfield to Chelmsford and to Southend. In this photograph we see an unidentified B1 on a Southend train arriving at Billericay in about 1953 prior to the electrification. *David Collins*

In this photograph taken between Billericay and Wickford, we see the uprights for the overhead gantries having been laid are being hoisted into position by use of a steam crane which can just be made out in the background. *David Collins*

In this photograph taken between Billericay and Wickford, we see the uprights for the overhead gantries being stabilised using in part power operated tools. The electrification was done within the time scale allotted and within budget. *David Collins*

With the uprights in position in this photograph that was taken in Billericay we see the crossbar of one of the overhead gantries being fixed into position. One has to say that compared with later years, the lack of hard hats and other safety equipment is noticeable. *David Collins*

With just over a week before the commencement of electric services between Liverpool Street and Southend, we find an unidentified K3 on a Down Southend train near Billericay on 23 December 1956. *Frank Church*

Whilst the existing Shenfield stock was used for the Chelmsford service, new 4-car emus were built for the service to Southend. In this photograph, taken not long after the start of the electrification, we see unit 05s leading a Liverpool Street train just having left Billericay. *David Collins*

The Southminster line also saw new trains when dmus took over the service on 17 September 1956. The decision to convert the Southminster line to diesel power was the reason for the trial of the diesel train on the line in 1953. On the same day the Romford to Upminster section of the LT&SR line went over to diesel operation. Diesel trains also took over a number of other services in the Eastern Counties.

There was an increase in the use of diesel shunters. Steam did not disappear from the electrified sections of line. Goods and parcels trains as well as excursion trains to and from the electrified sections continued to be operated by steam as did through trains originating or terminating beyond the electrified section of the main line as well as the Southminster line.

In the mid- to late 1950s, the Great Eastern section of British Railways was one of those treasure troves for those looking for antiquated motive power and rolling stock. There were still long funnelled locomotives dating back to the later part of the nineteenth century and early twentieth century hauling carriages and wagons of the same vintage working alongside the most modern motive power and rolling stock. All of that was to change under British Railways modernisation scheme.

The Derby Lightweight dmus were British Railways' first production dmus and first appeared in 1954 with the first ones operating on the GE section in September 1955. On 17 September 1956 they took over the working of the Wickford to Southminster line. One is seen at Woodham Ferrers on the first day of operation. *Frank Church*

Up to the mid- to late 1950s, the GE section of BR was a delight for those looking for types of locomotives which had mainly disappeared elsewhere. This photograph taken at Norwich on 18 May 1949 shows D16/3 No 62581 departing for Lowestoft with 10.40am ex York. In the background is Battle of Britain class No 34059 *Sir Archibald Sinclair* on the Up Norfolkman. *Ken Nunn*

B12/3s up until the end of 1956 were one of the principal types of locomotives on the Liverpool Street to Southend service. This photograph taken in the summer of 1953 shows No 61550 arriving at Wickford on a train bound for the seaside resort. *Frank Church*

By 1955, the E4 class locomotives were the last 2-4-0s working on BR. Amongst other lines, the Mildenhall branch was one of the lines that they worked. On 22 September 1956 No 62796 is seen at the terminus at Mildenhall waiting to depart for Cambridge. *Photomatic*

The class J15 were the backbone of the GE section from their introduction in 1883 until their final withdrawal in 1962. These locomotives could work all over the system. No 65464 is seen at Long Melford on the Stour Valley lines on 31 July 1958. *Frank Church*

On 25 January 1955, the government announced a £1,240 million 15-year budget for 'Better and Brighter railways'. Under the plan, £210 million would be spent on new tracks and signalling to raise speeds, £345 million on several thousand electric or diesel locomotives and track electrification, £285 million on modernising or replacing carriages by multiple unit electric or diesel trains and modernising stations and parcels depots, £365 million on remodelling freight services and marshalling yards and £35 million on ports, research, welfare and offices. In relation to the Eastern Region, it was proposed: on the Great Northern section to electrify from King's Cross and Moorgate to Hitchin and Letchworth including the Hertford loop and Doncaster and Leeds and possibly York; on the Great Eastern section to electrify to Chingford, Enfield, Hertford and Bishop's Stortford and to Ipswich; the LT&SR line would be electrified. The plan proposed the elimination of steam traction but according to the report in the *Daily Herald* of that day, some steam would last until 2000. The *Daily Mirror* of the same date says broadly the same thing, but that the extension of the electrification on the Great Eastern section to Ipswich would include the Clacton, Harwich and Felixstowe branches. In reading the summary of the report, there is no mention of the electrification system to be used, although one would assume that it would be the then existing systems, which in the case of the Great Eastern Section would be 1,500 volts dc overhead power. In March

1956 British Railways announced the decision to use a high voltage 50 cycle alternating current system of overhead electrification on amongst others the lines out of Liverpool Street. This meant that the existing lines of Liverpool Street and Fenchurch Street had to be converted to alternating current along with the trains using them.

The first tests of alternating current electrification on the Great Eastern section took place in March 1956 when the section of the overhead from Fenchurch Street to Bow Junction was fed electricity at 6,600 volts alternating current for establishing safety clearances. The train used was a former London and North Western Railway direct current emu dating from 1914 which been converted to run on alternating current in 1952 to run on the former Midland Railway branch from Lancaster to Morecambe and Heysham which had first been electrified in 1908. The *Locomotive Magazine* for January-February 1957 carried a photograph of the train at Fenchurch Street taken by G.M. Kitchenside.

The electrification to Hertford and Bishop's Stortford saw the reopening to passenger traffic of the Churchbury loop from Lower Edmonton to Cheshunt rather than the Lea Valley line; that service would be worked by diesel traction. The reason for the reopening was that since 1945 further development had taken place. The line was now to be called the Southbury line.

On the main line following a re-appraisal of the Modernisation Plan in 1959, it was decided to defer electrification beyond Colchester and on the Great Northern section until after 1964. The Government White Paper in which this was announced recommended that Bishop's Stortford to Cambridge be electrified as partial compensation. Because of spiralling operating deficits, this led to the abandonment for the time being of the latter proposal along with some other electrification proposals. Work on the remaining Great Eastern and LT&SR sections electrifications continued. Only the electrification of London Midland Region main lines from London to Birmingham, Crewe, Manchester and Liverpool survived of the proposed main line electrifications.

In order to test the new electrification system, British Railways needed a couple of lines on which to try it out. For the London Midland Region, this was the Styal Line near Manchester. For the Eastern Region, it was the line from Colchester to Clacton including the branches to St Botolph's station in Colchester and from Thorpe-le-Soken to Walton-on-the-Naze. This had the merits of having double- and single-track lines with a diesel operated branch line off the line at Wivenhoe and steam and diesel operated through services from London and other places as well excursion trains and goods trains.

The reason for choosing the new system was that it drew less current and needed fewer substations than the existing system of overhead electrification. Whilst the voltage of the new electrification system was to be 25,000 volts, where there was inadequate clearance above the wires such as tunnels and overbridges, a lower voltage of 6,250 volts was used. This was handy as it meant that the overhead gantries of the existing 1,500 electrification did not need to be replaced. Only on the section of line from Shenfield to Chelmsford was the latter done, the work being carried out between 12 September 1960 and 20 March 1961. During that time a replacement dmu shuttle service worked between the two places in addition to through trains.

The decision to electrify the Clacton and Walton lines was decided in late 1957 and in January 1959 trials began using some 4-car emus that been built for the forthcoming LT&SR line electrification. Public operation began on 16 March with a revised half hourly timetable coming into operation on 13 April. The 8-carriage trains ran from an electrified bay platform at Colchester and ran to Thorpe-le-Soken where they divided, with half going to Clacton and half going to Walton. In the reverse direction the reverse happened.

At Colchester, in connection with the forthcoming extension of the electrification, a fly-under from the Down main line to the Down Clacton line was constructed and was completed in 1962. At the same time the whole station was remodelled with a new station building on the north side of the lines.

Electrification work on the lines from Liverpool Street to Chingford, Enfield, Hertford East and Bishop's Stortford was begun in 1956 and the new services started on 21 November 1960 following the introduction of the new electric trains on Chingford and Enfield services in steam timings on 14 November. The last steam suburban train out of Liverpool Street was the 10.25pm to Hertford East on 20 November, hauled by class N7 locomotive No 69685. The last steam suburban train into Liverpool Street was the 9.40pm from Broxbourne on the same day, hauled by N7 No. 69718. During the period of the electrification, occasionally trains to Enfield were diverted to run via the original route via Angel Road. For the new electric services two types of train were provided. For the Chingford and Enfield services, 3-carriage trains of open stock which, unlike those provided for the Shenfield electrification, had slam doors as opposed to air operated sliding doors. For the unelectrified Lea Valley, a 3-carriage diesel version of the electric trains was provided. For the Bishop's Stortford and Hertford services 4-carriage trains were provided which were similar to those used on the Southend service, comprising a mixture of compartment and open carriages.

On the line from Liverpool Street to Shenfield and Southend conversion to alternating current took place between 4 and 6 November 1960. Prior to that, some of the Shenfield units and one of the Southend units had been converted to run on alternating current. This involved the units being fitted with a transformer and rectifier fed by 1,500-volt direct current. For the start of the new service, some of the converted Shenfield units and some of the units built for the LT&SR line were provided. These latter had been taken to Southend Victoria. Originally, diesel locomotives had been employed to do the job, but following a runaway and collision at Wickford on 1 November, class L1 steam locomotives were employed. This was because whilst the diesel locomotives had vacuum brakes, the electric units and the steam locomotives were equipped with air brakes. The conversion of the rest of the direct current units took some time. The trusty class L1 locomotives were employed to haul the units at Southend away for conversion. Whilst the line from Liverpool Street to Southend was converted to 6,250 volts, that between Shenfield and Chelmsford was converted to 25,000 volts. This took place between 12 September 1960 and 20 March 1961. Because of the two voltages, all the electric trains had to be dual voltage.

On the LT&SR line, electrification of the line other than the Romford to Upminster branch, the Thames Haven branch and the Tottenham and Forest Gate and Tottenham and Hampstead lines was completed with the first electric trains running in service on 6 November 1961 and the full service commencing on 18 June 1962.

With the spread of the electrification and the impending extension from Chelmsford to Colchester, more electric units were needed and so some more 4-car units were built, which, unlike the Shenfield, Southend and LT&SR units which had flat fronts, had piano style fronts like those built for the North East London electrification. A few units of the new type, but which had a luggage van in their formation for use on boat trains from Fenchurch Street to Tilbury, were also built.

On the North East London electrification all was not well with the trains provided for the services which had their electrical equipment supplied by GEC, as opposed to English Electric in the existing units, including the new units built for the existing lines. Until the problems were fixed, it was necessary to use some of the units built for the LT&SR line and some of the new units built for the existing electrified lines as mentioned earlier, as well as to borrow some 4-car units from the London Midland Region which had been built for local services out of Manchester. Some of the latter also turned up on services to Chelmsford and Southend.

On the main line, the gap in the electrification between Chelmsford and Colchester was closed on 18 June 1962. Until the new trains ordered for the service had been delivered and tested, some services were operated by diesel trains and others by outer suburban electric trains including the entire Sunday service. The idea of borrowing some electric locomotives from the London Midland Region to haul through trains from London was considered. Deliveries of the new electric trains began in late 1962 with the first one entering service on 7 January and the full electric service on 17 June 1963. The *Daily Herald* in its report of 8 January headed it 'Supertrain Flashes In'.

According to the newspaper, the trains were luxurious, had a griddle car which was a kind of buffet car and were capable of 90mph. On that latter the newspaper was wrong; they were capable 100mph.

The trains were different from other electric trains on the Eastern Region in that they were painted maroon as opposed to green and were gangwayed throughout, including between sets. The units comprised some 2-car and some 4-car units, some of which latter included a griddle car. In terms of luxury, in emus only the Southern Region's all Pullman Brighton Belle units dating from 1932 were comparable, but on the Clacton units, unlike the Brighton Belle, passengers did not have to pay a supplement to travel on them.

The following classes were put into service on the GE Section prior to the Beeching Report:

Classes 307, 302, 305 (3 and 4 Car), 308 (3 and 4 Car), 304 and 309.

There was one other electrification carried out during the period of this chapter and that was from Epping to Ongar which was inaugurated on 18 November 1957. Moreover, looking at it from the basis of the mid-1950s, it should never have been carried out and the section of line closed.

At the same time that the existing dc lines were converted to ac in 1960, all of the dc emus were converted to the new current. This involved something of a drastic rebuild. Rebuilt Shenfield unit No 023 leads a Liverpool Street train at Chelmsford in August 1961. *Frank Church*

Class 302 emus were an ac version of the dc units built for the Liverpool Street to Southend electrification of 1956. They first entered traffic in 1959 and were used all over the GE and LTS ac lines. A down Bishop's Stortford train is seen approaching Broxbourne Junction on 22 July 1970. *P.H. Groom*

Class 305 emus had GEC equipment. Not all was well with these trains and the problems had to be fixed. Here we see unit No 516 on a Bishop's Stortford to Liverpool Street train at Roydon in September of 1961. *Frank Church*

As well as new emus for the North East London electrification of 1960, a number of new emus were built for the existing lines. Class 308 units had English Electric equipment and No 156 is seen on a Hertford train approaching Broxbourne Junction on 17 August 1967. *P.H. Groom*

Whilst the problem was being fixed, some class 302 units intended for the LTS line electrification which commenced at the end of 1961 were used as were some class 304 units borrowed from the London Midland Region. Unit No 019 is seen at Shenfield on 12 March 1961. *Frank Church*

Although the electrification from London to Clacton and Walton had been completed by the summer of 1962, the class 309 emus that were designated to work the principle services did not enter service until 1963. One such train is seen passing Stratford on 10 July 1967. *P.H. Groom*

London Transport finally decided to electrify the remaining un-electrified section of the Central Line from Epping to Ongar and electric services commenced on 18 November 1957 using 2-car 1935 Tube Stock. Here is Epping with a train of Standard Tube Stock and a train of 1935 Tube Stock. *Frank Church*

This is North Weald on the first day of electric operation of the Epping to Ongar service. 1935 Tube Stock was the first tube stock to have its equipment under the floor of the driving cars as opposed to having an equipment compartment as in Standard Tube Stock. *Frank Church*

Under the pre-war plans for electrification, Ongar was to have a service of two trains per hour in the Monday to Saturdays peak hours and one or two trains per hour in the off-peak hours on those days and Sundays, all from Loughton.

Pre-war London Transport's Northern Line was to be extended from Highgate (now Archway) to Finchley, High Barnet and Edgware and from Finsbury Park via Highgate (ex GNR) to Alexandra Palace and East Finchley. The service on the latter section of line was to be fourteen trains per hour on Mondays to Saturdays peak from Moorgate to Highgate with seven going via East Finchley to High Barnet and seven to Alexandra Palace. On Mondays to Saturdays off peak, the service was to be twelve trains per hour with six going to East Finchley and six to Alexandra Palace. On Sundays, the service was to be eight trains per hour to East Finchley.

Although the electrification reached High Barnet in 1940 and Mill Hill East in 1941, the rest was not carried out. The service from Finsbury Park to Alexandra Palace was still steam operated and by 1953 it was decided to withdraw the service, which was running at peak hours only using rolling stock that was not of the best quality.

From the perspective of 1953, given that the line from Finsbury Park to East Finchley and Alexandra Palace ran through a populated urban area, it would make sense to complete the electrification. From the same perspective, given that the line from Epping to Ongar ran through a rural area and that Ongar had a smaller population than Dunmow which had lost its passenger service in 1952, it would make sense to close that section. However, as indicated, the opposite happened and London Transport persuaded the government to allow it to electrify to Ongar. Finsbury Park to Alexandra Palace passenger trains ceased running after Saturday, 3 July 1954.

The Epping to Ongar service saw was principally operated by LT 1935 Tube Stock but also Standard Tube Stock and the only use of a 3-car train of LT 1938 Stock Unit on the Central Line. On the main Central Line 1959 and 1962 Tube Stock replaced Standard Tube Stock.

British Railways in the main preferred diesel traction to electric traction as the alternative to steam as at the time it was not realised that diesel and petrol engines were just as polluting as steam engines. The Great Eastern section, because it was fairly self-contained, was chosen to be the first area of British Railways to be rid of steam traction.

The first main line diesel locomotives to enter service on the Great Eastern section were the Brush Type 2 A-1-A A-1-A locomotives in November 1957 after having been formally handed over to BR by the builders Brush on 31 October. The first recorded use of one was by the class leader No D5500 on the 10.36am Liverpool Street to Clacton train on 13 November. They were followed in March 1958 by the English Electric Type 4

On the London Transport Central Line, Standard and 1935 tube stocks were replaced by 1959 Tube Stock and 1962 Tube Stock. Here we see a train of 1962 Tube Stock at Epping in the summer of 1980 prior to its return journey to West Ruislip, the longest journey on the London underground. *Author*

1-Co-Co-1 locomotives. The first use of one on a passenger train was on 18 April when the class leader No D200 hauled a train from Liverpool Street to Norwich. It has to be said that the class was not the success it was meant to be and offered little advantage over a well driven Britannia class steam locomotive. These were followed by a variety of other classes of which the principal ones were the English Electric Type 3 Co-Co locomotives introduced in 1961 and the Brush Type 4 Co-Co locomotives introduced in 1962, although it was not until the beginning of 1965 that they took over the Liverpool Street to Norwich services. They were worthy successors to the Britannias. I would suggest that they did their finest express work on the GE.

The book *Great Eastern* by Cecil J. Allen published in 1959 by Ian Allan gives some interesting facts on the Great Eastern section half way between the announcement of the modernisation plan and the Beeching Report; in 1959, 39.6 per cent of the section's passenger mileage was worked by diesel traction, 38.9 per cent by steam traction and 21.5 per cent by electric traction.

The following classes of diesel locomotive saw service on the GE Section prior to the Beeching Report: 01, 03, 04, 06, 08, 10, 11, 15, 16, 20, 21, 24, 31, 37,40, 47, 53, D1/1, D1/3, D2/11, plus locomotives Nos D0226 and D0227.

Diesel locomotives of class 31 were the first main line diesel locomotives to work on the GE section and first went into service on 13 November 1957. Here we see class member No D5510 on the 10.30 Liverpool Street to Cromer service at Shenfield on 9 July 1958. *Ken Nunn*

Class 40 locomotives although first used on the GE section in 1958 showed few advantages over the Britannia class steam locomotives that they were intended to replace and only five worked on the section. One is seen on an Up express near Shenfield in 1959. *Frank Church*

The British Thomson-Houston class 15 locomotives were not fitted with train heating equipment and could only be used on passenger trains during the warmer months of the year. No D8220 is seen at Maldon on 6 August 1960 with the 3.41pm train from Witham deputising for a rail car because of an increase in passenger numbers attending the Maldon carnival that day. *Frank Church*

The North British class 16 locomotives were mainly used on local freight workings and the class comprised ten locomotives. On 14 June 1967, No D8405 is seen entering Temple Mills yard from the north passing Leyton Gas Works with a transfer freight. *P.H. Groom*

Class 37 first appeared at the end of 1960 and the first three locomotives (D6700-2) were allocated to Stratford depot. The class proved extremely useful. No D6722 is seen approaching Roydon with a Down Cambridge line morning express on 1 June 1966. *P.H. Groom*

The Brush built class 47s always looked better in their original two tone green livery and here we see No D1566 in its original colours north of Broxbourne Junction with a Down freight train on 28 August 1966. *P.H. Groom*

It is with the Liverpool Street to Norwich service that one associates class 47. I am tempted to say that this was, like the Britannia, where they did their finest work. Here No 47471 *Norman Tunna GC* awaits departure from Liverpool Street with a Norwich express in the early 1980s. *Author*

This photograph, which was taken on 16 July 1960 at Chelmsford, shows the railway in transition. Britannia class locomotive No 70000 *Britannia* on an Up train passes Derby/Sulzer diesel locomotive No D5039. *Frank Church*

The following classes of dmu saw service on the GE Section prior to the Beeching Report: 100, 101, 104, 105, 109, 116, 125, Derby Lightweight, Metro-Cammell Lightweight, Waggon und Maschinenbau four wheel railbuses.

Steam ceased officially working the Norwich services at the end of the summer 1961 timetable and by the start of the summer 1962 timetable only Stratford and March depots had allocations of steam locomotives. Apart from freight duties, steam was also employed on the relief Harwich boat trains and the North Woolwich to Palace Gates via Stratford service. There was the odd steam working to Norwich from London. The summer of 1962 briefly saw two new classes of steam locomotive put in service on the GE Section. Standard Class 2 MT 2 6 0 and Standard Class 4 MT 2 6 4 side tank. The latter transferred from the LTS Section following the completion of the electrification. I saw one of the former near Forest Gate in August 1962. The last steam workings in and out of Liverpool Street were on Sunday, 9 September 1962 by B1 class locomotives on Harwich relief boat trains. The locomotives in question were No 61375 on the last steam train out and No 61156 on the last steam train in. British Railways photographed both trains. The *Daily Herald* of Thursday, 6 September reported that the following Sunday, Liverpool Street station would see its last steam train. The *Daily Mirror* of Monday, 10 September reported that the last steam train into Liverpool Street station arrived

Metropolitan-Cammell was one of the first private manufacturers to build diesel multiple units. The first units appeared in 1955. In East Anglia they appeared in 2- and 3-car variants. A 2-car unit hauling a utility van is seen approaching Lowestoft in August 1968. *P.H. Groom*

The Craven 2-car dmus first appeared in 1958.The majority of the units were based at Norwich. Here we see a pair of units between Somerleyton and Oulton Broad on a Norwich to Lowestoft train on 8 August 1969. *P.H. Groom*

Only five Wickham two car dmus were built, all in 1957 and all only saw service in the Eastern Counties. On 18 June 1958 one of these units is seen working the 4.08pm train from Southminster to Wickford approaching Wickford. *Ken Nunn*

Until the Lea Valley line was electrified in 1969, Bishop's Stortford and Hertford trains ran via the reopened Southbury line. For the Lea Valley line some Rolls Royce 3 car dmus were provided. One such train is seen about to pass under the Kentish Town to Barking line on 11 July 1967. *P.H. Groom*

33 minutes late. On 9 September 1962, the last day of steam at Stratford, there were a total of forty-eight service steam locomotives as opposed to departmental steam locomotives at Stratford shed. There were sixteen B1s, two J19s, six J15s, eight L1s, eight 67/9s and eight N7s. After that date there was the odd steam working over the main lines. Some steam locomotives of Class B1 were used as stationary boilers for carriage warming and on one occasion one is known to have worked a passenger train on the East Suffolk line, the last one being No 61138 at Norwich. Only March remained open for steam where it survived until the end of November 1963 – the same month the only surviving steam locomotive at Stratford was withdrawn, Class Y4 0-4-0 side tank No 33 in departmental service formerly No 68129. When March closed to steam on 30 November 1963, there were a total of twenty-six service steam locomotives on the shed comprising twelve B1s, five O1s and nine Britannias. Of these, two O1s and the nine Britannias lingered on at the shed into December 1963 until being transferred elsewhere. The *Railway Magazine* for February 1964 recorded that the new diesel maintenance depot at March had been brought into use at the end of November 1963 and marked what was virtually the end of steam on the GE line. The same magazine reported that Stratford works was being dismantled and that the following steam locomotives were still there: B12 No 61572, Y4 No 33, J15s Nos 65445, 65462, 65464 and 65469 and N7 No 69621. It was understood that Nos 61572, 33 and 69621 were awaiting preservation. At March, other than workings over the GN and GE Joint Line, steam also worked the March to Wisbech goods service, the last scheduled steam working on the Great Eastern section. The *Railway Magazine* for September 1963 included a photograph taken by Dr Ian C. Allen at Wisbech East goods yard on 9 May of Class 04 diesel locomotive No D2201 having just brought in the daily goods from the Wisbech Harbour branch and Class B1 No 61204 about to leave with wagons for Whitemoor Yard. The caption noted that the return working was still a steam duty. There was one final use of steam on the Great Eastern section and that was at Lowestoft sleeper works where Departmental Y3 0-4-0 Sentinel locomotive No 40 formerly No 61873 remained in use until 1964. By a strange quirk, the last run of all in service on BR by a Standard Gauge steam locomotive, albeit as a light engine, finished on the GE when the last Britannia No 70013 *Oliver Cromwell*, following its participation in BR's last steam train on 11 August 1968, ran light from Lostock Hall to Norwich via Doncaster, leaving Lostock Hall on the evening of 11 August, arriving at Norwich on 12 August en route for preservation at Bressingham Gardens.

Oliver Cromwell was not the only former GE section locomotive to be preserved. Class mate No 70000 *Britannia* has also survived into preservation as has B1 No 61264 which first was shedded at Parkeston when built in December 1947. Of GER designed locomotives examples of classes B12, E4, J15, J17, J69 and Y5 have been preserved.

There were a couple of failures. The last Y6 was put aside at Stratford for about a year but was then broken up. A D16, or possibly a D15, was set aside for preservation, but unfortunately the word 'Save' or 'Preserve' was only written on one side of the boiler and in consequence the locomotive was scrapped. The last D15 was withdrawn from Stratford in 1952, whilst the last D16 was withdrawn from March in 1960. Given that according to John Scott-Morgan there was a bit of stink over the scrapping of the Y6 and the Claud Hamilton and which lead to the E4 being preserved, I would suggest that it was the D15. However, according to the *Railway Observer* of December 1960, the last surviving D16 was seen on the scrap roads at Stratford on 30 October 1960 with the words 'Do not scrap until further notice' scrawled on its tender. There are proposals to build a new D16, a new F5 and two new B17s. Now even some of the diesel locomotives and diesel and electric multiple units that worked on the GE have been preserved e.g. Class 15, 31, 47, 306 and 309 amongst others.

Incredibly, steam was outlasted by horse power on the GE section as it was not until 1967 that the last shunting horse on BR was withdrawn. According to the *Railway Magazine* for April 1967, Charlie a 24-year-old bay and white carthorse, who had spent the previous six years shunting horseboxes containing racehorses at Newmarket station, had just retired. The *Bury Free Press* of 17 February 1967 reported, 'He's The Last. Newmarket's "Charlie" a 24 year old bay and white carthorse is going to retire! He is the

In the summer of 1962, steam passenger working was confined to the North Woolwich-Palace Gates service and relief Harwich boat trains. Standard 4-2-6 4T No 80097 with another member of the class at North Woolwich on 3 July. Eight members of the class were based at Stratford that summer. *Photomatic*

On Sunday 9 September 1962, B1 class locomotive No 61375 awaits departure from Liverpool Street station with the relief boat train to Harwich Parkeston Quay. Sadly, this is the last time that a scheduled steam train will leave Liverpool Street station. *British Railways*

On 9 September there were eight N7 class locomotives left in service. All were withdrawn. Here we see a line-up of seven members of the class at Stratford on 27 September. Only one N7 has survived into preservation, No 69621 originally No 999E, the last locomotive built at Stratford. *P.H. Groom*

only survivor of the thousands of horses which during the past century have worked on the railway.' According to the *Illustrated London News* of 25 February 1967, he retired on 21 February and would spend his retirement at Frome in Somerset.

The period up to the publication of the Beeching Report in 1963 saw quite a number of passenger services withdrawn and in some instances complete closures of lines. Lines that the LNER had not been prepared to withdraw the passenger service from or completely close, British Railways were! The first line to lose its passenger service was the Kelvedon, Tiptree and Tollesbury Light Railway which closed to passengers on 7 May and beyond Tudwick Road Tiptree to goods on 29 October 1951. The section from Kelvedon to Tudwick Road closed on 10 October 1962. On 2 July passenger services were withdrawn between Felixstowe Beach and Felixstowe Pier. On August 1951 the line from Wymondham to Forncett which had lost its passenger service in 1939 was closed completely.

1952 saw more closures. On 3 March 1952, Bishop's Stortford to Dunmow and Braintree closed to passengers except for excursions which lasted until 1964. The *Herts and Essex Observer* carried an article headed 'Flyer makes its last trip'. The article gave a description of not only the last passenger train over the line, but also that several people spent the day travelling over the line taking photographs and collecting souvenirs. Heacham to Burnham Market and Wells closed to passengers on 31 May 1952, between Burnham Market and Wells goods ceased on 30 January 1953 and did not reopen after flood damage except for drainage trains. The *Lynn Advertiser* of 10 June reported that a Mr Tom Fuller of 'The Drift' who would be 90 that August had waved to both the first and last trains on the line. On 28 July, the Mid Suffolk Light Railway closed to all traffic. According to the *Diss Express* of 1 August, the event was a happy occasion. To mourn the line's passing there were elements of celebration. For the last train of all from Haughley to Laxfield, staff from East Suffolk County Council at County Hall in Ipswich dressed up in Edwardian clothes. After that there were a few trains over the line in connection with the removal of items of equipment as late as 30 August 1953 prior to demolition. On 15 September, the line from Elsenham to Thaxted closed to passengers. Goods traffic followed on 1 June 1953. 15 September saw Wroxham to County School closed to passengers. The section from Reepham to Foulsham closed completely. The section was partially re-laid in 1960 with the Themelthorpe Curve to connect with the now goods-only former Midland and Great Northern Joint Railway line to Norwich. The date of reopening was 12 September 1960. On 3 November, Wickham Market to Framlingham closed to passengers except for excursions.

1953 brought more closures. Tivetshall to Beccles closed to passengers on 5 January 1953 and from Harleston to Bungay for goods on 1 February 1960. The *Diss Express* of 9 January 1953 carried a report of the closure including the mock funeral held at

F5 No 67211 heads a train at Hockerill Halt on the Bishop's Stortford to Braintree line on 1 March 1952. Sadly, though, this was the last day of normal passenger services on the line. Excursion trains continued on the line until August 1964. *Frank Church*

The end of passenger services did not necessarily mean the end of goods services. This photograph, taken at Dunmow on 16 August 1956, shows two goods trains passing. It was the motor lorry and Dr Beeching that killed station to station goods traffic. The line slowly closed from 1966 to 1972. *Frank Church*

Harleston station. Woodham Ferrers to Maldon West closed 1 April 1953. Maldon West to Maldon East closed 1 September 1954, reopened 3 January 1957, closed 31 January 1959. The passenger service had been withdrawn in 1939 at the start of the Second World War. On the Norfolk and Suffolk Joint Railway, Cromer Beach to Mundesley closed completely 17 April 1953. On the Norfolk–Suffolk borders, Thetford to Bury St Edmunds closed to passengers on 8 June 1953 and goods 27 June 1960. The final closure of 1953 was Yarmouth Beach to Gorleston on the Midland and Great Northern Joint Railway, closed completely 21 September 1953. In 1954, Cromer Junction to Cromer High closed to passengers on 20 September 1954 and to goods on 7 March 1960.

Cromer Beach was used by passenger and goods services respectively after those dates. 1955 saw the closure of the spur to Chatteris dock off the St Ives to March line via Chatteris. On 17 September 1956 Warboys to Ramsey closed to goods. In 1957 excursion traffic ceased on the Ely to St Ives line.

The following year, goods traffic ceased between Bluntisham and Sutton on 6 October. 1959 saw a spate of closures, principally large parts of the former Midland and Great Northern Joint Railway on 1 March 1959. Only the section from Cromer Beach to Melton Constable retained its passenger service. Some parts did keep their goods service. The same year saw the closure of the section of the Great Northern and Great Eastern joint line from Huntingdon to St Ives on 11 September followed by the section of line from Yarmouth South Town to Beccles for passenger and through goods traffic on 1 November. On 30 November, goods traffic was withdrawn between Leiston and Aldeburgh, but passenger traffic remained open. Finally for that year, a sea route closed. The Harwich to Antwerp full passenger service had ceased in February 1950. The service had lost money heavily between the wars and ran at a loss since resuming after the end of the Second World War. The ships used on it were unsuitable as they did not comply with modern conditions. A cargo liner with passenger accommodation for twelve passengers, the SS *Dewsbury* took over the service. The new service was hardly well advertised. The *Daily Herald* of 24 November 1956 reported that Julian Ridsdale, the MP for Harwich, said in the House of Commons on 23 November 1956 that the passenger service had hardly been advertised and there was no proper provision for the issue of tickets. British Railways said that 70,000 timetables and 30,000 brochures had been issued to stations and travel agents that year alone. British Railways denied that bookings were discouraged. On average, only five passengers used the service in winter and nine in summer. British Railways did not say whether this was per sailing or those numbers for all of the winter and all of the summer. The service was not advertised. The service finally ceased on 31 January 1959. 7 March 1960 saw the closure of the goods only Snape branch.

1961 saw the closure to passenger traffic between Bury St Edmunds and Long Melford on 10 April and goods traffic between Lavenham and Long Melford on the same day.

1 January 1962 saw the withdrawal of passenger services between Chappel and Haverhill over the former Colne Valley and Halstead Railway. On the same day, goods services were withdrawn from the section of that line between Yeldham and Haverhill. On 18 June of the same year, passenger services were withdrawn between Cambridge and Mildenhall via Fordham.

The final pre-Beeching service withdrawal was the line from Seven Sisters to Palace Gates, which lost its passenger service on 7 January 1963. Since 23 March 1951, the service had been peak hours only. Prior to the end of steam at Stratford on 9 September 1962, the service from North Woolwich to Palace Gates had been almost the last suburban line in London to be steam worked. Only the Clapham Junction to Kensington Olympia service remained steam worked longer.

It is possible, if a report in *Railways* for July 1951 can be accepted as correct, that BR were also contemplating withdrawing more passenger services in East Anglia including the Saffron Walden branch and the Witham to Maldon East branch. The list as it applies to the East Anglia is as follows: Bishop's Stortford–Braintree and Bocking; Wickham Market–Framlingham; Mildenhall–Barnwell; Long Melford–Bury St Edmunds; Wells–Heacham; Thetford–Bury St Edmunds; Witham–Maldon (East); Bartlow–Audley End; Shelford–Haverhill; Sudbury (Suffolk)–Haverhill; Beccles–Tivetshall.

6 February 1952 saw the death of George VI at Sandringham and the succession of Elizabeth II. One of her first duties was on 11 February was to meet the special train carrying the body of her father at King's Cross. The train was hauled from Wolferton to Kings Lynn by Class B2 locomotive No 61617 *Ford Castle* and from Kings Lynn to King's Cross behind Britannia Class locomotive No 70000 *Britannia*. The late king's body was taken to Westminster where after three days lying in state it was taken to Paddington where it went by special train to Windsor hauled by Castle class locomotive No 7013 *Bristol Castle* in the guise of No 4082 *Windsor Castle* which had hauled George V's funeral train in 1936, but was at the time undergoing overhaul at Swindon Works.

On 11 January1961, while the queen was travelling from London to Sandringham in a royal saloon attached to the rear of the 4.36 pm train from Liverpool Street to Kings Lynn (The Fenman) the diesel locomotive hauling the train, Brush Type 2 No D5667, failed 300 yards south of Audley End due to a pump taking oil to main bearings failing and blocked the main line. A steam locomotive in the form of a B1 was sent from Cambridge to rescue the train which got underway after a delay of 56 minutes. Mr W.G. Thorpe, the Traffic Manager of the Great Eastern Line, who was travelling with the queen, apologised for the hold up. According to the *Daily Herald* of Friday, 13 January, when the queen returned to London on the following Monday, the train would be hauled by a Britannia class steam locomotive. Stan Fenn, the driver whose diesel locomotive unfortunately broke down, would be driving the Britannia hauling the train taking the queen back to London. Stan had said, 'You can bet the Britannia won't let the Queen down.'

1952 and 1962 saw two smogs. That of 1952 lasted from 5 to 9 December and killed at least 4,000 people whilst that of 1962 lasted from 4 to 7 December and killed between 300 and 700 people. During both these occasions, train services were severely delayed.

1953 saw the East Coast floods. On the night of Saturday, 31 January/Sunday, 1 February, high winds and severe gales caused the sea on the east coast of England to rise several feet higher than predicted, with the gales whipping up wave action. The floods killed 307 people. All of the railways in the Eastern Counties were affected. In West Norfolk, the main line between London, Kings Lynn and Hunstanton was breached in several places north of Kings Lynn, and south of Kings Lynn by the flooding of the River Ouse at Magdalen Road. At South Lynn, on the former Midland and Great Northern Joint Railway, the station and the marshalling yard were flooded. At Wells-next-the-Sea, the station was flooded. On the line from Heacham to Burnham Market and Wells, which had closed to passengers on 31 May 1952, the section of line near Holkham was so severely damaged that the section from Burnham Market to Wells did not reopen except for drainage trains. Wells station reopened on 4 February and the main line to Hunstanton on 11 February. At Lowestoft, the station and other railway premises were flooded. Both Yarmouth South Town and Yarmouth Vauxhall stations were flooded. At the former, the motive power depot was also flooded. Flooding occurred on the line from Yarmouth Vauxhall to Reedham at Berney Arms, whilst the main line from Yarmouth South Town to London was flooded near Belton and Aldeby. The Lowestoft to Norwich line was flooded in several places at Haddiscoe. The damage at Yarmouth was relatively slight and was repaired within a few days, but that at Haddiscoe took a fortnight to repair. Slight flooding occurred on the Snape branch and the East Suffolk line between Melton and Woodbridge. At Felixstowe, both Pier and Beach stations were flooded. The line from Manningtree to Harwich was damaged at several places between Wrabness and Harwich. Harwich, Dovercourt and Parkeston stations were cut off or under water. Parkeston motive power depot was flooded. Despite some damage to the quays, services to the Continent were maintained at Parkeston without interruption. The line between Wrabness and Parkeston was restored on

5 February, but normal working to Harwich was not resumed until 23 February. The 120 ton double track bridge ramp of the Harwich to Zeebrugge train ferry was severely damaged when the Essex Ferry was lifted to an abnormal height on the flood tide and was not fully restored until 5 March. The line from Colchester to Clacton and Walton-on-the-Naze was flooded between Hythe and Wivenhoe, but services were restored within a few days. Three miles of the line from Wivenhoe to Brightlingsea were washed away and the line was not reopened until 7 December. Canvey Island in the Thames Estuary was very severely flooded with much loss of life. The former LT&SR was flooded between Benfleet and Leigh. Prior to single track working being resumed between the two stations on 6 February and double track working on 9 February, shuttle services were run from Fenchurch Street to Benfleet and Leigh to Shoeburyness. As the former GER line was not affected by the floods and there was not sufficient rolling stock to maintain the required additional trains to London, a shuttle service of steam trains was put on from Southend to Shenfield, where a non-stop service of electric trains was put on to Fenchurch Street. This commenced on 2 February and was maintained until 9 February. From then until 18 February when full services were restored between Fenchurch Street and Shoeburyness, four relief steam trains were run from Fenchurch Street to Southend via Shenfield. Tilbury Riverside station was flooded and a length of track near Low Street was damaged. The branch line to Thames Haven was flooded and at Purfleet two miles of line were rendered unusable when the adjacent industrial estate was flooded. The track at Low Street was restored on 9 February, but that at Purfleet was not restored until 19 February. During that time, a shuttle service was maintained between Purfleet and Barking and Tilbury and Upminster via the single track line from Upminster to Grays. This line was also used by ocean liner specials to Tilbury on their resumption two days after the flood, and heavy goods trains to the Thames Haven branch when that was restored. In the London area, the running lines and sidings at Canning Town and Stratford Market were flooded and the Blackwall branch was blocked. There was no serious damage and services were quickly restored. Even the Royal Train was affected by the floods. According to the *British Railways Eastern Region Magazine* for April 1953, because of the flooding on the Kings Lynn, Downham Market and Ely line, the Royal train conveying the Queen and the Duke of Edinburgh back from Sandringham to London was diverted from Kings Lynn to South Lynn and thence along the former Midland and Great Northern Railway through Wisbech to Peterborough, then up the main line to King's Cross.

In September 1958, the weather caused more damage to the railways. During the evening of Friday, 5 September, violent thunderstorms accompanied by torrential rain swept over southern England causing widespread damage to the railways in the Home

Counties. Between 8 and 9pm, the recorder at a metrological station in Harrow picked up 1,470 lightning flashes within a 10 to 15 mile radius and observers at the station reckoned it to be one of the most spectacular storms of the century. In Essex, flooding occurred on the former LT&SR at the bridge carrying Timberlog Lane over the railway between Laindon and Pitsea. Part of the cutting collapsed, bringing many hundreds of tons of mud onto the railway. Ballast was washed away for a considerable distance between Upminster and Laindon. Similar damage occurred on the line from Upminster via Ockendon to Grays. Between Pitsea and Stanford-le-Hope there was extensive wash away of track. Nearly 100 signal and track failures were reported throughout the line. There were ten trains en route which were brought to a stand at stations and held there until adequate linking road services could be provided. In many stations the water rose to platform level and in some instances the lighting failed. Refreshment rooms were kept open later than normally or opened specially. As Upminster had no refreshment room, arrangements were made to open a private café outside the station to serve passengers. Army vehicles were obtained to clear 300 passengers from a train stranded at Laindon and were later used to run a road shuttle service between Pitsea and Upminster. Buses were obtained from all local sources, but the buses had problems as many vehicles were stranded by flooding on the main roads. About 4,000 passengers were conveyed by the linking road services and were able to complete their journeys before the morning. At this time, Saturday morning working was quite common, so someone staying a bit late after work on Friday and got caught out by the storm would not have got much sleep that night. The lines to Tilbury, the line through Ockendon, the sections between Upminster and Laindon and Pitsea and Standford-le-Hope were restored the following day whilst the section between Laindon and Pitsea was not restored until late Sunday afternoon. On the former GER line, there was slight flooding at Clapton and Seven Sisters. At Brentwood, the line was flooded twice and twice the water fell sufficiently for trains to pass at very reduced speeds. At New Hall near Chelmsford a landslip at first blocked only the Down line, but later blocked both lines. During the night of 5-6 September, Down trains could not get beyond Chelmsford nor could Up trains get into the station. At times, trains could not pass through Brentwood in either direction. Movement was also restricted or even prohibited by a queue of trains on both lines and particularly the Down line. Trains stuck in the queue west of Brentwood were gradually worked into the stations. Some of the trains were already in the stations. Passengers from the trains were transferred to road services to continue their journeys. A shuttle service was started between Gidea Park and Liverpool Street and many passengers were brought to the terminus, where tea and food were distributed and arrangements made with London Transport to take the passengers home. Road services were run between

Gidea Park and Witham to connect with the trains to Ipswich and Clacton standing on the other side of the landslip. A special road service was run between Gidea Park and Shenfield to connect with trains on the Southend branch. At Brentwood, the Up electric and Down main lines were restored at 12.30 and 12.50am respectively and the Down electric and Up main at 6.30am on 6 September. The landslip at New Hall was cleared by 9.30am on the same morning with the aid of soldiers from Chelmsford barracks. By 10am all suburban services were running more or less normally, but main line trains on the Norwich line continued to be subject to delay throughout the day.

The winter of 1962-63 was one of the coldest winters on record in Britain. It was popularly known as the 'Big Freeze'. Snow first fell on 12-13 December 1962. There was heavy snow late on 26-27 December. Temperatures plummeted. Although there was a brief thaw lasting three days, from 25 January snow continued to fall into February. It was not until 6 March that there was a morning in 1963 without frost, when a gradual thaw set in, fortunately without flooding. It is difficult to judge what precisely happened on the railways during the 'Big Freeze'. The *Daily Herald* of 27 February said that diesel locomotives failed very badly during the 'Big Freeze', but that electric locomotives and dmus stood up to the cold weather. The newspaper said that fuel oil solidified in ordinary diesels. According to the newspaper, the overhead electric system that was in use in East Anglia and Essex worked virtually without a hitch during the freeze. According to the *Railway Observer* for March 1963, during the previous January, GE passenger services were remarkably good. Operating difficulties occurred when there were power cuts on the national grid supply. During January current was cut off three times between Chelmsford and Witham. Fortunately, two of the occasions were on Saturdays. Main line trains stopped at intermediate stations and electric trains were cut back to Shenfield. On 29 January, the afternoon railbus from Audley End to Haverhill got stuck in a snow drift outside Haverhill station. It was eventually freed and ended up being pushed by the guard, four platelayers and some helpful passengers. Two days later, the weather got the better of it and for a few days Class 03 No D2048 with two coaches took over. As class 03s were not equipped for train heating, the journey must have been rather cold.

On 7 March 1950, there was a collision at Witham which resulted in the deaths of two people. At 3.11am, the 11pm express from Peterborough to London via Ipswich hauled by B1 class locomotive No 61057 over-ran all signals at Rivenhall and collided at about 60mph with the 7.45pm Class A mineral freight train from Whitemoor to Witham hauled by a 2-8-0 locomotive with left hand drive. There was fog. In the collision, the fireman of the express and the guard of the freight train were both killed. On the express, there were about twenty passengers and postal staff, seven of whom received minor injuries. The driver and the second guard of the express both received injuries, the former seriously. The main cause of the accident was driver error, excessive speed and the secondary cause was an error by the signalman in the fog. Locomotive No 61057 was scrapped.

On the Central Line, there was a collision between two trains at Stratford on Wednesday, 8 April 1953. At 6.56pm, an eastbound train running under the 'Stop and Proceed' rule collided at about 20mph with a stationary train in the tunnel between Stratford and Leyton. Twelve passengers were killed. Four passengers and the driver of the train proceeding under the 'Stop and Proceed' rule received serious injuries and were detained in hospital. Forty-one passengers were slightly injured or received shock. According to the accident report:

> The removal of the wrecked coaches from the tube was a difficult and lengthy operation and consequently it was not possible for normal working to be resumed until 10.00 a.m. on Friday, 10th April. In the meantime services between Liverpool Street and Leytonstone were augmented during the peak periods by special bus services, and on the Thursday evening and the Friday morning additional train services were operated by the Eastern Region, British Railways, between Liverpool Street, Stratford, and – Ilford'.

The cause of the accident was driver error and excessive speed.

From 29 May to 14 June 1955, there was a strike by the drivers' and firemen's union ASLEF. The cause of the strike was the failure of the Railway Staff National Tribunal to agree to the union's claim for higher wages for certain grades of footplatemen. Not all footplatemen belonged to ASLEF. Some belonged to the National Union of Railwaymen (NUR). In consequence, not all footplatemen came out on strike. For example, the *Lynn Advertiser* of Friday, 3 June reported that at Lynn (GE) and South Lynn (M&GN) 243 ASLEF men were on strike the previous day. Eight reported for duty. Thirty footplatemen belonging to the NUR went to work, as did seven non-unionists. The train service that was provided was somewhat limited. In Essex, the strike is best remembered for the appearance of Britannia Class locomotives on some of the Southend trains that did run. 29 May 1955, the first day of the strike, was Whit Sunday. Whit week was not from the public's point of view the best time for a strike – even if ASLEF had a justifiable case. Coach operators and bus operators unquestionably benefited from the extra trade generated. The strike also caused bitterness between those footplatemen who struck and those who did not.

During the period of transition from steam to diesel and electrics, according to Richard Hardy in *Steam in the Blood* (Ian Allan 1971), Jimmy Groom, a boilermaker, who was the Chairman of the Workshop Committee at Stratford and a very able man, set up with management blessing a small training school for boilermakers and fitters who had the right aptitude to convert to the electrical side.

The 1950s to early 1960s were the peak period for named trains on the Great Eastern Section. 1950 saw the introduction of the 'Broadsman' between London and Cromer. The train left Cromer in the morning and returned from London in the evening. 1958 saw the introduction of the 'Essex Coast Express' between London and Clacton with a portion for Walton-on-the-Naze which was detached or joined at Thorpe-le-Soken. The train left Clacton and Walton-on-the Naze in the morning and returned from London in the evening. The other titled trains were the 'Continentals'. These were the 'Hook Continental', the 'Day Continental' and the 'Scandinavian'. Unfortunately, in June 1962 following a speed up of services the 'East Anglian', the 'Norfolkman' and the 'Broadsman' disappeared from the timetables. The 'Continentals', the 'Fenman' and the 'Essex Coast Express' survived longer.

In 1950, the Sandringham Hotel in Hunstanton was sold to Hunstanton Urban District Council which used it as offices and a library until 1959 when it was converted into flats. The building was demolished in 1967.

At Felixstowe, the Felix Hotel was sold to Fisons in 1952. In the 1980s the building – by then renamed Harvest House – was converted into apartments.

1955 saw the publication by Ian Allan of the first edition of Cecil J. Allen's *The Great Eastern Railway*. This was the first and until quite recently the only history of the GER. Cecil J. Allen was a former employee of the Company.

1962 saw the centenary of the formation of the GER and the *Railway Magazine* for July and August of that year carried a two part article on the Railway by B.D.J. Walsh, who had previously written a number of articles on the GER in the *Magazine* and in 1973 would become the first President of the Great Eastern Railway Society. *British Railways Eastern Region Magazine* for August 1962 carried a very short article on the centenary of the GER by the railway author C. Hamilton Ellis.

Chapter 5

From the Beeching Report to the Elizabeth Line

The most important things that happened between the end of steam and the completion of CrossRail 1, or rather the Elizabeth Line as it is now known, were the infamous Beeching Report of 1963, the electrification of most of the surviving un-electrified suburban lines, the completion of the electrification of the main lines and the privatisation of British Railways, or British Rail as it had been rebranded.

The Beeching Report was actually in two parts. Part 1 was 'The Reshaping of British Railways' and came out in 1963 on 27 March. Part 2 was 'The Development of Major Railway Trunk Routes' and came out in February 1965. Part 1 was the more famous, or should one say 'infamous' part.

Dr Richard Beeching, later Lord Beeching, was a physicist and engineer and was a director of Imperial Chemicals Industry (ICI). He was appointed Chairman of British Railways by the Minister of Transport, Ernest Marples, on 15 March 1961. It has been suggested that it may not be entirely coincidental that whilst Dr Beeching was closing railway lines, the government was providing funding for the construction of motorways, which were being built by companies in which Marples had an interest.

'The Reshaping of British Railways' is notorious because of the number of lines that it recommended for closure. Below is a list of those in the Eastern Counties and North East London to be either withdrawn or modified:

Passenger services to be withdrawn.
London Broad Street to Richmond.
London St Pancras to Barking (Local Service).
Westerfield to Yarmouth South Town
Shelford to Marks Tey
Saxmundham to Aldeburgh
Audley End to Bartlow
Cambridge to St Ives and March
Swaffham to Thetford

Dereham to Wells-Next-The-Sea
Sheringham to Melton Constable
North Walsham to Mundesley-on-Sea
St Margarets to Buntingford
Romford to Upminster
Witham to Maldon (East) and Heybridge
Witham to Braintree and Bocking
Wivenhoe to Brightlingsea
Passenger services to be modified
Oxford to Bletchley and Cambridge
London Broad Street to Watford
Ipswich to Norwich (Local services)
Cambridge to Ely and Kings Lynn
Bishop's Stortford to Cambridge
Ely to Norwich
Cambridge to Ipswich
Ely to Newmarket
Norwich to Dereham and King's Lynn
Norwich to Sheringham
Passenger services under consideration for withdrawal before the formulation of the report.
Palace Gates to Stratford (Already withdrawn)

Beeching also envisaged container Freightliner trains serving the domestic freight market. By 1968, BR had developed seventeen purpose-built depots. The most profitable routes, though, were those servicing the country's major ports and in particular to and from Europe and Ireland in addition to import/export traffic to the rest of the world. The Transport Act 1968 recognised that pattern of profitability and Freightliner became a separate listed commercial company which was wholly owned by the UK government, which leased its UK domestic transport from BR. At the end of the 1960s, Freightliner operated twenty-eight terminals and served fifty-six routes. The shift of the Company's focus from the original domestic freight market to the international market serviced via ports continued over the next 30 years and many of the original domestic depots which did not service port traffic either never opened or eventually closed, such as King's Cross. At the same time, investment in seaport depots and specifically Southampton and Harwich and at Felixstowe, at which latter place Beeching's plan had never envisaged a depot, continued at an increased pace.

The Aldeburgh branch closed to passengers in 1966, but part of it remains open beyond Leiston to serve Sizewell Nuclear Power Station. Here is Leiston Station on 14 June 2024. *Author*

In 'The Development of Major Railway Trunk Routes' only the line from London to Colchester and Ipswich to Norwich was selected for development.

In looking at 'The Reshaping of British Railways' and comparing it with the present network, there are certain differences in that certain lines down for closure have fully or partially remained open. Equally, there are lines that were not down for closure that were closed or partially closed and other lines that were not in the report that were closed. For example, Witham to Braintree and Romford to Upminster remain open. Oxford to Bletchley and Bedford to Cambridge were closed as was Norwich to Dereham and Kings Lynn to Hunstanton.

To give a flavour of local reaction to the report here are some examples. The front page of the *Saffron Walden Weekly News* of Friday, 29 March 1963 began 'Mayor Describes Proposal As "A Severe Blow" WALDEN STATION TO BE CLOSED About 300 Tickets Are Issued Daily'.

The front page of the *Lynn Advertiser* of the same day began 'Dr Beeching's rail "pill" is swallowed and brings signs of quick relief MOST W NORFOLK SERVICES ESCAPE AXING.'

According to the *Bury Free Press* of that date, 'Passengers are a dead loss so Beeching's bitter pill goes all out for bulk freight RAIL AXE MISSES BURY But smaller stations may have to go.'

The *Herts and Essex Observer* for that day said, 'BUNTINGFORD AND WALDEN LINES TO BE AXED Big cuts in coal depots.'

These headlines reflected that the report proposed the development of bulk freight by rail, but also that many small stations would be closed.

According to H.C. Casserley in *Railways Since 1939* (David and Charles 1972), some of the figures that were produced by the accountants to enable Dr Beeching to justify his decisions were, if not 'cooked', then at the least very misleading. One of the rural branch lines on the GE Section that was not included in the report was Wickford to Southminster. Had the passenger service on the Southminster branch been withdrawn it would have been necessary to keep the line open for freight, principally to serve Bradwell Nuclear Power Station which had begun generating electricity in 1962. Understandably, a fightback took place against the cuts. Some were successful and some were unsuccessful. To give two examples, on the East Suffolk Line, the Branch Line Reinvigoration Society asked people to use the line more often so that it could be saved. According to John M. Cooper in *The East Suffolk Railway* (Oakwood 1982), on 10 September 1965 campaigners met to discuss evidence to be placed before the Transport Users Consultative Committee (TUCC) inquiry to be held on 28 September. Cooper says that Mr Godfrey, the Secretary of the Lowestoft branch of the NUR, said that the NUR had asked British Railways to close signalboxes already disused on Sundays. The signalbox at Beccles South could be shut at a capital cost of £3,000 but BR was paid £4,000 to keep it open. Whilst the Southern Region was boosting sugar beet traffic, the Eastern Region was reluctant to carry it since the wagons were useless for the rest of the year. Through freight traffic that could have used the East Suffolk line was instead being sent via Norwich. At the inquiry, objections were heard. Already 1,914 people had written objecting to the closure of the line. On Christmas Eve the TUCC recommended that the Ipswich to Lowestoft line be kept open, but that the Aldeburgh branch be closed. Barbara Castle, the Minister of Transport, announced on 29 June 1966 that the line must be kept open. It became essential to reduce the cost of operating the line to a minimum and this was done by introducing conductor guard working on the line from 7 March 1967. On 12 September 1966, the Aldeburgh branch was closed to passenger traffic. In November 1966, the through local service from Ipswich to Yarmouth via Beccles ceased. The line from Lowestoft to Yarmouth, which had formerly been part of the Norfolk and Suffolk Joint Committee, closed on 4 May 1970. In the 1980s, singling of parts of the line took place. These were Woodbridge to Saxmundham and Halesworth to Oulton Broad North Junction. At Beccles on 10 September 2012, a new passing loop and a reinstated second platform was opened. In 1984, the line was resignalled using the Radio Electronic Token Block (RETB). This resulted in the closure of all conventional signal boxes. The RETB controlling signal box was at Saxmundham.

Had the campaign to keep the East Suffolk line open been unsuccessful, part of the line would have had to remain open to Saxmundham and the Aldeburgh branch as far as Leiston to serve Sizewell Nuclear Power Station, later Sizewell A, for which construction was started in 1961 and was commissioned in 1966. Unless Westerfield had been made the rail head, for the power station to have had a railway running through Woodbridge solely used for transporting nuclear waste flasks would have jarred considerably with the inhabitants of that town.

According to Denis Swindale in *Branch Lines to Maldon* (EARM 1978), at Maldon in Essex on 24 June 1963, the local Trades Council called a public meeting in the Moot Hall in the town in an effort to stimulate reaction to the proposed closure of the town's railway. At the same time, the Maldon and Witham Railway Campaign Committee came into being. Unfortunately, Maldon Rural District Council declined to give their support. Equally if not more damaging was when the East Anglian TUCC said that except at peak hours the bus services provided by the Eastern National Omnibus Company provided a reasonable and adequate alternative. Despite the Campaign Committee having achieved a delay of several months, on 11 August 1964 the official notification of the closure was issued by the TUCC. Ernest Marples accepted the TUCC's findings and BR announced that the branch would be closed subject to the granting of licences for additional buses by the Traffic Commissioners. A condition of the closure was that six additional limited stop buses should run each day between Witham and Maldon to meet early morning and evening traffic demands. As well as the existing route between Maldon and Witham, there were two routes to Chelmsford, one via Danbury and the other via Hatfield Peverel, the latter having been acquired by Eastern National when it took over Moore's of Kelvedon on 3 February 1963. Unfortunately, at the time Eastern National was suffering from severe staff shortages, which meant that it was impossible for it to maintain its schedules. Despite this, Mr R.E. Handley, the Traffic Manager of Eastern National, said that the Company hoped to start the new service in September as Maldon bus depot did not have a staff shortage. He was of the opinion that there would not be a lot of passengers on the new service, which would be run on a subsidy from BR and would be cheaper than running the branch line at a loss. The Mayor of Maldon and the Chairman of the Railway Campaign Committee, Councillor W.S. Hutchinson, said that closure was 'a disastrous and retrograde step' and felt that the TUCC had not looked far enough ahead, feeling that closure would have an adverse effect on the proposed increase in population in Maldon. He felt that the additional bus services would have looked after commuters, but not the general travelling public. A request for support was made by those opposing the closure to the local Member of Parliament for Maldon, Brian Harrison. Harrison gave his support, but this was somewhat tainted as earlier he had supported the Beeching Plan. He felt that the campaign had been started too late. Despite the strong opposition, it was clear that BR intended to withdraw the passenger service. Because of an embargo, the TUCC's decision was held back until 22 August. *The Times* of 24 August reported 'Train Service To End.--The Eastern Region, British Railways, announced on Saturday that the passenger train service between Witham and Maldon in Essex, will be withdrawn from September 7'. Prior to closure, a telegram was sent to Dr Beeching inviting him 'to attend the funeral of the Maldon-Witham passenger rail service at Maldon East Station, Essex at 8.13 pm on Sunday September 6th'. The event was a somewhat muted affair. On the last passenger train to Witham, there were only about 100 people. More joined at Witham for the last train to Maldon. When the train reached Maldon there was a speech by the Mayor to the effect that the new bus services would be monitored closely to see that they matched up with what had been promised. According to the *Maldon and Burnham Standard*, 'Maldon's rail service ended oh so quietly'. This was not quite the end of Maldon's railway, as the goods service lingered on until 15 April 1966, with the official closure taking place three days later. Prior to final closure a return Sunday school excursion had run to Walton-on-the-Naze on 13 June 1965. The last passenger trains on the branch. The replacement limited stop bus service survived until 1970, when it was withdrawn on 2 January. The service was locally known as the 'Ghost Service' as, although it started from Maldon Bus Depot, it was not allowed to pick up passengers until it was at Station Road near Maldon East Station. Since the closure, there have been calls to reopen the line or failing that the line from Woodham Ferrers. But there have also been those in Maldon who oppose reopening, even though considerable development has taken place there.

The following list of closure dates of lines post Beeching up to privatisation. includes goods services, although the Report was only concerned with passenger services.

The first closure was in 1963 but was not in the Beeching Report. This was Newstead Lane to Runton West Junction on the former Norfolk and Suffolk Joint Line which closed 21 April to all traffic.

The autumn of 1963 saw the winding up of the Southwold Railway over 34 years since the last train had run and over 20 years since the Railway had been demolished in the Second World War.

1964 saw a spate of closures. On the former Midland and Great Northern Joint Railway Sheringham to Melton Constable closed to passengers on 6 April and to goods on 28 December.

Thetford to Watton and Swaffham closed to passengers throughout and to goods between Thetford and Watton on 15 June. Goods traffic between Swaffham and Watton survived until 19 April 1965. 15 June 1964 also saw Wivenhoe to Brightlingsea closed to all traffic.

13 July saw goods traffic withdrawn between Somersham and Warboys, Three Horseshoes Junction to Benwick as well as Fordham to Mildenhall, Mellis to Eye and Ely to Sutton.

On 3 August Bungay to Ditchingham closed to goods.

7 September saw the Witham to Maldon line closing to passenger, with the line formally being closed to goods on 18 April 1966. The last goods train running on 15 April. At Witham a short stretch of line remained open to serve a factory until 1982, albeit operated by the factory's own motive power. 7 September 1964 also saw Audley End to Bartlow closed to passengers with goods following on 28 December.

North Walsham to Mundesley on the former Norfolk and Suffolk Joint Line closed to passengers on 5 October and to goods on 28 December. 5 October also saw the Dereham to Wells line closed to passengers on 5 October with goods services between Fakenham and Wells ceasing from 31 October. Also on 5 October, the section of line from St Ives to the mill at Bluntisham was closed to goods traffic.

On 31 October the line from County School to Foulsham was closed to goods traffic.

The passenger service from St Margarets to Buntingford ceased on 16 November followed by goods traffic on 20 September 1965.

Goods services south of Sudbury other than a daily conditional train ceased on 2 November. This train ceased on 28 December along with goods services between Heacham and Burnham Market and Halstead and Yeldham on the former Colne Valley and Halstead Railway.

Goods services on the original line to Enfield ceased on 7 December 1964. On 28 December through traffic over the Palace Gates branch ceased.

1965 saw Haddiscoe to Aldeby closed to goods in February followed by Wickham Market to Framlingham, Abbey to Stoke Ferry, Bury St Edmunds to Lavenham, Fordham to Burwell, Beccles to Ditchingham and Chapel to Halstead on 19 April.

Goods workings over the Hainault Loop ceased after 3 October.

1966 saw goods workings cease over the line to Loughton, Epping and Ongar other than to Leyton on 18 April. Leyton closed to goods on 6 May 1968.

18 April also saw the connection to the East London Railway closed at East London Junction, Shoreditch.

On 18 April, Tivetshall to Harleston closed to goods, thus bringing an end to the Waveney Valley line. 18 April also saw the start of closing the Bishop's Stortford to Dunmow and Braintree line when the section from Dunmow to Felstead closed when it was found that it would cost £120,000 to make the viaduct at Dunmow safe for continuing use.

Braintree to Felstead and Easton Lodge to Dunmow closed on 1 April 1969.

Bishop's Stortford to Easton Lodge remained open to serve Geest's banana factory at the latter place and this closed on 17 February 1972. After closure and before the track was lifted, an enthusiasts' trip formed of two brake vans and Class locomotive No 5637 ran from Bishop's Stortford to Easton Lodge and back on 27 July1972.

23 May saw the closure of the Wisbech and Upwell tramway to goods traffic with the last train running on 20 May.

On 12 September passenger services ceased between Saxmundham and Aldeburgh. Goods traffic other than that for Sizewell Nuclear Power Station ceased on the same day.

It was not only lines that were closing. Stations on those lines that were open were either closed or lost their goods facilities. To list all would take a long time.

1967 saw the withdrawal of passenger services between Sudbury and Shelford on 6 March. As indicated that whole line from Marks Tey to Shelford had been down for closure. Despite a spirited campaign to save the whole line the Minister of Transport closed the aforementioned section and left Marks Tey to Sudbury open.

Goods traffic on the section from Shelford to Sudbury had ceased on 31 October 1966.

6 March 1967 also saw the March to St Ives section of the Great Northern and Great Eastern Joint Line closed.

On the Felixstowe branch the daily passenger services between Felixstowe Town and Felixstowe Beach which since 2 November 1959 had been summer only were withdrawn on 11 September 1967. Whilst the line through to the docks remained open, goods facilities at both Felixstowe Town and Felixstowe Beach had closed on 5 December 1966.

1 January 1968 saw the withdrawal of passenger services between Cambridge and Oxford except for the section between Bedford and Bletchley. Most local goods facilities were closed on 18 April 1966. This line had not been proposed for closure by Dr Beeching.

9 September 1968 passenger and goods services withdrawn from the line from Kings Lynn to Dereham except for a 3-mile section from Kings Lynn to Middleton which remained open for sand traffic.

The same day, the line from March to Magdalen Road via Wisbech closed to all traffic between Magdalen Road and Wisbech and passenger traffic between March and Wisbech. Freight traffic remained until 2000. The line is still in existence and there have been attempts to reopen it.

On 5 May 1969 passenger services ceased between Kings Lynn and Hunstanton. Goods traffic had ceased on 28 December 1964.

6 October 1969 saw the end of passenger services between Wymondham and Dereham.

During the 1960s the various lines to the London Docks lost their goods traffic.

4 May 1970 saw the closure of the former Norfolk and Suffolk Joint Line between Yarmouth and Lowestoft to passengers. Goods traffic had ceased on 3 July 1967 except at Lowestoft North where it ceased on 6 November that year.

Until 31 May 1970, some passenger workings by BR ran to Epping. These ceased after that date and the connection to the Loughton and Epping lines was taken out on 2 October 1972, thus severing the lines from the national network. Whilst some trains were only for staff, others were for the general public. One of the weekdays early morning east bound trains started from Stratford BR and on Sunday mornings there were two trains in each direction between Liverpool Street and Epping. As by the beginning of 1970 all the suburban trains out of Liverpool Street were worked by emus, these trains worked by dmus were the last non-electric suburban trains out of Liverpool Street.

On 6 October 1970 the line from St Ives to Cambridge was closed to passenger traffic and although there were campaigns in the 1970s to reopen it, the only remaining rail traffic on the line was a freight service to Chivers in Histon which ran until 1983 and a contract to ferry sand from ARC at Fen Drayton which continued in operation until May 1992. On 2 October the line from Home to Ramsey North closed to goods.

At Whitemoor Marshalling Yard, as freight began to be carried in trainloads, the use of the Yard declined beginning in the 1970s and on 27 January 1972 the Down Yard was closed with the Up Yard taking its trains. For a time Whitemoor became a Freightliner centre, but in 1990 that too closed and all that remained was a small wagon repair facility. Any freight sorting that required to be done was done in the sidings to the east of the station. H M Prison Whitemoor was built on part of the site.

At this point it is convenient to mention closures in the London Docklands, where, beginning in the 1960s, the various local goods depots started to close as BR began to withdraw from single wagon load traffic, which was much better suited to road transport. The introduction of container traffic depots further downstream such as at Tilbury resulted in the almost overnight closure of the docks.

On the Gallions branch, Cory's traffic ceased in 1967 bringing an end to the line's commercial traffic.

On the Becton branch, traffic ceased when the last trainload of pitch left Becton Gasworks in December 1970. Final closure came on 22 February 1971.

North Woolwich closed to goods traffic on 7 December 1970.

On the former North London Railway Poplar branch goods traffic ceased in 1980.

On the former London and Blackwall Railway the junction to the Blackwall branch at Stepney had been disconnected in 1951, leaving the only access via the Limehouse Curve, which was abandoned in 1963 just after the last train ran on 5 November 1962. Until 1968 access for the occasional goods services to Blackwall and North Greenwich was via the former North London Railway at Poplar.

On 5 January 1981, in connection with the electrification of the Midland Line from Moorgate and St Pancras to Bedford the connection to the Tottenham and Hampstead line at Kentish Town was closed and the service diverted to run from Barking to Gospel Oak.

Fakenham lost its goods service on 1 January 1980, whilst Ryburgh followed on 1 January 1981. Wymondham via Dereham to North Elham followed on 12 October 1989.

Denver to Abbey closed for freight in 1982 along with the privately owned Wissington Light Railway which served a sugar beet factory at Wissington.

The line from Wroxham to Lenwade closed on 6 January 1982; following the cessation of traffic in 1983 a weed-killing train ran and the track was lifted in 1983.

On the LT&SR Line, Tilbury Riverside Station closed to passengers on 30 November 1992.

The last closure of a line in pre privatisation days was the section of the Central Line from Epping to Ongar which closed on 30 September 1994. For years, traffic remained very light on this very rural section of the Underground. London Transport had previously tried to close it on a number of occasions before finally succeeding.

The Beeching report had included a reduction in freight services, especially the marshalling yards, to concentrate on long distance bulk transport. The period after Beeching saw not only the closure of stations on lines that remained opened, many of the stations that remained open lost their goods facilities with road haulage taking over. With the closure of the goods yards came the end of the pick-up goods train. This decreased the need for some of the lower powered diesel locomotives and ultimately led to their withdrawal. The closure dates of goods yards are too numerous to mention.

In 1977 two Class 47 locomotives, Nos 47163 and 47164, were painted by Stratford TMD with silver roofs and other decorations including a full body height Union Flag on each side, in celebration of the Queen's Silver Jubilee.

In 1982 there had been severe threat to the railways in the form of the Serpell Report, which fortunately never got implemented. The Report was produced by a committee chaired by Sir David Serpell, who had been the first Permanent Secretary of the Department of the Environment on its creation in 1970. The Report had been commissioned by the government of Margaret Thatcher to examine the state and long-term prospects of Great Britain's railway system. The Report was in two parts. The first part gave a detailed description of the state of BR in 1982. The second looked at various options for a future rail network in 1992 and made comparisons between each option and the continuation of the existing network. Under the worst one, all that would have been left in East Anglia would have been the lines from Liverpool Street to Southend and to Norwich via Ipswich.

Starting on 6 January 1969 a limited LTS Section service was resumed into Liverpool Street via Forest Gate Junction, although one Up Sunday evening train had run from 3 November 1968.

1965 had seen the completion of a new container terminal at Felixstowe docks. This was served by Freightliner trains and helped to contribute to the docks handling 2,019,270 tons in 1969 – more than nine times the traffic of ten years earlier. On 13 May 1970, a new direct line to Felixstowe Docks was opened using the same alignment that had been used between 1877 and 1898 and removed the need for trains to reverse at Felixstowe Town. The section from Felixstowe Town to where it joined the reopened old alignment was closed on the same day.

There was another reopening when on 14 May 1979 a service from Camden Road on the North London Line to North Woolwich was started. This involved the reopening to passenger traffic of the line east of Dalston Junction to Victoria Park and Stratford. Initially, the service was worked by dmus, but on 14 May 1985 the service was electrified on the third rail system using Southern Region 2-car emus.

The Felixstowe Dock and Railway Company in 1981 obtained an Act of Parliament which allowed it to construct 1.61 miles of new railway. The first part to come into use was the extension of the existing dock lines to a new Northern Freightliner Terminal. In March 1986, work started on the remainder of the work. The new work saw the extension of the line from the Northern Freightliner Terminal to Trimley station. This opened on 16 February 1987. The construction work involved heavy earthworks and cost the Company £2 million, but as it would reduce road traffic, the Company received a 40 per cent grant under Section 8 of the Railways Act 1974.

There were even some station reopenings. For example, on the East Suffolk Line, Melton between Woodbridge and Wickham Market was reopened on 3 September 1984.

Between 1 September 1968 and 23 July 1971, the Victoria Line was opened in stages from Walthamstow to Brixton via King's Cross and Victoria. The origins of the line go back to the County of London Plan published in 1943 for a tube railway from Victoria to Walthamstow. In 1955, a private bill was introduced into parliament for a line from Victoria to Walthamstow. Originally, it was proposed that the line would terminate on the surface at Wood Street station in Walthamstow rather than Hoe Street but the section east of Hoe Street was abandoned on the grounds that, following the disruption caused by the Chingford electrification, further disruption at Wood Street was unacceptable. Although initial construction started in January 1960, it was not until 20 August 1962 that the line gained parliamentary approval. In Walthamstow, the terminus at Walthamstow Hoe Street station was renamed Walthamstow Central. During the planning stages the line was known as Route C, but it was named the Victoria Line by David McKenna from British Transport Advertising and seconded by the Chairman of London Transport Sir John Elliot. In March 1966, approval was given for the extension to Brixton. Serving not only Walthamstow, but also Tottenham Black Horse Road, Tottenham Hale and Seven Sisters, the line when opened from Walthamstow to Victoria on 7 March 1969 diverted some traffic away from the North East London section suburban lines.

In 1964/5, an extension of the GE electrification from Colchester to Ipswich, Harwich and Felixstowe for passenger and freight traffic was appraised. Freight traffic from the London Midland Region would have been worked over the cross-London link provided by an electrification of the North London line at ac current to Gospel Oak and then via the electrification of the Tottenham and Hampstead and the Tottenham and Forest Gate lines to Barking and Tilbury. It was also proposed to electrify from Copper Mill Junction Tottenham to Stratford including part of Temple Mills Yard to permit electric freight working from the LMR to GE. Unfortunately, poor financial returns and competing demands saw the scheme put to one side, Freightliner traffic did not start until 1965 and the growth of Felixstowe as a container port could not have been foreseen.

In 1964, there was a proposal to electrify the Southminster branch using battery operated trains. At the time, BR was looking at automatic train operation and research was conducted by British Railways (Electrical) Research Division (Electrical Research Division). The report was produced by H.I. Andrews and H.H. Ogilvy and dated 14 April 1964. The Southminster line was chosen as it was near to BR Headquarters in London. What was proposed were two 2-car battery electric units. The system to be used was a semi-conductor system on the lines that were being introduced in West Germany. It would give a power saving of 20 per cent over the existing battery electric system that was being used by battery electric trains on the Scottish Region. The trains would be charged from short lengths of live rail at Wickford and Southminster to which contact would be made when the trains were stationary. The live rails would be supplied by 100 Kw electricity from the national grid through a transformer energising at 500 volts ac. This would give the railcars a wider range of operation with a smaller battery, though the bulk of the power would be drawn at night when cheap rate electricity was available. The trains would be operated by automatic control through a continuous induction system actuated by two insulated wires along the centre of the track. The trains would have a crew of two. A guard who would push a button to start the train and would also stop the train in an emergency. The other member of staff would be a travelling ticket clerk as it was intended to close all the ticket offices and make all the stations unstaffed halts, except for Southminster where there would be a small number of staff to maintain the trains. The two trains would have American style headlights. The three daily goods trains would continue to be operated by diesel locomotives and the appropriate eight locomotives would be fitted with an indicating device activated from the track system advising the driver to proceed. On entering the branch, a small indicating device would be attached to the last vehicle of the train, together with the tail lamp. All the signal boxes and the passing loops at Woodham Ferrers and Burnham would be closed, leaving only the passing loop at Fambridge. The existing signal boxes would be reduced to ground frame status, used by pick up goods trains only and operated by the guard. The two level crossings on the line at Woodham Ferrers and Althorne would be converted to the automatically operated boom type. Nothing came of the proposal.

London Transport was also interested in automatic train operation, intending to use it on the Victoria Line. From 5 April 1964, the Woodford to Hainault section of the Central Line was operated with this equipment for an extensive period using 1960 Tube Stock motor cars and Standard Tube Stock trailer cars. When each 1967 Tube Stock train intended for the Victoria Line was delivered, it was run for three weeks in test on the service.

The next section of line to be electrified was the Lea Valley Line. Authorisation for this was given in April 1967. According to the *Herts and Essex Observer* of Friday

14 April 1967, work on electrifying the 9 miles from Copper Mill Junction Tottenham to Cheshunt would start in the autumn and was expected to be finished by spring 1968 and cost £1.25 million. It took until May 1969 for the electrification to be completed, the new service coming into operation on 5 May. With the electrification of the Lea Valley Line and the end on 31 May 1970 of the Sundays only diesel trains from Liverpool Street to Epping, all suburban trains out of Liverpool Street were now worked by electric traction. 5 May 1969 also saw the electrification of the section from Seven Sisters Junction via South Tottenham on the former Tottenham and Hampstead Junction Railway to Tottenham South Junction completed. This was mainly used for stock transfers.

During the 1970s, the principal focus on electrification by British Railways' Eastern Region was the Great Northern suburban services. This was in two stages. The first, which commenced on 3 November 1976, was from Moorgate to Welwyn Garden City and Hertford North over the former London Transport Great Northern and City Line which had been built to main line dimension unlike the rest of the tube lines. The line had been built by the Great Northern and City Railway from Finsbury Park to Moorgate with the intention that its electric locomotives would haul Great Northern Railway trains to the City from Finsbury Park. The line had opened in 1904, but at the time was not able to fulfil its objective. The second stage was from King's Cross to Finsbury Park and from Welwyn Garden City and Hertford North to Stevenage and thence via Hitchin to Royston which commenced on 6 February 1978. A dmu shuttle service ran between Royston and Cambridge and through trains from King's Cross to Cambridge were withdrawn.

The only section of the GE to be electrified in the 1970s was the branch line from Witham to Braintree. Unlike Maldon, Braintree had a Campaign Committee which had been formed in 1962, before the Report, to promote the growth of passenger traffic. In September 1966, the Committee's efforts had been rewarded when BR announced that the line had been reprieved. Starting in 1967, the Committee, in its newsletter to various season ticket holders, called for through trains from London to Braintree either by diesel power or by having the branch electrified. Passenger numbers rose from 153,000 in 1962 to 427,000 in 1972 and 575,000 in 1975. At that point, BR considered traffic on the line to be sufficient to warrant electrification. As the branch would be powered from the main line and thus not require a separate feeder station, the budget for the electrification was only £306,000. Work on the electrification started in early autumn of 1976. Following an inspection of the work by the Department of Transport's Railway Inspectors Majors C.F. Rose and E. Holden, BR announced Monday 3 October 1977 as the provisional start date for the start of the electric service. The Railway Campaign

Committee made arrangements with BR to run a special excursion train to London on Saturday, 1 October. At Braintree station there would be a musical display and a tape cutting ceremony. Things did not go to plan. There was a union dispute and everything had to be cancelled. Quietly, on Monday 31 October – four weeks late – the first electric train left Braintree.

By the latter part of the 1970s, BR had revised the clearances for 25,000 volts ac electrification and it was decided to convert all of the 6,250 sections to the higher voltage. This was finally achieved in March 1989.

According to Ian Cowley in *Anglia East: The Transformation of A Railway*, in the early 1970s the plans of 1964/5 were looked at again. By that time, Freightliner traffic had not grown sufficiently to offset the general decline in freight traffic, so the cross London link was abandoned and the new proposal relied on passenger traffic, with freight traffic limited to spare time in the locomotives' passenger diagrams. Electrification to Ipswich and Harwich was considered, with push-pull working between London and Norwich. In order to minimise the time taken to change locomotives at Ipswich, it was proposed to split the Norwich bound trains at the former place with the diesel locomotive taking the front five carriages only to Norwich. In the reverse direction, the diesel would push its train back to Ipswich to join the three or 4-carriages with the electric locomotive attached. The high cost of the driving trailers ruled against this, and the planners decided to electrify all the way to Norwich.

In November 1977, following the recommendations of a Select Committee on Nationalised Industries, the government announced its intention to review with the BR Board the general case for further main line electrification on the basis of an up-to-date appreciation that it expected to shortly receive from the BR Board. The appreciation duly arrived in the form of a discussion paper entitled 'Railway Electrification'. This showed that, while the cost per train mile was £0.85 for electric traction, that for diesel traction was £1.82. Even after the capital and maintenance charges for electrification were considered, electric traction still had an advantage of £0.56 per mile.

First, something had to be done about the signalling north of Colchester and Bishop's Stortford. It needed renewal. I remember travelling from London to Cambridge in October 1977 in a second class side corridor compartment carriage with arm rests to the seats and but for the diesel locomotive, north of Bishop's Stortford I could have been in steam days with a B1 at the head of the train rather than the Class 37. Additionally, the section from Bishop's Stortford to Cambridge required some track realignment to raise speeds from 70 to 90mph in some locations and ten overbridges required clearance work. North of Colchester, apart from the signalling and judicious track rationalisation, the other major work was Ipswich tunnel which had to be re-laid with slab track for clearance purposes.

In 1978, the scheme for the resignalling and track rationalisation was submitted to the BR Board and was approved. This was followed at the end of 1980 by proposals for the electrification from Bishop's Stortford to Cambridge and Colchester to Norwich and Manningtree to Harwich as well as the Royston to Cambridge section of the GN Line, the idea being to start work on the Bishop's Stortford to Cambridge section first as work on track renewal and signalling was more pressing at Cambridge. Furthermore, the M11 motorway threatened BR's market and there were plans in existence to transfer the Bedford to St Pancras electrification team to Cambridge. By electrifying the Royston to Cambridge section first, it was proposed to divert the main London to Cambridge service to King's Cross to enable work to proceed on the Bishop's Stortford to Cambridge section. However, the financial return on the Colchester to Norwich and Manningtree to Harwich sections was more attractive than that on the Royston to Cambridge and Bishop's Stortford to Cambridge sections, leading the government to reject Royston to Cambridge and give priority to approval to Colchester to Norwich and Manningtree to Harwich. In December 1981, the Department of Transport gave qualified approval for the latter, but subject to the continued viability of the proposals in the light of the reversed order of the work. This was subsequently confirmed and in September 1982 the final approval for the work to proceed was given by the BR Board. Following the deletion of proposals for emu depot facilities at Cambridge, approval was given for the electrification of the Bishop's Stortford to Cambridge section on 16 January 1984.

The work was carried out in stages. The electrification from Colchester to Ipswich was inaugurated on 11 May 1985, although the first public working by electric traction had taken place on 1 May. Class 81 locomotives dating from 1959 to 1964 were originally envisaged, but rejected on grounds of poor performance, so the more reliable Class 86 locomotives dating from 1965 to 1966 were selected instead. Class member No.86259 *Peter Pan* had the first public working of the Class on the GE Section on 1 May on the 9.30 a.m. from Liverpool Street to Norwich as far as Ipswich. On 7 August 1986 there was a modest extension of the electrification to Stowmarket. This was a peak hour only working using a Class 309 emu set. In the summer of 1985, because of rolling stock shortages, some extra boat trains were formed of class 309 units which worked under their own power from Liverpool Street to Colchester and vice versa and were hauled by diesel locomotives for the leg to and from Harwich. On 12 May 1986, Manningtree to Harwich was electrified, followed on 11 May 1987 by Stowmarket to Norwich with the full electric service from London to Norwich and Bishop's Stortford to Cambridge. The first electric train had run from London to Cambridge on 17 January that year, whilst on 6 April the first electric trains had reached Norwich. Through trains to Kings Lynn involved a change of locomotive at Cambridge and some diesel working into Liverpool Street by Class 47 locomotives continued until 1990. On 4 March that year approval had been given for the electrification from Royston to Cambridge which came into operation on 16 May 1988. Unfortunately, despite the route being longer than that from Liverpool Street, the service provided was faster.

There was other electrification. To some extent this was connected with the rebuilding or rather the redevelopment of Liverpool Street station. The work involved the closing and demolition of Broad Street station and diverting the Richmond service to North Woolwich via a newly electrified section of line from Dalston to North Woolwich and building a curve from London Fields on the Cambridge line to enable a peak hour service from Watford Junction to London continue. With the electrification of the North Woolwich line, Stratford depot would only have responsibility for maintaining dmus on

Class 86 electric locomotives were first built in 1965 for the London Midland Region and came to the GE section with first stage of the Norwich, Harwich and Cambridge electrification in 1985. No 86246 *Royal Anglian Regiment* pauses at Ipswich whilst working 1P33 1140 Norwich-London Liverpool Street on 25 October 2003. *Scott Borthwick*

the Romford to Upminster and Wickford to Southminster lines. Electrification seemed the most sensible answer. The electrification to North Woolwich was inaugurated on 11 May 1985. Approval for the electrification to Southminster was given in January 1984, followed by that for Romford to Upminster in June of that year, both being inaugurated on 12 May 1986. Whilst existing ac emus worked the Romford to Upminster and the Southminster branches, Southern Region Class 416 2 car units worked the North Woolwich service, the only use of Southern Region emus on the GE.

On 30 June 1986, in connection with rebuilding of Liverpool Street station and the closure of Broad Street station, an electrified single track curve was opened from London Fields to Dalston Kingsland on the North London Line. The curve was used by some peak hour trains from Liverpool Street to Watford until 28 September 1992. The curve was known as the Graham Road Curve.

Under the electrification of the West Coast Main Line in the 1960s, ac overhead electrification had been extended to Camden Road on the North London Line on 18 November 1965. On 14 April 1986, the ac electrification was extended to Stratford. This meant that the section from Camden Road to Stratford was equipped with both dc third rail electrification and ac overhead electrification.

The 2-car units of class 416 were first built in 1955 for the Southern Region and were the only Southern Region emus to work on the GE section taking over the Richmond to North Woolwich service in 1986. One such unit is seen at North Woolwich in the late 1980s. *Author.*

On 4 September 1989, the section to Coppermill North Junction was electrified at 25,000 volts overhead followed on 8 October 1989 by the section from Temple Mills East Junction to Stratford.

Along with the electrification, there were new electric trains. The 4-car Class 312 emus which were gangwayed between carriages within the set had first been built in 1975 but did not enter service until 1977. The 4-car Class 315 emus had first entered service in 1980 and like Class 312 were gangwayed within the set. These trains, like Class 306 which they replaced, had sliding doors. Non-gangwayed trains of which some carriages had compartments were becoming outdated by the beginning of the 1980s and work started converting Class 307, 308 and 305 4-car units and 30 Class 302 units to being all open carriages ganwayed within the sets. This started in 1981. It was a pretty drastic move. In the Class 302 units which were not converted, some of the compartment carriages were converted to open carriages. In them you could see in the roofs where the compartments had been – not the most elegant interior design! Further new ac emus on the GE Section were 310, 317, 321 and 322. Class 321 which first entered service in 1988 were the first outer suburban/main line units on the GE to have sliding doors. The units were a very great success with some remaining in service until 2023.

For the sake of completeness, I will mention the classes of dmu that have appeared on the GE Section. They were 150, 153, 155, 156, 158, 170 and 172.

Class 312 emus were first built in 1975 but did not enter public service until 1977. The class was unlike the preceding 4-car emus on the GE section gangwayed within each unit. A member of the class is seen leaving Chelmsford for Liverpool Street in the early 1980s. *Author*

The 4-car emus of class 315 were the replacements for the original Shenfield units of class 306. Though originally only working Liverpool Street to Shenfield, they later extended their field of operations. Nos 315824 and 315835 are seen arriving at Stratford on the 14.14 Shenfield to Liverpool Street service on 16 November 2016. *Brian Garrett*

By the early 1980s, non-gangwayed trains were out of fashion and British Rail commenced rebuilding its emus with internal gangways. Class 307 having first been rebuilt from dc traction to ac traction now saw a further rebuild. No 121 heads a train into Wickford in the mid-1980s. *Author*

Class 310 emus first entered service in 1965 on the London Midland Region and were originally gangwayed between pairs of carriages. They were later rebuilt to be gangwayed within the set and transferred to the GE section. A pair is seen entering Billericay on a London train in the mid-1980s. *Author*

Class 317 4-car units had first appeared in 1981 for the Midland suburban service. They were later displaced by class 319 to the LNW, GN and GE sections. Unit No 317654 passes Bethnal Green on the 12 42 Liverpool Street to Hertford East service on 6 April 2019. *Brian Garrett*

The 2-car class 156 or Super Sprinter first went into service in 1987 and replaced first generation dmus and locomotive hauled trains on some services. Unit No 156407 is seen arriving at Norwich on 1 April 2019 with the 16.49 train from Sheringham. *Brian Garrett*

The 2-car class 158 or Express Sprinter first entered service in 1990 and their appearance in East Anglia was on inter regional trains. On 4 April 2019 East Midlands Trains unit No 158780 arrives at Norwich on a Liverpool Lime Street to Norwich train. *Brian Garrett*

Class 170 3-car dmus were first built in 1998 and entered service in 1999. On 12 March 2017 unit No 170202 departs from Ipswich with the 8.30 Harwich International to Cambridge service. *Brian Garrett*

Just north of Bishop's Stortford but within the county of Essex is Stansted Airport. The airport was first built as RAF Stansted during the Second World War and opened in early July 1943. It was first used by the United States Army Air Force. To cut a long story short, civilian commercial air traffic started in 1966. To serve the airport, a branch line from Stansted Mountfichet just north of Bishop's Stortford to Stansted Airport was constructed and was opened on 29 January 1991. The airport was and is served by a dedicated service from Liverpool Street. It is worth mentioning that Chris Green and Mike Vincent in *The Network SouthEast Story* (OPC 2014) state that there was a proposal to link Stansted Airport to the Thameslink service, which at that time linked Bedford to Brighton via Farringdon in Central London. The proposal was to link Kentish Town to Tottenham Hale via reopened chords lines at the two stations.

On 7 February 1989, electrification was authorised to the section from Cambridge to Kings Lynn via Ely. The work involved singling the track north of Ely between Littleport and Downham Market and Watlington to Kings Lynn. After 12 May 1990 until the inauguration of the electrification, all through trains south of Cambridge ceased. Class 47 No 47581 *Great Eastern* hauled the last scheduled diesel trains into and out of Liverpool Street on 12 May – 9am Kings Lynn to Liverpool Street and 6.32pm Liverpool Street to Kings Lynn. On the train to Kings Lynn, the locomotive carried a headboard which read 'Farewell to Stratford Passenger Locos – Last Scheduled Diesel Service From Liverpool Street 12th May 1990'. The departure screens at Liverpool Street announced the last diesel hauled trains with the numbers and names of the locomotives, Class No 47576 *Kings Lynn* being the other diesel locomotive working the service that day. During the interim there was Fenland Steam Weekend on 19 and 20 October 1991, when special trains were hauled by either A3 Class No 4472 *Flying Scotsman*, still in its elegant single chimney condition, rebuilt West Country Class No 34027 *Taw Valley* and Britannia Class No 70000 *Britannia*. I travelled on the special trains on 19 October. I went out from Cambridge behind *Taw Valley* which carried the headboard for the *Golden Arrow* and came back behind *Flying Scotsman*. The electrification was inaugurated on 22 August 1992. Other than a couple of peak hour trains to Liverpool Street, all trains ran through to King's Cross. Given that King's Cross has got hold of the Cambridge and Kings Lynn services, no doubt when Ely to Norwich is electrified King's Cross will become the main station for Norwich with a faster service over a longer route.

Had privatisation not occurred, there were plans for further electrification. These were Gospel Oak to Barking, which occurred after privatisation, and Marks Tey to Sudbury, which at the time of writing has not happened.

1966 saw the publication of Cecil J. Allen's *The London and North Eastern Railway*. The book is something of a disappointment in that Allen skirts over the Second World War and assumes that readers will have or will acquire a copy of Norman Crump's *By Rail To Victory*. Michael Bonavia's three volume history of the Company published in 1982–3 is considerably better. Both Allen and Bonavia had worked for the Company.

The rebuilding of Liverpool Street station was, together with the completion of main line and suburban electrification, one of the most significant events relating to the GE Section. In 1973, BR, London Transport, the Great London Council and the Department of the Environment produced a report which examined the modernisation of London's transport. The report recommended that high priority be given to reconstructing Liverpool Street and Broad Street stations and that it be financed through property development on the site. In 1975, BR announced plans to demolish and redevelop both stations. Under the plans, Broad Street would have been closed and trains diverted to Liverpool Street via the Graham Road Curve. All of Liverpool Street station as it then was would have been demolished in the same way that in the 1960s Euston Station had been redeveloped. The proposal for the demolition of the station caused considerable public opposition and a campaign started, led by Sir John Betjeman, which led to a public inquiry which lasted from November 1976 to February 1977. The inquiry recommended that, whilst the eastern train shed roof be demolished, the western train shed roof should be retained and be repaired and reinforced. The work to do this took place between 1982 and 1984 with the repairs to the main roof being completed in 1987. The original plans for the station had included adding two additional tracks into the station and increasing the number of platforms from eighteen to twenty-two. The whole station still to be at the existing level of Liverpool Street Station. In 1983/4 the development was reassessed and it was decided to retain the existing six tracks out of the station and to not increase the number of platforms, in combination with resignalling. The result was a station confined to the Liverpool Street site with an increase in ground space for redevelopment. In 1985, BR signed an agreement with the developers Rosehaugh Stanhope and work on the office development, which was known as Broadgate, started. As mentioned, the work in connection with the redevelopment included the construction of the Graham Road Curve which opened in June 1986 and saw the final closure of Broad Street Station on 30 June 1986. The redeveloped station had a single concourse at the head of the platforms and entrances from Bishopsgate and Liverpool Street as well as a bus interchange in the south west corner of the station. The Broadgate development, which was constructed between 1985 and 1991 had 2.6 million sqft of office space on the site of Broad Street Station and above the tracks at Liverpool Street Station. The proceeds from the Broadgate development were used to fund the modernisation of Liverpool Street Station. In 1988, there was a proposal by London Regional Transport and MEPC to demolish the arcade above the Underground station and develop the site into a five-storey block of offices and shops. However, a petition to save the arcade signed by more 6,000 people resulted in it being saved.

Fenchurch Street station was also rebuilt. At the end of the 1980s, the station was carrying 50,000 passengers a day using infrastructure that was 50 years old. In 1994, shortly before rail privatisation, the station was closed for eight weeks to replace signals, track and electrification works. The cost of this was £83 million.

1982 saw the sectorisation of British Rail. Under this, three passenger sectors were created: InterCity; London and South East, later renamed Network South East; and Provincial, later named Regional Railways. In the east of England, InterCity operated the Colchester main line expresses including Harwich boat trains and local services north of Colchester. Network South East operated all suburban services and main line trains including local services, to Cambridge, Kings Lynn, Clacton, Walton and Sudbury. Regional Railways trains operated into East Anglia but did not operate any internally. There was also Scotrail which looked after passenger services operation exclusively in Scotland. Freight traffic was also divided into sectors. Trainload Freight took trainload goods, Railfreight took non-trainload goods, Freightliner took intermodal traffic and Rail Express Systems took parcels traffic. In connection with Network SouthEast, Chris

Green and Mike Vincent tell a lovely story in their book *The Network SouthEast Story*. Chris Green, who was the Sector Director of Network SouthEast from 1986 to 1991, had been struck by the impact of red lampposts at his local B&Q warehouse. The Stations Group of Network South East decided to paint every lamppost across the sector bright red. In doing this, Britain nearly ran out of red paint! In Brentwood the contractors were instructed to paint the lampposts red. A slight problem arose. All the lampposts in the town were painted red – except those at the railway station. It was not only lampposts that were painted red. The platform seats were painted red as well as ticket collecting booths.

In 1988, the Eastern Region, which in 1967 had absorbed the North Eastern Region, was divided with the creation of the new Anglia Region. The new Region covered the Eastern Counties and had its boundary points between Peterborough and Whittlesea, Royston and Meldreth, Harringay Stadium and Crouch Hill and Caledonian Road and Camden Road.

In the London Docklands, efforts to redevelop the docks began almost as soon as they had closed. However, it took a decade for most of the plans to get beyond the drawing board and another decade for them to take full effect.

To serve the Docklands, public transport was needed. This initially came in the form of the Docklands Light Railway. What emerged was a third rail automated railway running from Island Gardens on the site of the old North Greenwich station to West India Quay, where the railway branched in two. One branch went via Limehouse (formerly Stepney East) to Tower Gateway, which was virtually on the site of the old Minories station, near Tower Hill Underground station and used most of the southernmost pair of the two tracks from Fenchurch Street to Limehouse. The other branch went to Stratford via Poplar, Devons Road and Bow Church and from Bow Junction ran alongside the GE mainline. At Stratford, it used one of the unused bay platforms intended for the never-operated shuttle service to Fenchurch Street that had been intended under the original proposals for the London to Shenfield electrification. Although the 2-car trains were fully automated and were controlled by computer, they did have a member of staff called a train captain whose job it was to patrol the train, checking tickets, making announcements, controlling the doors by closing them automatically prior to starting and being able to drive the train in the event of the failure of the equipment or in an emergency. The new railway, which cost £77 million, was constructed between 1985 and 1987 and was formally opened on 30 July 1987 by the Queen, with public services beginning on 31 August. The railway was initially operated by London Transport.

Prior to rail privatisation, a number of extensions were opened. These were to Bank via a new tunnel, whilst still leaving Tower Gateway operational and which opened in

1991. This required additional trains suitable to work through the tunnel. The other extension was to Becton via a branch from Poplar which opened in March 1994.

In 1990, the former East London Railway became a separate line in its own right, instead of being the East London Section of the Metropolitan Line. Meanwhile the surviving named trains ceased to exist.

There were changes to the shipping side of the railway. Just prior to the Beeching Report, the following services operated out of Harwich, firstly to the Hook of Holland jointly between BR and the Zeeland Steamship Company. Secondly to Esjberg by the United Steamship Company Limited of Copenhagen.

1968 saw the shipping interests of British Rail adopt the name Sealink for marketing purposes. In preparation for the privatisation of BR's fleet, the ownership was transferred to Sealink UK, which on 27 July 1984 was sold for £66 million to the Bermuda-based Sea Containers, which renamed it Sealink British Ferries. In 1991, Sea Containers sold it to the Swedish-owned Stena Line, who changed the name to Sealink Stena Line and then a few years later to Stena Sealink Line.

In 1964, another train ferry had entered service – *Cambridge Ferry*, built by Hawthorne Leslie's yard on the Tyne. Following modifications to the sterns of *Essex Ferry* and *Norfolk Ferry* in October 1967, a secondary train ferry service opened from Harwich to Dunkirk. *Cambridge Ferry* was later modified.

In 1980, the government started to put pressure on the nationalised industries for wasting taxpayer's money. In May 1981, the *Alpha Express,* which had been built in 1973 as the *Stena Shipper* by A. Vuyk & Zonen's Scheepswerven, Amsterdam, was sent to Smith's Dock, Middlesbrough, Tyne and Wear for conversion to a train ferry. The ship had received its new name when it had been chartered to Aghiris Lines, Piraeus in 1977. In 1979, following the bankruptcy of Aghiris Lines, the ship was arrested at Mombasa in Kenya. In August 1981, the ship was chartered by Sealink and renamed *Speedlink Vanguard* with a capacity for 56 railway wagons.

Later, further cost cutting feasibility studies were considered which included basing all train ferry traffic through one English port and one Continental port using two new purpose-built train ferries and new ferry terminals. Unfortunately, on purely geographical grounds Harwich did not stand a chance of winning the competition, as Dover was much closer to any Continental port with a shorter sea voyage enabling more trips per day per vessel. So the Dover-Dunkirk route was selected, though only one new train ferry was built. On 29 January 1987, *Speedlink Vanguard* brought the end of train ferry services from Harwich when it left the port for the last time. The previous year had seen cargo levels reach record breaking levels. The Dover to Dunkirk train ferry did not last that much longer, as the opening of the Channel Tunnel in 1994 meant that most of the freight that was carried on the train ferry was re-routed through the tunnel. In December 1995 the train ferry ceased operation.

Away from train ferries, 1964 had seen the first roll-on-roll-off ship enter service serving Harwich when United Steamship Company's ship the *England* entered service on the route to Esjberg. 1964 also saw the Zim Israel Navigation Company start a weekly service from Harwich to Hamburg. Zim later joined forces with the Star Shipping Agency; although traffic increased slightly, the service only lasted ten months.

24 May1966 had seen Prinz Ferries start a service from Harwich to Bremerhaven in Germany or West German as it was prior to reunification. From 1 January 1969 to 30 April 1979, the service used Navy Yard Wharf instead of Parkeston Quay.

10 May 1967 saw Fred Olsen Lines start a new service from Harwich to Kristiansands in Norway.

On 29 May 1968, the Belgian Marine Administration started a service from Harwich to Ostend. Sadly, the service only lasted until 10 September 1973.

1970 saw Hamburg added to places served by Prinz Ferries from Harwich.

In 1977 Oslo was added to the list of places served by Fred Olson Line.

The link between Parkston Quay and Germany was restarted on 1 May 1979.

In 1981, the United Steamship Company (DFDS) took over Prinz Ferries and Tor Line.

Tor Line transferred its Gothenburg passenger service from Felixstowe to Parkeston Quay on 1 May 1983.

Between 1982 and 1983, DFDS passenger services were branded as DFDS Danish Seaways. Initially, it operated to the following places from Harwich: Esjberg, Gothenburg, Hamburg, Bremerhaven, but the service to Bremerhaven ceased on 17 December 1982.

In 1988, DFDS rebranded itself Scandinavian Seaways.

Beginning in 1968 with the introduction of car ferries, Sealink services and those of the Zeeland Steamship Company were amalgamated but remaining separate. In 1989 Stena acquired the Dutch company.

In 1997, a new ship entered service between Harwich and the Hook of Holland. This was the *Stena Discovery*. This was a high-speed ship capable of 40 knots. This compared to the 19 knots of the *Stena Europe* which I sailed on from Harwich to the Hook of Holland in September 1994.

The train ferry was not the only thing to cease. 11 May 1990 saw the end of the Peterborough section of the East Anglian TPO. The main East Anglian TPO survived into privatisation.

In the 1960s, railway preservation which had begun with the Talyllyn Railway in Mid Wales in 1951 really got off the ground. Even before the 1960s there had been a preservation society formed in East Anglia. Following the closure of much of former Midland and Great Northern Joint Railway at the end of February 1959, the Midland & Great Northern Joint Railways Preservation Society was formed in April of that year. Initially it hoped to save the 22-mile long North Walsham to Yarmouth section, then the North Walsham to Aylsham section, and then the section between Themelthorpe and Melton Constable. When those plans proved impossible, attention was turned to the 3-mile section of line between Sheringham and Weybourne, although at that time Sheringham to Melton Constable via Weybourne was still open. In 1963, the Society formed the North Norfolk Railways Limited. Initially, as it did not own any railway, to preserve and operate the line it was required to be titled Central Norfolk Enterprises. At that time, Sheringham station was still being used by British Rail services. By the time the purchase of the line had been completed, track lifting had taken place at Weybourne, and some way towards Sheringham. In 1965, work started on rebuilding the line. Following its closure and replacement by a halt on the other side of the level crossing at Sheringham, in 1967 Sheringham station was leased by the society. At first, trains were only operated for members. Operations over the line were later authorised through a Light Railway Order, the first of these issued in 1975 under the control of British Rail, and independently from 1976. In 1978, the Railway opened to the public.

Only one J15 has survived into preservation and resides on the North Norfolk Railway. The locomotive, GER No 564/7564/5462/65462 is seen at Sheringham on 31 May 1983 awaiting departure for the short run to Weybourne. The locomotive first entered traffic in preservation in 1978. *Author*

In 1987, an Amendment Order was issued in relation to the extension of the NNR to a new station site at Holt, using a parcel of land originally purchased as the junction for the never-built Blakeney branch.

Following the closure in 1967 of the line between Sudbury and Shelford, the Stour Valley Railway Preservation Society was formed in 1968. Its aim was to preserve the 3-mile stretch of line from Sudbury to Long Melford. Unfortunately, a lack of funding meant this project proved unsuccessful and the line was lost. The section of line is now a footpath which can also be used by cyclists. In 1969, the Society re-established itself at Chappel and Wakes Colne Station after securing a lease from British Rail for the derelict goods yard, goods shed, signal box and station buildings, with the first steaming taking place that year. During the early 1980s, the site changed to become a public attraction, or living archive for the benefit and enjoyment of the whole community. In 1986, the Stour Valley Railway Preservation Society became the East Anglian Railway Museum, to confirm its focus on representing the railway history of the Eastern Counties. In 1987, the Museum was able to purchase the Chappel site from the British Railway Property Board, part funded by the sale of a locomotive to a consortium of members.

In 1973, at Castle Hedingham, served by the former Colne Valley and Halstead Railway, the Colne Valley Railway Company Ltd acquired land for a railway from the landowner who had bought it from BR. In 1974, a volunteers' supporters' body, the Colne Valley Railway Preservation Society (CVRPS), was formed. As the track and infrastructure of the railway had been taken up in the late 1960s, there was no remaining infrastructure onsite. The original Sible and Castle Hedingham station 1 mile away was taken down carefully brick by brick, the bricks numbered, and the structure transported to the new site where it was subsequently reconstructed.

1973 also saw the formation of the Great Eastern Railway Society. Its purpose is to promote a widespread interest in the GER including its ancestors and successors and to encourage and to coordinate research into the Railway's history and also provide a permanent record of the results. The person initially responsible for the forming of the Society was Terry Simister, who had placed an advert in the *Railway Modeller*, with the inaugural meeting being held in his house in Chelmsford on 15 June 1973. The Society's first President was Bernard Walsh, one of the eminent enthusiasts and historians of the GER. The Society has gone on to great things, including creating an archive which is held in the Essex Record Office and reprinting or making available either electronically or in CD form various magazines such as the *Great Eastern Railway Magazine*, *Railway and Travel Monthly*, the *LNER Magazine* and the *British Railways Eastern Region Magazine*, *Railways* and the *Locomotive Magazine* amongst others as well as inspiring the North Eastern Railway Association to make available on CD the *North Eastern Railway Magazine.*

In the north of Norfolk, a local railway enthusiast Lieutenant Commander Roy Francis, who had already built and opened the 10¼in gauge Wells Harbour Railway in 1976, in 1979 set about restoration of the railway service south from Wells, towards Walsingham. The ground works and track laying took three years to complete, and the railway was opened on 6 April 1982. The railway was built to the same gauge as the Wells Harbour Railway.

The Bure Valley Railway is a 15in gauge railway running from Wroxham to Aylesham on the trackbed of the closed line from Wroxham to County School. Following closure in 1982 and the lifting of the track in 1983, the trackbed was purchased by Broadland District Council, who initially had plans to develop it as a long-distance footpath. In 1986, however, the idea of using part of the closed line as an operational railway was considered. Following a comparative study between the proposed Bure Valley Railway and the long-established Romney, Hythe and Dymchurch Railway in Kent, with various mitigations required of the new company, consent was given for the rebuilding of the line in 1987, despite local objections and with complaints from residents of Buxton with Lamas initially seeing plans for a restored station in the village dropped. On 10 July 1990, the Railway opened. Initially, whilst owning its own rolling stock and prior to it obtaining its own motive power, some locomotives were hired from the Romney Hythe and Dymchurch Railway.

The origins of the Mid-Norfolk Railway can be found in pre-privatisation days, with the formation of the Wymondham, Dereham and Fakenham Railway Action Committee in 1974 following an unsuccessful attempt to restore passenger services between Wymondham and Fakenham. In 1978, rumours started to spread of the closure of the Ryburgh to Fakenham section and so the Fakenham and Dereham Railway Society (F&DRS) was formed with the aim of operating the section after closure by BR. This was a forerunner of the Mid-Norfolk Railway.

Starting in 1976 there were and have been a number of steam-hauled trains on the main line. The first was with the no longer existing former Southern Railway S15 4 6 0 No 841 *Greene King.* Equally, there are or have been a number of places where steam locomotives associated with the East of England are or were displayed. The only one at present is Bressingham Gardens near Diss, but at North Woolwich from 1984 until 2008 the original station buildings and one disused platform served as the North Woolwich Old Station Museum, dedicated to the history of the GER. Displayed outside was the last surviving Y5 Class saddle tank No 229 which had been sold out of service in 1918, but had survived long enough to be preserved. At Burnham-on-Crouch, John

Only four original GER locomotives have survived into preservation of which the most interesting survivor is GER class 209/ LNER class Y5 No 229 which was sold out of service in 1918. It is seen at the former North Woolwich station museum where it resided from 1984 to 2008. *Author*

Jolly opened a museum which included a running line at the end of August 1989. The Museum reputedly has the largest collection of small artefacts outside the National Railway Museum.

Some projects that were proposed pre-privatisation did not materialise until afterwards. The origins of the Jubilee Line go back to the late 1960s/early 1970s. In 1969, powers were obtained to build the first stage of what was the known as the Fleet Line. This was to take over the Stanmore to Baker Street section of the Bakerloo Line and then run via Bond Street and Green Park to Charing Cross. In 1971, work started on the construction of the first stage. From Charing Cross the line was to run via Aldwych, Ludgate Circus and Canon Street to Fenchurch Street. From there it would go to Surrey Docks on the East London Line and take over both New Cross branches of that line with an extension from New Cross to Lewisham. Powers to build these two stages were obtained in 1971 and 1972. Things got rather complicated as in 1973 it was proposed to rename the line the River Line and extend it Fenchurch Street to Thamesmead via St Katharine Docks, Wapping, Surrey Docks North, Millwall North Greenwich, Custom House, Silvertown and Woolwich Arsenal. In the end, prior to privatisation all that was constructed was the first section to Charing Cross plus some tunnel beyond that, extending nearly to Aldwych and a bit of tunnel at New Cross as well as the shell of the upper stage of Fenchurch Street tube station. In 1977, the Silver Jubilee of the Queen's accession to the throne, the line was renamed the Jubilee Line and was opened by the Prince of Wales, now Charles III, on 30 April 1979, with passenger services operating from 1 May 1979. In the late 1980s, prompted by the proposed development of the London Docklands and Canary Wharf, Olympia and York, the developers of the latter, proposed a Waterloo and Greenwich Railway to run from Waterloo to Greenwich via London Bridge and Canary Wharf. London Transport resisted this and preferred to wait for the results of studies into new railway construction. One of these was the East London Railway Study. This recommended an extension of the Jubilee line from Green Park via Westminster and to follow the route of the proposed Waterloo and Greenwich Railway to Greenwich before continuing to Stratford via Canning Town, running alongside the North London Line. In 1990, powers were obtained to extend the line to Stratford from Green Park via Westminster, London Bridge and North Greenwich.

The origins of CrossRail or what is now known as the Elizabeth Line go back to a proposal in the Central London Rail Study of 1989 for an East–West Crossrail. According to the CrossRail Information Brochure dated 1991, the line would have run from Shenfield in the east to Stratford before going underground via Liverpool Street, Farringdon, Tottenham Court Road and Bond Street to Paddington where just beyond it would surface with one branch going to Reading via Slough with a branch from Hayes and Harlington to Heathrow Airport and the other branch going via Harrow-on-the-Hill to Rickmansworth, and Amersham to Aylesbury with a branch from Chalfont and Latimer to Chesham. In that same year, a private bill promoted by London Underground and British Rail and supported by the government was submitted to parliament for the scheme including the new underground line from Liverpool Street to Paddington. Unfortunately, the bill was rejected in 1994 by the Private Bill Committee on the grounds that a case had not been made. The government, though, did issue 'Safeguarding Directions', protecting the route from any development that would jeopardise future schemes.

The period between the Beeching Report and privatisation saw quite a lot of industrial action. Sometimes rather than a strike this took the form of work to rules and overtime bans which in some ways were worse than a strike as at least with a full-scale strike one knew what was not running. With an overtime ban and a work to rule one had to believe that something would run. Some lines were hit harder than others. Main lines fared better than suburban lines. The early to mid-1970s were particularly bad. Travelling was hell! It was during one in 1972 that what is believed to be the only known working in scheduled Liverpool Street to Southend passenger service and return of a Class 309 emu or Clacton unit took place on 12 April 1972 according to the *Railway Magazine* for June 1972. To give an example of how bad things could get, according to the *Railway Observer* of April 1973, on 20 February 1973 only three trains left Southend for Liverpool Street between 8.30am and 3.30pm. Another event, but not mentioned in the *Railway Observer*, is that once the Chelmsford signalman arranged for the morning boat train from Harwich to make an unscheduled stop at Chelmsford to enable waiting passengers to get on it. From what I have heard, the driver of the boat train was not particularly pleased with the signalman – even if the waiting passengers were. On 10 April 1972 I had to go to London for a job interview. Having waited some time for a train at Billericay station and a train not turning up, I went and got a refund of my ticket from the ticket office. That also shows how bad things were.

1982 was a particularly bad year. On 28 and 29 June there was a strike by the NUR over BR's refusal to improve a 5 per cent pay offer which was frozen until September and tied to productivity. Because of public hostility and a lack of support from the railwaymen, the strike was called off at the Union's Conference, held at Plymouth. At the same time there was a strike on the London Underground which had started on 22 June over cuts in services and which was called off at the same time as the strike on BR. From personal memory, there were no trains running into Liverpool Street or Fenchurch Street on 28 June, but there were on 29 June. No sooner had the NUR called off its strike than the train drivers' union ASLEF called one commencing on 5 July over flexible rostering. On 18 July, the strike was called off. During that time, some trains did run driven by NUR or non-union drivers. From personal observation I know that a pair of Class 315 emus once worked an all-stations train from Liverpool Street to Clacton and that some Southend line trains were operated by 3-car dmus of Class 104. A lot of trains on the Southend line during the 1982 ASLEF strike were worked by Class 315 units, but I also remember travelling on a Class 312 unit. Living where I do, I am able to use either Billericay on the Southend line or Chelmsford on the main line.

In the summer and very early autumn of 1994, there was a series of strikes by signallers who were members of the Rail, Maritime Transport Union (RMT) over pay. The RMT was an amalgamation of the National Union of Railwaymen and the National Union of Seamen.

The weather also played havoc. On the night of 15-16 October 1987, there was a terrible storm, causing significant damage to infrastructure. Trees were uprooted and some still remain where they fell to this day. Trains were disrupted by trees falling on the line or overhead power cables coming down. At the time it was regarded as a hurricane. And it was. It got into British folklore. According to the *Railway Observer* of December 1987 there were no trains running out of Liverpool Street until late in the day on 16 October when there was an occasional service to Shenfield. On 17 October, a limited stopping service was run between Liverpool Street and Shenfield formed of locomotive hauled rakes of three or four coaches. One gets the impression that diesel locomotives were used as the *Observer* mentions class 47 No 47630 being used. Although most services had been restored on 19 October it was not until later in the week that full services were resumed. On 25 January 1990 there was an even worse storm which again caused disruption to transport. This could also be regarded as a hurricane.

On Friday 5 December 1964 there was a fire at Bishopsgate Goods Depot, which unfortunately claimed the lives of two HM Customs officers working at the site. The fire was one of the biggest peacetime fires in Britain. It caused £5 million worth of damage. 300 railway wagons and 60 motor vehicles were destroyed. Flames reached 100 feet in the air and could be seen ten miles away.

The first call was received by the London County Council Fire Brigade headquarters fire control room at 6.20am from a passer-by dialling 999 from an exchange telephone. Another call was received four minutes later and a further six calls with the last at 6.58am. A total of 45 pumping appliances, 10 turntable ladders and 13 other specialist fire engines with 235 London firemen were employed to fight the blaze.

As the goods depot was only a quarter of a mile from Liverpool Street station and because many of the passenger lines passed close to the walls of the Goods Depot which were in danger of falling, there was serious interruption to services. Some Colchester and Southend lines trains were terminated at Stratford and some were diverted to Fenchurch Street. Chingford, Enfield, Hertford, Bishop's Stortford, Cambridge and King's Lynn trains were not affected. It was not until a week later that normal services were resumed. The 1,200 men employed at the depot were directed to other depots which were handling the goods traffic. BR Eastern Region had, prior to the fire, decided to close the sundries section of the freight service from Bishopsgate within the following few months. Owing to the destruction of all material evidence by the fire it was impossible to establish its cause.

In 1983, the Liverpool Street Hotel was sold off to a private company; it is now the Andaz Liverpool Street.

With the modernisation of the railways there was a lot of rationalisation of signalling, including the replacement of semaphore signals by colour light signals. The number of signal boxes was reduced, with control being transferred to a smaller number of centralised signalling centres. Stations were also modernised. Some of these modernisations were not tasteful, with some buildings of historic architectural interest being destroyed. There were and are instances of station buildings being replaced by basic shelters more suitable for a bus route or a pleasing building having a modern extension stuck on it.

Margaret Thatcher, despite what has been said about her, did not believe in the privatisation of the railways or the Post Office. The idea of a couple of experimental privatisations was, I understand, considered, one being the LTS Section. John Major, who succeeded Mrs Thatcher as Prime Minister in 1990, did believe in the privatisation of the railways and the Post Office. What had once been a unified system was now split up into myriad companies. Railtrack looked after the infrastructure except for a few major stations. In 2002, Railtrack was renationalised as Network Rail. There were separate freight operators and separate passenger operators. Everything was owned by a franchise. Privatisation took place between 1996 and 1997.

For freight, you had Mendip Rail which still operates aggregate trains from quarries in the Mendip Hills in Southwest England, to London and Southeast England. This is owned by Aggregate Industries (formerly Foster Yeoman) and Hanson Aggregates (previously ARC). DC Rail (legally Devon and Cornwall Railways Ltd) originally owned by British American Railway Services, a subsidiary of Iowa Pacific Holdings, a pure freight operating company. Direct Rail Services, which is state owned and is a subsidiary of British Nuclear Fuels, is responsible for the transporting of nuclear material. DB Cargo UK (which was formerly DB Schenker Rail UK and earlier English, Welsh & Scottish Railway [EWS]), is a rail freight company and is owned by the German Deutsche Bahn. EWS was owned by Wisconsin Central. Freightliner Group is a rail freight company and is owned by the American holding company Genesee & Wyoming. Another freight company is GB Railfreight.

Initially, the following companies operated passenger services in the east of England. Silverlink, owned by National Express, operated suburban services out of Euston station, the North London line and the Gospel Oak to Barking Line. West Anglia Great Northern, owned by National Express, operated suburban and some main line services out of King's Cross and Moorgate and the west side of Liverpool Street. First Great Eastern owned by First Group operated suburban services including branch lines and some main line services out of the east side of Liverpool Street plus the Romford to Upminster line. Anglia Railways, owned by GB Railways, operated the main line services from Liverpool Street to Norwich and the Harwich boat trains and all branch lines and cross country lines east and north of Ipswich.c2c started off as LTS Rail operated the former LTS Section. The franchise was originally owned by Prism which sold it in 2000 to National Express and 2017 it was sold to Trenitalia. It has not been specified what c2c stands for, with the marketing material stating 'c2c could stand for coast to capital, or capital to coast'. Central Trains, owned by National Express, operated cross-country services into East Anglia. Given that a few c2c trains operated into Liverpool Street, there were now four train companies operating into the station. *Bradshaw's Railway Companion* for 1841 showed only two railway companies operating into Shoreditch station. In 2004, all of the principal companies operating out of Liverpool Street were combined into one company – National Express East Anglia or, as it branded itself, One. This was sense as with c2c there were only two companies operating out of Liverpool Street.

In 2007, the London Overground was formed to initially take over the suburban services from Euston to Watford plus the North London Line and the Gospel Oak to Barking Line. In 2008, National Express East Anglia had changed its branding from One to National Express East Anglia. In 2012, the franchise owner was changed to the Dutch Nederlandse Spoorwegen and it was operated as a subsidiary of this under the name Greater Anglia. In 2015 London Overground took over the Liverpool Street to Enfield Town, Cheshunt via Seven Sisters and Chingford services as well as the Romford to Upminster Line. It was originally operated for Transport for London (TfL) by MTR but from November 2016 by Arriva Rail London. Also in 2015 the local service between Liverpool Street and Shenfield was transferred to Transport for London Rail in preparation for the Elizabeth Line services. In May 2022, the service was branded the Elizabeth Line. After early November 2022 and the start of services through to Paddington, only a few Elizabeth Line services used Liverpool Street main line station. The concession was and is operated by MTR.

In November 2007, Central Trains was split up. The Liverpool–Nottingham–Norwich service and local trains in the East Midlands were combined with Midland Mainline services to form East Midlands Trains, whilst the Cardiff–Birmingham–Nottingham and Birmingham–Stansted Airport Citylink services, were merged with former Virgin CrossCountry services except for the Birmingham/Manchester to Scotland services to form CrossCountry, which is owned by Arriva UK Trains.

Following the split of the Liverpool Street services to National Express East Anglia in 2004, West Anglia Great Northern carried on until 2006 when it became part of First Capital Connect which was owned by First Group. This operated services from Luton and Bedford via Central London using the connection from Farringdon to Blackfriars to Sutton, Wimbledon and Brighton, also services from Moorgate and King's Cross to Welwyn Garden City, Hertford North, Stevenage, Peterborough, Cambridge and Kings Lynn. In 2014, the services were taken over by the Govia-owned Govia Thameslink. The new franchise also included the former Southern Franchise.

In 2018 the former Great Northern Line was connected to the cross London line via Farringdon and Blackfriars.

Away from the main line there were further extensions to the Docklands Light Railway. On 20 November 1999, an extension was opened to Lewisham via Greenwich. In order for the line to reach Greenwich and Lewisham, a new railway was built from just south of the Crossharbour reversing sidings before dropping gently to Mudchute where a station at street level replaced the one on the former London and Blackwall Railway viaduct. From there it went in a tunnel following the route of the viaduct where a shallow subsurface station at Island Gardens replaced the existing high level one and then in a tunnel under the Thames via a subsurface station at Cutty Sark in the centre of Greenwich before surfacing at Greenwich station and from there it ran on a viaduct to Deptford Bridge before descending at street level to Elverston Road close to Lewisham town centre before terminating between and below the main station platforms at Lewisham station.

On 2 December 2005, a branch was opened from Canning Town to King George V via London City Airport. On 12 January 2009, the line was extended under the Thames to Woolwich Arsenal.

On the main line, in 2001, Stratford locomotive depot closed. This was used for the construction of the new international station on High Speed One (HS1) between St Pancras and the Channel Tunnel. A new diesel depot was opened at nearby Temple Mills. This new depot only lasted a few years as changes to the freight market saw it close. It was demolished and was replaced by Orient Way Carriage Sidings, which were the replacement for Thornton Fields Carriage sidings which was being developed as part of the 2012 London Olympic site. The site of Stratford depot is today occupied by Stratford International station and Westfield Stratford City shopping centre. Temple Mills Depot in Leyton is now used for storage and servicing of Eurostar trains and the off-peak berthing of Class 395 South Eastern high-speed trains.

Briefly, High Speed 1 (HS1) from St Pancras to the Channel Tunnel replaced the existing route to the Channel Tunnel from Waterloo via existing lines. I did use the latter quite a bit on holidays to the Continent. HS1 opened in two stages, the first in 2003 and the second in 2007 when services out of Waterloo ceased, despite in the early 1990s a lot of money having been spent on rebuilding part of Waterloo station. One wonders how successful the Channel Tunnel will be now that Britain has left the European Union. Will it survive as a route to the Continent or will it close?

Stratford International Station was not part of the government's original plans for HS1 and despite its name, international trains have never stopped there. On the other hand, it does provide an easier and quicker way of getting from parts of Essex, Hertfordshire, Suffolk and Norfolk to Kent.

To serve Stratford International, the Docklands Light Railway was extended from Canning Town to Stratford using part of the North Woolwich branch to a station across the road from the International station. In order to allow the conversion of the North Woolwich Line between Stratford and Canning Town to a DLR line, the line was closed on 9 December 2006. After the opening of the DLR extension to London City Airport in 2005, the area was better served by more frequent services from King George V DLR station. The DLR extension to Stratford International station opened in August 2011.

This was not the only opening in 2011. Southend Airport, which originated as an airfield in the First World War used by the Royal Flying Corps and also the Royal Naval Air Service, was officially opened as a municipal airport in 1935. During the Second World War it again became a military airfield used by the Royal Air Force. The idea for a railway station was first proposed in 1935. It was not until 1997, after Southend Borough Council had sold the airport to Regional Airports Ltd, that planning permission was obtained from Rochford District Council. In December 2008 the airport was bought by the Stobart Group who began to advance the project, and construction began in late 2009. The station was originally planned to open in 2009, but the opening date was postponed several times. In June 2011, trains began stopping at the station, but passengers were not permitted to get off. On 18 July 2011, the station was opened to the public by the Transport Minister Theresa Villers. No longer would intending travellers have to get off at Rochford and make their way to the airport despite the railway running right beside it. In 2012, a new terminal building adjoining the station was opened.

Authorisation for the Jubilee Line extension to Stratford was granted in 1990. The cost of the extension was estimated at £2.1 billion, of which Olympia and York, the developers of Canary Wharf, would contribute £400 million. In the end, partly because of huge cost overruns during its construction, it ended up costing £3.5 bn. A station was originally planned at Blackwall, however, this was replaced by diverting the line between Canary Wharf and Stratford underneath the Thames to serve the Greenwich peninsula at North Greenwich. Construction of the extension officially started in December 1993. It was expected to take 53 months, but tunnelling was delayed after a collapse in October 1994 during the Heathrow Express project, which used the same new Austrian tunnelling method. The extension was opened in stages, from Stratford to North Greenwich on 14 May 1999, from North Greenwich to Waterloo on 19 August and from Waterloo to Green Park on 7 October. The section of the Jubilee Line from Green Park to Charing Cross closed 19 November. Given the money that had been spent previously, including building the line to Charing Cross and the station and the tunnels of the authorised second stage to Aldwych, it could be held that a lot of money had been wasted.

9 December 2012 had seen what could best be described as the completion of the 'Outer Circle'. The project began as an engineering project to extend the East London Line and make it part of the London Overground. This was done by re-opening some sections of disused railway and by converting the track electrification from the third and fourth rail system to the third-rail system, plus altering signalling, lineside signage and communication systems, etc. to mainline standards. The work, which cost about £1m, started in 2005. It was carried out in two phases, the first of which was completed on 23 May 2010 and involved extending the East London Line north to Dalston Junction and southward from New Cross Gate to West Croydon and Crystal Palace. Earlier, in conjunction with the work, Shoreditch station had closed on 9 June 2006. It was replaced by a new station at Shoreditch High Street. On 28 February 2011, the line was extended at its northern end to Highbury and Islington on the North London Line. Finally on 9 December 2012 under the second stage, a branch was connected from Surrey Quays, formerly Surrey Docks, station to the South London Line. This enables with one change at Highbury and Islington or Clapham Junction a complete circuit of London. It is worth pointing out that since 2009, the Circle Line is no longer a full circle as trains run from Edgware Road via Victoria, Aldgate and Moorgate and Edgware Road to Hammersmith and vice versa.

Crossrail had not totally died. In 2001, Cross London Rail Links (CLRL), which was a joint venture between TfL and the Department for Transport, was formed to develop and promote the Crossrail scheme and also a scheme for a line from Wimbledon to Hackney. While CLRL was promoting the Crossrail project, in 2002 GB Railways put forward a scheme called Super Crossrail which would link regional stations such as Cambridge, Guildford, Oxford, Milton Keynes Central, Southend Victoria and Ipswich via a west–east rail tunnel through central London. In 2004, another proposal named Superlink was promoted by a group of senior railway managers. This would have towns including Cambridge, Ipswich, Southend-on-Sea, Pitsea, Reading, Basingstoke and Northampton. Both these other two schemes were rejected following evaluation by CLRL.

The Crossrail Bill, which was a hybrid bill, went through parliament and the Crossrail Act 2008 received its Royal Assent in July of that year. As authorised, Crossrail was to run from Shenfield via Whitechapel, Liverpool Street and Paddington to Reading. There would be branches from Abbey Wood to Whitechapel and Hayes and Harlington to Heathrow. Due to contractual conflicts with the then Chiltern line franchise and the Metropolitan Line Public Private Partnership, the Aylesbury and Chesham option was discounted, leaving stations north of Amersham reliant on diesel traction. In September 2009, TfL was loaned £1 billion towards the project by the European Investment Bank. Construction work began in 2009 at Canary Wharf. In 2015 the local service between Liverpool Street and Shenfield was transferred to TfL Rail with the services from Paddington to Heathrow and Paddington to Reading following in 2018 and 2019 respectively. In 2017, the new trains for the service had entered service between Liverpool Street and Shenfield.

It was hoped to open the core section of the line in December 2018, but in August of that year it was announced that completion was delayed and that the line would not open before autumn 2019. Further delays occurred and it was not until 22 May 2022 that services began between Paddington and Abbey Wood. The line was renamed the Elizabeth Line in honour of Queen Elizabeth who celebrated her Platinum Jubilee that year. On 6 November 2022, services began between Reading and Heathrow and Abbey Wood and Paddington and Shenfield plus a few services serving Liverpool Street main line station to and from Gidea Park and Shenfield. 21 May 2023 saw the full route opening for passenger trains.

Extensions to the line could come in the form of one to Ebbsfleet and Gravesend. In March of 2019, the government committed £4.8 million on exploratory work into the extension to Gravesend as part of the Thames Estuary 2050 Growth Commission. Southend-on-Sea City Council would like to see the line extended to Southend from Shenfield and there is a proposal to build a connecting line from Heathrow to Staines.

There was further electrification in the London area and an extension of an existing line. Prior to the privatisation of BR, the line from Gospel Oak to Barking had been proposed for electrification, but initially under privatisation this did not happen. After TfL took over the line in 2007 as part of the London Overground in order to increase the capacity of the line from six trains per hour to eight trains per hour, the line was closed for most of September 2008 for upgrading work which was carried out by Network Rail. This work did not include electrification, which was ruled out on grounds of cost and the difficulty of electrifying a line with so many viaducts and bridges. However, Network Rail's Network Route Utilisation Strategy, published in October 2009, showed a benefit–cost ratio for the scheme of 2.4:1. In 2011, Network Rail proposed the electrification of the line in Control Period 5 (CP5), but in July 2012, the Secretary of State for Transport Justine Greening said that the electrification was not included in the High Level Output Specification for CP5, and that any funds would need to be provided by TfL The Mayor of London, Boris Johnson, indicated that he felt that funding for the electrification was a matter for the Department of Transport and in August he wrote to the Secretary of State for Transport seeking a way forward. In reply, she committed her officials to support work with TfL, Network Rail, train operators and other industry parties to see if a viable way could be found to bridge the funding gap. There was a difference of opinion as to how much the electrification would cost as in November of that year, *Modern Railways* magazine reported that the Department for Transport had ruled out the work on the basis of an estimated cost of £90 million, which contrasted to an estimate of £40 million by TfL.

Finally, in June 2013 it was announced that £115 million of funding for electrification was being made available as part of upgrades to rail infrastructure included in the government's 2013 spending round. At the same time, it was announced by TfL that they had obtained a £90 million commitment from the Chancellor of the Exchequer and the Secretary of State for Transport for the electrification. In September 2015, the contract to electrify the line was awarded by Network Rail to J. Murphy and Sons. During the period of the electrification, there were part and full closures of the line from June 2016 to February 2017, followed by further already planned evening and weekend works which lasted until June 2017. There then followed around four months of commissioning work before the electric wires could be turned on in order that the Class 710 trains that were intended for the line could run. By mid-January 2018, the line was completely electrified, but the trains were not ready. The first test of an electric train had taken place on 8 January 2018 and the first revenue earning electric train over the line was a freight train on 4 July, which probably did not please any waiting passengers who saw it, having been promised electric passenger trains nearly six months earlier. Meanwhile the Class 172 dmus that operated the service were needed by West Midlands Trains and so three Class 378 emus shortened from 5 to 4-carriages to provide an interim service until the Class 710 emus entered service were moved from other parts of the London Overground. The first passenger-carrying electric train entered service on 28 January 2019, over one year late. As six trains per hour were needed to run the service for a time there was a mixed diesel and electric service. However, with the 2-carriage Class 172 dmus being needed in the West Midlands, when the last of these left London Overground on 15 March the service frequency was reduced to two trains per hour which certainly did not please passengers. Finally, on 23 May 2019, the first two Class 710 emus entered service. It was not until June that the full timetable of four trains per hour was restored. By August, all the new Class 710 emus were in service and to compensate the passengers, TfL offered them a month's free travel. Thus ended the saga of the electrification of the Gospel Oak to Barking Line. This was not the end of the line, as on 18 July 2022 the line was extended southeast by 2.8 miles from the terminus at Barking to serve the Barking Riverside regeneration area. The extension had been proposed in the mid-2010s following the cancellation of the proposed DLR extension to Dagenham Dock, Approval for the extension was given in 2017, and construction started in late 2018. The line runs partially alongside the existing former LTS line and then on a new viaduct to the Barking Riverside station.

On the North London Line, the section from Acton Central was gradually converted over the years to 25,000 volts ac overhead supply leaving only the section west from Acton Central to Richmond on 750 volts dc third rail. This is because the section from Gunnersbury is shared with the London Underground's District Line which is equipped for both third rail running by Overground trains and third and fourth rail running by Underground trains. North London line trains have to able to operate on ac overhead power and dc third rail power.

Away from the London area, there was new construction at Cambridge and on the East Suffolk and Felixstowe lines.

At Cambridge, an island platform was constructed on the eastern side of the station and was brought into use in December 2011. This ended Cambridge's unique status on the main lines in the east of England of having only one long platform, albeit one with bays and a crossover in the middle. In May 2017, a new station named Cambridge North was opened in the suburb of Chesterton to serve Cambridge Science Park.

In 1997, Railtrack initiated an upgrading of the Felixstowe branch line. This was in anticipation of it receiving increased revenue from freight train operators. At Derby Road, the passing loop was extended so that two container trains could pass. The signalling was replaced and transferred to the control of Colchester Power Signalling Box. The line speed was increased, the aim being to allow an hourly passenger train service to operate whilst accommodating more freight trains. The line as far as Felixstowe Beach was maintained to passenger standard should there be a resumption of the service there in the future. Electrification was again considered, as most Freightliner trains were by then being worked by electric locomotives to Ipswich, where they had to be changed to diesel for the short trip to Felixstowe, but the cost of this could not be justified. The work which cost £8 million was completed by June 1999. It is clear that even in the 1970s BR did consider that it might electrify to Felixstowe as the Class 312 emus included Felixstowe in the places on their destination blinds.

2008 saw the Secretary of State for Transport approve the 'Felixstowe Branch Line and Ipswich Yard Improvement Order'. This empowered the rebuilding of Ipswich Yard and the laying of a second track for 4.44 miles from Trimley westwards to Levington.

During the 2012 Summer Olympics, held principally in east London, Freightliner diverted ten Felixstowe trains each day through either Cambridge or Ely in order to free up capacity at Stratford, which was next to the main venue for the games.

Network Rail in 2011 submitted plans for a new double track curve at Ipswich which was to be known as the Bacon Factory Curve and was built on part of the site of a former Harris meat factory. The curve avoided the necessity of any train running between Felixstowe and the Ely Line having to reverse in Ipswich Upper Yard. Construction work started early in 2013 and was completed in March 2014, the first train running over the new curve on 24 March. The purpose of the new curve was one of a number of enhancements between Felixstowe and Nuneaton, their purpose being to allow trains to reach the West Coast Main Line without travelling over congested lines in the London area.

October 2017 saw final approval given for a £60.4 million project which included doubling between Trimley station and Grimston Lane foot crossing. Work on the project started on 7 April 2018 and was predicted to end in autumn 2019, but it was completed by May 2019 and saw changes to the infrastructure at Trimley station where trains from the Felixstowe direction could now access the disused platform road and the establishment of a double track as far as a new junction called Gun Lane Junction just over a mile west of Trimley station. Both of the lines can be worked bi-directionally. With the increase in freight traffic that resulted from the additional capacity, a number of level crossings were either abolished or were upgraded to improve safety.

Up to October 2012, the section of the East Suffolk line from Westerfield to Oulton Broad was signalled using RETB which was controlled from Saxmundham. However, due to radio frequency licensing issues, and the imminent beginning of an hourly train service on the line, which would have been beyond the capacity of RETB, Track Circuit Block signalling (using AzLM axle counters) was introduced to replace the RETB system after the last train ran on 19 October 2012. The new signalling came into operation on 23 October 2012 and was controlled from the existing signal box at Saxmundham. On 10 December 2012, a new passing loop and reinstated second platform was opened at Beccles. This resulted in an hourly service over the East Suffolk line being introduced.

The other notable event was the reopening to passengers of Soham station in Cambridgeshire. Soham, on the Ipswich to Ely line, had closed to passengers on 13 September 1965. Following many years of local campaigning, a new station was opened on the site of the original station on 13 December 2021.

The period since privatisation saw the end of the Travelling Post Offices on the night of 25-26 July 2003. According to information from David Scudamore, the last Up East Anglian TPO departing Norwich at 7.52 pm on 25 July to PRDC (Princess Royal Distribution Centre) at Wembley was hauled by Class 67 locomotive No 67029. The last Down East Anglian TPO from PRDC to Norwich was hauled by 67027 *Rising Star* and the loco carried the headboard 'Last Norwich TPO – Sorted'. The train arrived at Norwich on 26 July at 2.41am, 28 minutes earlier than its booked arrival time of 3.5am.

8 January 2020 had seen the first Class 745 FLIRT emu enter service between London and Norwich. 24 March 2020 saw the end of locomotive powered passenger trains on the national railway system in East Anglia after nearly 161 years. Locomotive No 90001 had the distinction of working the last scheduled locomotive propelled trains on the GE when it worked the 7.30pm Liverpool Street to Norwich train. Whilst the new trains are very efficient, something has been lost with the end of locomotive powered trains. Named power cars do not have the same appeal as a named locomotive whatever its means of propulsion.

Since privatisation the only new class of electric locomotive to see service on the GE Section was Class 90 in 2005.

Since the mid-1970s the following new classes of diesel locomotive have appeared on the GE Section: 56, 57, 58, 60, 66, 67, 70.

Since privatisation the following classes of emu have appeared on the GE Section. Some of these are dual power. 345, 357, 360, 365, 378, 379, 387, 710, 720, 745, 755.

Beginning in 2013 under the Renatus project, thirty-one Class 321 units were upgraded. The upgrade included the fitting of air conditioning.

Class 90 first appeared on the GE Section in 2005 on transfer from the LNW section and displaced class 86. The appropriately named No 90008 *The East Anglian* stands at Ipswich on 2 April 2019 on the 10.30 Norwich to Liverpool Street service. *Brian Garrett*

Class 70 Co-Co which were first built in 2008 by General Electric and are not the most attractive looking locomotives. On 16 March 2017, No 70017 passes Trimley with the 22.50 Didcot to Felixstowe container train. *Brian Garrett*

The General Motors class 66 diesel locomotives first entered service on the British railway network in 1998 and have worked all over the country. In this photograph taken at Margaretting on 19 May 2023, we see one such locomotive heading an Up freight. *Author*

Class 360 4-car emus were first built in 2002 and entered service on the GE Colchester main line and electrified branches east of Shenfield in 2003. No 360107 passes Brantham on 6 July 2004 whilst working the 15.30 Ipswich-London Liverpool Street service. *Scott Borthwick*

Class 379 4-car emus were first built in 2010 and entered service in 2011 on the Cambridge main line. Units Nos 379019 and 379001 are seen passing Bethnal Green on 12.25 Liverpool Street to Stansted Airport service on 6 April 2019. *Brian Garrett*

Starting in 2013, a total of thirty-one class 321 emus were upgraded under the Renatus project which included air conditioning. On 4 April 2019, newly refurbished unit No 321313 stands ready to depart Ipswich with a service for Liverpool Street. *Brian Garrett*

Class 345 9-car emus were first built in 2015 and entered service in 2017. One such unit is seen passing Bethnal Green on 6 April 2019 working a Shenfield to Liverpool Street service. These units operate the Elizabeth Line service. *Brian Garrett.*

Class 720 5-car emus entered service in 2020 and work all of the suburban service of Greater Anglia. They worked their first services from Liverpool Street commencing on 26 November 2020. Two units are seen on an up train at Margaretting on 19 May 2023. *Author*

Class 745 12-car emus entered service with Greater Anglia in 2020 and have replaced the final locomotive propelled trains in East Anglia – the Liverpool Street to Norwich service. Here we see a unit on an up express at Margaretting on 19 May 2023. *Author*

On the LT Central Line 1992 Tube Stock and on the Jubilee Line 1996 Tube Stock
On the DLR P86, P89, B90, B92, B2K, B07, B23

2012 had seen the 150th anniversary of the formation of the GER. There were various events to commemorate this. My own personal memory has nothing to do with celebrations. I had a week's holiday in Norfolk in the middle of June. I was staying in Norwich. On Sunday 17 June, I took a trip on the Mid-Norfolk Railway from Dereham to Wymondham. At Dereham station, as the train arrived I thought the locomotive was an LMS Class 2 Ivatt design 2-6-0. But no, it was a British Railways Class 2-2-6-0 No 78019. I got a very slight bit sentimental having last seen one of these locomotives on the GE Section in August 1962. You could say the years rolled back. Perhaps for a short while it was 1962 again. A little bit of steam had made its way back to Norfolk to help out that summer. Needless to say, I enjoyed my journey to Wymondham Abbey and back as well as looking at the Abbey and having a nice meal in a nearby thatched pub.

Returning to preservation, properly. As mentioned, on what has become the Mid-Norfolk Railway, the section of line from Ryburgh to Fakenham was closed to goods services on 1 January 1980, followed on 1 January 1981 by the section from North Elham to Ryburgh. However, in May 1982 a weed killing train ran to Ryburgh followed in

The Mid Norfolk Railway is the longest preserved railway in the east of England. With a little bit of imagination, one could imagine that this scene of Standard 2MT No 78019 entering Dereham on 17 June 2012 was taken in 1962 as five members of the class were shedded at Stratford that summer. *Author*

August of that year by a track recording train. After that the section was officially closed. On 12 October 1989, the section from Wymondham via Dereham to North Elham was closed to goods traffic.

Following the closure of the line from North Elham to Ryburgh, the Fakenham and Dereham Railway Society (F&DRS) decided to concentrate on the Wymondham to Dereham section. In 1983 it successfully negotiated the lease on part of the station and yard at Hardingham where some track was laid in the yard, a Ruston diesel locomotive was acquired and a small museum was set up in the building. However, the rent and rates were higher than income and in 1986 when BR decided to auction off the site, the F&DRS decided to cut its losses and moved to a temporary site down the line at Yaxham. Shortly afterwards, Breckland District Council enquired about a railway presence at their proposed Heritage Centre at County School. The F&DRS moved in and laid tracks, relaid the level crossing and established a thriving railway centre there.

It was the hope that when a rail centre was operating at County School, it could be linked again to the BR line at North Elmham so as to connect with chartered trains on the branch. The dream was shattered when in June 1989 the complete closure of the line was announced. The likelihood of being able to get the funds together to purchase a 17½ mile stretch of line was almost unthinkable. A sudden surge of interest however kept the idea alive. It was agreed that all of the organisations that were interested in saving the line should meet and so the Mid-Norfolk Railway Project (MNRP) was born.

The MNRP's original idea was to set up a company to try to raise capital to purchase all, or part, of the line. Interest from local councils was now much greater than it was in the past and many people asked to be kept in touch with events.

Things got a bit complicated. In 1989, responding to the approaching closure of the entire branch between Wymondham, Dereham and North Elmham, the Great Eastern Railway (1989) Limited had been formed to save the line. The F&DRS backed this scheme, and signed its lease of County School station over to the company.

Meanwhile, in the hope that the line could be purchased, and because of the need for a big supporting society, the decision was made that the unification of the various groups with an interest in the line would be a good thing. The groups amalgamated in 1990 and shortly afterwards the F&DRS voted to change its name to the Mid-Norfolk Railway Society (MNRS). At County School, where a short running line had been established, this was extended over ½ mile in the direction of North Elmham, and a collection of rolling stock was built up. The first passenger train, a Mk2 brake coach converted to work as a Driving Brake Standard open with an industrial diesel locomotive, operated at the County School site on 2 November 1991.

In 1991 the managing director of the GER (1989) Ltd. stated that he had raised much of the finance required to purchase the line and that it was the company's intention to provide a regular passenger train service over the line by 1993.

In the early 1990s, the GER (1989) Ltd, contrary to the earlier announcements relating to the future of the line, announced plans to lift the railway between Dereham and Wymondham. At this point, the MNRS withdrew their support for the GER (1989) Ltd and made their own bid for the line.

In 1994, British Railways Property Board granted the MNRS access to the railway line between Wymondham and North Elmham on a temporary 'care and maintenance' basis. The reason for this was in response to increasing levels of vandalism occurring at the site. The problem had worsened after the GER (1989) Ltd had lifted the track between Norwich Road level crossing and a point just north of the Automatic Open Level Crossings. In December 1994, Class 20 diesels were moved by road from County School to the truncated railhead at Dereham. On Christmas Eve, with permission from British Rail, both locomotives made their way along the line to Yaxham station.

In 1995, GER (1989) Ltd was in trouble and the Yorkshire Bank called in the receivers to solve concerns with the Company. In June 1995, Breckland District Council informed the receivers that they wanted GER (1989) Ltd to give up the lease for County School station in order that they could review their operations in respect of the site. GER (1989) Ltd said that they were attracting 12,000 visitors a year to the site, announced their intention to contest the decision. Things got murky. In July 1995 the police were called in to investigate the sudden and unauthorised road transfer of two Mid-Norfolk Railway Society Mk 2 coaches to a nearby breaker's yard at Lenwade. Breckland District Council in July 1996 issued a threat to stop trains running at County School station, because it was found that someone other than the leaseholder was operating trains at the site, the lease being non-transferable. In November 1996, in order to prevent the stripping of the property after having served an eviction order on GER (1989) Ltd in-mid October, Breckland District Council brought in 24-hour security guards at the County School site. County School station was then boarded up and GER (1989) Ltd rolling stock was concentrated in the isolated yard prior to disposal or scrapping. All track north of the station platforms was lifted, and the site was left to become derelict.

In 1995 the Mid-Norfolk Railway Preservation Trust (MNRPT) had been formed. The Trust's aims of the new charity were:

> To preserve and to renovate, reconstruct and operate for the benefit of the people of the County of Norfolk and of the nation at large, whatever of the historical, architectural and constructional heritage that may exist of the permanent way,

> track, buildings (including any buildings as defined in Section 336(1) of the Town And Country Planning Act 1990), bridges, operating equipment and rolling stock once forming part of or connected with or adjacent to the GER line running between County School at North Elmham in the County of Norfolk and Wymondham in the County of Norfolk.

In July 1995, two Mk2 coaches were transferred by road from County School railway station to the truncated railhead at Dereham. Here they were placed between the already present Class 20 locomotives. These coaches were then hauled to the MNR's temporary base at Yaxham. On 17 August a further three coaches were delivered.

On 29 November 1995 Chris Hall, HM Principal Inspecting Officer of Railways inspected the section of the railway between Yaxham station and a temporary halt built beside a footpath crossing on the Rash's Green industrial estate in Dereham. Permission to operate passenger trains over this section was granted from Saturday 23 December 1995. Sixty-three trains, each composed of the five Mk2 coaches topped and tailed by the Class 20s, were operated between that date and 14 January 1996. In October 1995, Breckland District Council had established a rail working party to consider purchasing the line from British Rail, then leasing it out to a rail group – of which the Mid-Norfolk Railway was the preferred lessee. On 11 April 1998, the Mid-Norfolk Railway Preservation Trust bought the line between Wymondham and Dereham for £100,000. This included the Dereham station buildings and the 6.5 acre goods yard. The BR Property Board also sold the MNRPT the 4½ miles of track between Dereham and North Elmham for £25,000. On 17 March 1998, the MNRPT had signed a Tenancy at Will agreement with Breckland District Council to take over the station and trackbed at County School. The purpose of the agreement was to allow the railway to take control of the station until it could afford to buy it outright and followed on from the removal of the remaining rolling stock associated with the defunct GER (1989) Ltd from the site.

The original Dereham station was re-opened to passengers on Saturday 26 July 1997, with the first services being operated by 1890-built Manning Wardle 0-6-0ST *Sir Berkeley*, which had been hired from the Keighley and Worth Valley Railway in Yorkshire. On 23 September 1997, the British Railways Board (Residuary) Limited transferred the line between Wymondham and Dereham to the MNRPT. The first preservation-era train to operate between Dereham and Wymondham was on 8 February 1998, when a works train ran as part of preparations for a March freight test train The first commercial freight train operated on 8 July 1998. On 2 May 1999, passenger services between Dereham and Wymondham commenced, with the opening of Wymondham Abbey railway station near the Abbey. Initially, the services were operated by diesel traction, but, following the completion of infrastructure work such as the replacement of the water tower at Dereham and the provision of an inspection pit, steam passenger services returned to the Dereham to Wymondham Abbey section on Sunday 30 April 2006.

The current position is as follows. The 11½ mile section of line between Dereham and Wymondham is in regular use. A further 3½ miles to Worthing are passed for operation, but are only used for passengers during special events and for works trains enabling the reconditioning of the derelict line further north. The company also owns the next 2½ miles of disused line from Worthing to County School station near North Elmham, although a section of about one mile lacks track between North Elmham and County School. Beyond the railway's holding, the trackbed is mostly intact from County School to Fakenham, and is reserved by the council for railway use. There is a proposal for a station at Wymondham Junction adjacent to main line passenger station.

The Mid-Norfolk Railway facilitates commercial freight trains, using its connection with the National Rail network at Wymondham. Dereham station yard has been used as a servicing depot by Direct Rail Services since 2007 and for storage of Network Rail track plant since 2008.

North Norfolk District Council has listed Fakenham and Great Ryburgh as potential freight hubs, subject to them being linked to the Mid-Norfolk Railway at County School.

After several attempts to close it, finally on 30 September 1994 the line from Epping to Ongar was closed. The line was making a loss of £7 for each passenger journey and was in need of some expensive maintenance work. As early as the end of the 1970s/ beginning of the 1980s, realising that the line would close, a preservation society was formed but nothing came of this. On the other hand, it may have generated some extra traffic over the line as people who would not have otherwise travelled on the line, including myself, did. I did my trip in the summer of 1980. All that happened was that Blake Hall, which was the least used station on the line and reputed to have only seventeen passengers a day, officially closed on 2 November 1981, with the last train calling at the station on 31 October 1981. Prior to the closure, the Ongar Railway Preservation Society had been formed to operate the line. The idea was that during weekdays it would provide a commuter and community service and at weekends a heritage line. Things did not go the Society's way and in 1998 the line was sold to Pilot Developments (later Epping Ongar Railway Ltd). The Ongar Railway Preservation Society entered a bid of £325,000 for the line, but Pilot Developments convinced London Underground to accept its slightly higher offer after the bidding deadline. The Independent politician Martin Bell described the deal as 'the most controversial land deal in the constituency for years', alleging a conflict of interest with local politicians. Bell was not even the member for the constituency in which the line was situated. Glenda Jackson, the Transport Minister in the Department of Environment, Transport and the Regions was slammed by the Ongar Railway Preservation Society after she had said that she did not believe that there were any grounds for a judicial review on the sale of the line. On Sunday, 10 October 2004, line was reopened by the Epping Ongar Railway Volunteer Society and provided an hourly service between Ongar and North Weald. Shortly afterwards the line was extended to Coopersale, although there are no boarding or alighting facilities there. From 22 January to 9 April 2006, the line was shut down for engineering works. After that date, Ongar station remained closed for engineering works and general maintenance. It reopened on 28 May 2006 without the use of the station buildings. 2007 saw a change of ownership. It was decided to suspend the operation of trains and to concentrate on improving the track, the reason being in order to undertake the major engineering works to secure its long-term future and facilitate the return of steam to the line, including restoration of station buildings, run-round loops, full signalling, and coal and water facilities. Services resumed on 25 May 2012, coinciding with the 150th year since the GER was formed. The Railway operates steam- and diesel-hauled trains between Ongar and North Weald, a diesel shuttle from North Weald to Coopersale Lane, and heritage bus services connecting with surrounding towns and the Central line at Epping as although the line runs to Epping there no interchange facilities. It is intended to extend trains to a new platform called Epping Glade near the London Underground's Epping station.

Other preservation projects include the Southwold Railway Society, which was formed in 1994. Amongst other things, it was formed to investigate the possibility of re-establishing part of the line and to promote this if re-establishment was shown to be possible.

In 2006, the Southwold Railway Trust was established. Its objective was to promote awareness of the heritage of the Southwold Railway, to preserve any remaining artefacts and to instigate the re-instatement of the railway as a local community and public amenity connecting Southwold to the main line railway at Halesworth. In June 2012, the Trust submitted a planning application with a view to recreating a new station close to the original station site in Wenhaston. The plans included a new station building based on the design of the original, plus a workshop and visitor centre building. The proposals also include the reopening of a ½ mile section of the original railway towards Blythburgh.

At Brockford in Suffolk, a section of the former Mid Suffolk Light Railway has been reopened by the Mid Suffolk Light Railway.

In Norfolk, the Whitwell and Reepham Railway Preservation Society Limited has been formed. Based at Whitwell and Reepham station on the closed Melton Constable to Norwich City line, its aims are firstly, to return the station to its original layout by re-laying track and restoring the station buildings. Secondly, to extend the line along Marriott's Way long-distance footpath, cycle-path and bridleway to re-create the 7 miles from Themelthorpe curve to Reepham railway station and thirdly to link up with either the North Norfolk Railway or Mid-Norfolk Railway.

4 September 2009 saw a very special train arrive at Liverpool Street. This was a private train which was one of four which ran from Prague in the Czech Republic via Cologne, Rotterdam, the Hook of Holland and Harwich. It was in tribute to Sir Nicholas Winton who had saved Jewish refugee children from Czechoslovakia. On the English leg, the train was hauled by the recently built Peppercorn A1 No 60163 *Tornado*. At Liverpool Street, the train was met by Sir Nicholas Winton who at the time was 100 years old. He died in 2015.

Sadly the years have seen decline on the maritime front and all of the DFDS services from Harwich have ceased.

In 1999, the Harwich to Gothenburg service ceased. In March 2002 the German terminus of the route from Harwich was changed from Hamburg to Cuxhaven. In November 2005, because of competition from low-cost airlines and the cessation in 1999 of on-board duty-free sales between EU countries, the service ceased.

In 2007, the *Stena Discovery* was taken off the Harwich to the Hook of Holland route and replaced by a conventional ship. In truth, I get the impression that the ship had a few problems. Being a twin-hulled ship, it could not cope so well with the rougher weather. One night I was at Liverpool Street station in 2004 waiting to get a train home from work and I heard it announced that because of rough weather that evening's sailing had been cancelled and the passengers were being taken by coach through the Channel Tunnel!

With the sailing of Sunday 29 September 2014 of the 5.15pm *Sirena Seaways* to Esjberg the end of the service to Denmark came to an end after just over 140 years.

In Holland, the railway line from the Hook of Holland was closed on 1 April 2017 and reopened on 30 September 2019 as the western terminus of Rotterdam Metro Line B, something of a comedown for the line which was once served by the Rheingold Express and whose route from the mid-1960s to the early 1980s was Geneva–Basel–Freiburg–Baden-Baden–Karlsruhe–Mannheim–Mainz–Cologne–Düsseldorf–Duisburg–Utrecht and then in separate trains continuing (still as the Rheingold) to both the Hook of Holland and Amsterdam. I am tempted to wonder how long the service from Harwich to the Hook of Holland will survive, at least for foot passengers.

As mentioned, the use of locomotives to propel passenger trains on the GE Section came to an end on Tuesday 24 March 2020 when Class 90 No 90001 worked the 7.30pm

Liverpool Street to Norwich train. Thus ended just over 180 years and 9 months of scheduled locomotive propelled trains on the GE section. For the rest of that week, a locomotive propelled set was kept in reserve should the need arise. Somehow multiple unit trains generally do not have the same appeal as locomotive propelled trains.

Greater Anglia ceased running services north of Ely from 21 May 2023. As the through trains to Kings Lynn only ran in peak hours, this meant that the last through trains to and from Kings Lynn ceased on 19 May.

And then there was COVID 19, which, although not like it was in 2020 and 2021, is still with us. The virus first began circulating in the country in early 2020 and by March 2020 widespread health measures were introduced. People were told to stop at home other than for one hour's exercise a day unless they had a valid reason to go out. I would suggest that it was easier living in the country than in a town to find a valid reason to go out. On the railways and buses and other public transport, services were cut. I did not travel on a train between early 2020 and late 2021. People were encouraged where possible to work from home. Schools went to on-line teaching. To give an example, in the year prior to the pandemic, Liverpool Street was the third-busiest railway station in the United Kingdom after Waterloo and Victoria stations in London with an estimated 66 million entries/exits. In the financial year 2020/21 entries/exits fell to 11.2 million – a drop of 83 per cent. Whilst I appreciate very much that there was much sadness over the loss of loved ones by the pandemic, equally, it gave people time to take stock of things. People got used to working from home and did not want to go back to travelling to work every day on crowded trains. Some people found new careers for themselves. It has taken some time, but rail travel has now recovered to pre pandemic levels. According to the Office of Rail and Road Liverpool Street is now the busiest station in the United Kingdom. It is not only rail travel. Southend Airport suffered worse than any airport in the country.

What of the future?

There is a proposal for a north to south CrossRail. The proposal goes back to the 1970s and to describe its history would take too long, beyond saying that the original idea was for a Chelsea–Hackney or Chelney line. In its present proposal, it is intended to run from Epsom, Chessington South, Hampton Court and Shepperton via Raynes Park, Clapham Junction, Victoria, Tottenham Court Road, a joint Euston St Pancras station and the Angel (Islington) to Dalston where one branch would go to New Southgate and the other to Broxbourne. There is also a potential branch from south of Dalston to Hackney Central/Hackney Downs. At the opening ceremony of the Elizabeth line in May 2022, the prime minister and former Mayor of London Boris Johnson said that 'the government should be getting on with building Crossrail 2', but he also clarified that the business case would need to be written and put forward by TfL. In 2014, when he was Mayor of London Boris Johnson had called for the future line to be called the

Churchill Line after Winston Churchill. Of course, ultimately everything depends on political will and money.

In Cambridgeshire, there is a proposal to reopen the March to Wisbech line. Between March and Wisbech the line is intact but following the closure to passengers in 1968 Wisbech East Station was lost to redevelopment and in 2001 the station site was obliterated by a housing development. The track now ends at Weasenham Lane level crossing following the tarmacking over of the rails from the crossing in 2005. Beyond that point, the old Wisbech East Goods Yard was last used in 2000. Three years after the last train ran from Wisbech, the remaining three sidings were lifted. Most of the yard area now forms the factory and car park extension.

Network Rail in a review response in 2022 identified a number of areas which it said needed deeper consideration before proposals could be assessed further. Particularly it highlighted that any Wisbech–Cambridge service plans would rely on train paths being available through Ely, without the proposals for reopening having considered whether this could be achieved. According to the *New Civil Engineer* for 21 November 2023, Network Rail is considering plans to re-open the March to Wisbech line.

Another idea is the Norfolk Orbital Railway – as the Holt, Melton Constable and Fakenham Railway Company is proposed to link the North Norfolk Railway at its Holt station via Fakenham to join the Mid Norfolk Railway at Dereham. It remains to be seen whether this project comes to fruition.

Another proposal, but which is going ahead, is East West Rail to link Oxford and Cambridge again by a direct rail route. Whilst the line from Oxford to Bedford via Bletchley exists still, the section of the former route to Cambridge no longer does and at the time of writing has not yet been decided.

There are calls for the line from Cambridge to Haverhill to be reopened.

Just north of Chelmsford, a new station is going to be built to serve the development to be called Beaulieu Park to be completed in 2025 and open in 2026.

At Cambridge, adjacent to Addenbrooke's Hospital and Cambridge Biomedical Centre, a new station called Cambridge South is planned to open in 2025.

It is a pity that when work starts on Sizewell C that the Leiston branch cannot be upgraded to take passenger trains once more and a new station be built at Leiston to enable a regular passenger service to be operated over the line.

It is a pity that a London facing curve a cannot be built at Marks Tey off the Sudbury branch to permit through running from London to Sudbury.

Sellar, the developer of the building known as 'The Shard', beginning in 2021 proposed a £1.5bn redevelopment of Liverpool Street Station. The plan includes removing the 1980s roof and original station entrance and constructing a 10-storey hotel and office block. Understandably, this created an outcry. According to the *Guardian* of 23 November 2022, Historic England, the government's heritage agency, said it was 'deeply concerned' about the plans. The Victorian Society, a charity which campaigns for nineteenth-century and Edwardian buildings, said the redevelopment will 'irreparably damage its character and architectural and historical significance'. According to *The Railway Observer* for March 2023, Historic England has listed the 1992 train shed grade 2 and the hotel grade 2*. This means that any work can only be done with the consent of the planning authority.

There are proposals to renew the signalling in and around the Cambridge area and enhance capacity in the Ely area.

In early July 2023, the government was putting pressure on the Rail Delivery Group (RDG) and rail operators to make sweeping cost-cutting measures across the country after the industry was battered by a lack of travel during the COVID pandemic. On 5 July, the Group, together with English rail operators, announced their intentions to shut the ticket offices, with public consultations being launched. On Greater Anglia only at London Liverpool Street, Chelmsford, Colchester, Ipswich, Norwich, Stansted Airport and Cambridge would Customer Information Centres would sell a 'full range of products', and help customers with 'more complex transactions'. Of the remaining forty-seven stations, some would have staff available for similar hours as at present, but some would see the number of staffed hours reduced. According to Greater Anglia, this approach was already in place at Bury St. Edmunds and Cambridge North stations and had 'proved to be successful and well received by passengers'. What was appalling is that large towns such as Lowestoft, Yarmouth, Ely, Harlow and Southend would be left without ticket offices. Not only would Southend not have a ticket office at its Greater Anglia station, but as the rival c2c line was closing all its ticket offices there would be no ticket offices at the town's stations. Following protests, the government thankfully reversed the decision on 31 October 2023. Another bad idea that was fortunately cancelled was to end one day travel cards to London. Had this been implemented, it would have meant that one would have had to buy a separate ticket at the entry point to TfL services rather than having a through ticket from a National Rail station. This would have meant anyone going for a day out in London on to the TfL network would have incurred extra costs than at present.

As I have said, I am cynical enough to believe that should the line from Ely to Norwich via Thetford be electrified, I am quite sure King's Cross will become the main London station for Norwich.

30 November 2023 and 30 June 2024 respectively saw the publication of the first and second volumes of this author's history of the Great Eastern Railway of which this book is the third volume.

As to what the future holds for the former GER only time will tell.

Appendix

Motive Power that at one time worked on GE Section

Ex GER

Class	First Built	Last Withdrawn/ Rebuilt	Comment
B12 4-6-0	1911	1961	Some rebuilt with round topped fireboxes commencing in 1932. Ten additional locomotives built in 1928 by Beyer Peacock of Manchester.
D13 4-4-0	1886	1944	Built as 2-4-0 rebuilt to 4 4 0 in 1905
D14 4-4-0	1900	1931	Rebuilt to D15
D15 4-4-0	1903	1952	Some rebuilt from D14 and some rebuilt to D16
D16 4-4-0	1922	1960	Prototype rebuilt from D15. Some rebuilt with round topped fireboxes commencing in 1933 The class leader No 8900/2600 was named *Claud Hamilton*, but on its withdrawal in 1947 the name was transferred to No 2546
E4 2-4-0	1891	1959	Last 2-4-0s in mainland Britain
F3 2-4-2T	1893	1953	
F4 2-4-2T	1884	1956	
F5 2-4-2T	1903	1958	
F6 2-4-2T	1904	1958	
F7 2-4-2T	1909	1948	
G4 0-4-4T	1898	1938	
J14 0-6-0	1893	1925	
J15 0-6-0	1883	1962	
J16 0-6-0	1900	1932	
J17 0-6-0	1902	1962	
J18 0-6-0	1912	1936	Rebuilt to J19

J19 0-6-0	1916	1962	Rebuilt with round topped fireboxes commencing in 1935.
J20 0-6-0	1920	1962	Rebuilt with round topped fireboxes commencing in 1943.
J65 0-6-0 T	1889	1956	
J66 0-6-0 T	1886	1962	
J67 0-6-0 T	1890	1958	
J68 0-6-0 T	1912	1961	
J69 0-6-0 T	1890	1962	
J70 0-6-0 T	1903	1955	Tram locomotives
J92 0-6-0 CRANE TANK	1868	1952	Crane tanks. first classified Z4, but reclassified J92 in 1927
N7 0-6-2 T	1915	1962	In addition to those on order by the GER 112 more built by the LNER between 1925 and 1928. 40 from the former Great Central Railway works at Gorton in Manchester, 32 from the former Great Northern Railway works at Doncaster, 20 from Robert Stephenson and Company and 20 from William Beardmore and Company. Some rebuilt or built with round topped fireboxes. Rebuilding of Belpaire fireboxed locomotives to round topped fireboxed locomotives commenced in 1940.
Y4 0-4-0T	1913	1963	Last ex GER locomotive in service
Y5 0-4-0ST	1874	1948	
Y6 0-4-0	1883	1952	Tram locomotives
Y11 0-4-0	1919	1956	Petrol locomotive
A 0-4-0 ST	1872	1922	Still in existence on 1 January 1923 and scrapped that year

Ex C,V&HR

Class	First Built	Last Withdrawn/ Rebuilt	Comment
F9 2-4-2T	1897	1930	
N18 0-6-2T	1908	1928	
Z6 0-4-2T	1877	1923	Class No not confirmed

Ex MSLR

Class	First Built	Last Withdrawn/ Rebuilt	Comment
J64 0-6-0T	1904	1929	

Ex GNR

Class	First Built	Last Withdrawn/ Rebuilt	Comment
D1 4-4-0	1911	1950	According to the Locomotives of the LNER published by the RCTS some members of the class worked on the Great Eastern section from 1932 until final withdrawal in 1950
D3 4-4-0	1896	1952	After takeover of working of M&GNJTR some were transferred to that section, but there were occasional transfers to the GE Section.
J50 0-6-0T	1922	1965	First allocated to GE Section in 1930. On GE Section until 1961
K1 2-6-0	1912	1937	Rebuilt to K2 First worked on GE Section in 1923
K2 2-6-0	1913	1962	First worked on GE Section in 1924
K3 2-6-0	1920	1962	First worked on GE Section in 1925 at March, but not until 1938 they were authorised to work further south on the Section.
N1 0-6-2 T	1906	1959	From 1950 when some shopped at Stratford before returned to their home shed they were run in on empty stock workings into and out of Liverpool Street station.
N2 0-6-2 T	1920	1962	
O2 2-8-0	1921	1963	First worked on GE Section in 1932

Ex GCR

Class	First Built	Last Withdrawn/ Rebuilt	Comment
A5 4-6-2T	1911	1960	Worked principally in Norfolk in the early to late 1950s. in 1951 some worked the Liverpool Street to Southend service whilst the turntable at Liverpool Street was being modified to take the Britannia Class locomotives.
B4 4-6-0	1906	1950	For short period commencing in 1923 some B4 4 6 0s built in 1906 worked on the Great Northern and Great Eastern Joint Line. In the period 1933-5 three Nos 6095 and 6103-4 were stationed at March. Whilst they did not normally work south of Cambridge they did occasionally reached Norwich via the curve north of Ely. The three normally worked northwards over the GN and GE Joint Line.
B8 4-6-0	1913	1949	Worked over GN&GE Jt line in 1923 and 1924-6. Allocated to March
C4 4-4-2	1903	1950	In the mid to late 1930s the members of the class worked a diagram from March to Wisbech, thence to Ely and return.
C14 4-4-2T	1907	1960	From 1934 onwards 12 4 4 2 side tanks of Class C14 were allocated to the Great Eastern section. Remained on GE Section until 1950.
D9 4-4-0	1901	1950	The class was first allocated to the GE Section in 1934 and remained on it until 1946.

F2 2-4-2T	1896	1950	Four push pull fitted F2 2-4-2 side tanks dating from 1898 were allocated the Norwich area of Great Eastern Section in the 1930s to replace the Clayton and Shuttleworth steam railcars. Others followed during the Second World War to Yarmouth South Town and for a time in 1941-2 two engines were transferred from Norwich to Stratford to work the Epping to Ongar service before being transferred to King's Cross to work the Alexandra Palace branch.
J10 0-6-0	1892	1961	Thirteen J10s were allocated to the GE area between 1925 and 1933. They were seen regularly at Cambridge, Lowestoft, March, Norwich, and Peterborough sheds.
J11 0-6-0	1901	1962	In 1927 26 members were allocated the GE Section to replace some withdrawn ex GE J15s. They remained on the section for only a short time and had all returned to their home section by January 1933.
L1 later L3 2-6-4T	1914	1956	Allocated to March 1929-31 to works transfer freights Peterborough to Whitemoor.
O4 2-8-0	1911	1966	Originally allocated to March to work GN and GE Joint Line. Not passed to work south of March until March 1929.
S1 0-8-4T	1908 and 1932	1957	Was on section from July 1932 to December 1949.

Ex NER

Class	First Built	Last Withdrawn/ Rebuilt	Comment
G5 0-4-4T	1894	1958	Two were transferred in 1938 to work the Seven Sisters to Palace Gates service. In 1944 they were joined by another member of the class. Latterly they worked the Saffron Walden branch and were withdrawn in 1956.
J21 0-6-0	1886	1961	During the mid-1930s, some Class J21s built between 1886 and 1894 were allocated to the Great Eastern section, where they remained until the end of 1937.
J26 0-6-0	1904	1962	No 379. According to the RCTS *History of the Locomotives of the LNER* this was from December 1926 to July 1928.
J27 0-6-0	1906	1967	In 1926, twelve superheated J27s 0-6-0s which were built between 1906 and 1922 having been displaced from the North Eastern section by the arrival of the first J39 Class 0-6-0s moved to the Great Eastern section where they worked alongside former GER 0-6-0s. The class remained on the section until 1943.
J72 0-6-0T	1898	1967	Two at Ipswich from May 1950 to February 1952.
T1 4-8-0T	1909	1961	No 1656 was sent to the newly-built Whitemoor Yard at March in 1929. In 1932 this was replaced by class members Nos 1355 and 1358 which in turn were displaced by Class S1 0 8 4Ts in 1934.
EB1 Bo Bo	1914	1964	Electric locomotive. Used as depot shunter at Ilford Last ran in November 1960.

Ex NBR

Class	First Built	Last Withdrawn/ Rebuilt	Comment
J 37 0-6-0	1914	1967	Only NBR steam locomotive to work on GE Section in 1926 - No 9454
Y11 0-4-0	1921	1956	Petrol locomotive

New LNER

Class	First Built	Last Withdrawn/ Rebuilt	Comment
B1 4-6-0	1942	1967	
B2 4-6-0	1945	1959	2 cylinder rebuilt of B17
B17 4-6-0	1928	1960	3 cylinders. 2 streamlined in 1937 for East Anglian train. Streamlining removed in 1951.
K1 2-6-0	1945/1949	1967	Prototype rebuilt from Class K4 locomotive. Last LNER designed locomotive in service.
K5 2-6-0	1945	1959	Rebuild of K3
L1 2-6-4 T	1945	1962	
O1 2-8-0	1944	1965	Rebuilt of O4
O6 2-8-0	1943	1968	LMS Stanier 8F introduced 1935. On LNER 1943 to 1948.
O7 2-8-0	1943	1967	Riddles Austerity 2-8-0. LNER purchased 200 in 1946. LNER classed them O7 in January 1947.
Q1 0-8-0T	1942	1959	Tank locomotive rebuild of Q4 tender locomotive.
V1 2-6-2 T	1930	1961	
V2 2-6-2	1936	1965	Allocated March for GN&GE Joint Line. One once worked to Ipswich on a troop train en route to Parkestone and one worked into Liverpool Street on clearance trials. The class was permitted to work from Whitemoor to Stratford.

Class	First Built	Last Withdrawn/ Rebuilt	Comment
V3 2-6-2T	1939	1963	Some rebuilt from V1
V4 2-6-2	1941	1957	Only had brief stay on GE section in 1941-42
Y1 0-4-0T	1927	1963	One-speed Sentinel Shunter
Y3 0-4-0T	1927	1964	Two-speed Sentinel Shunter
Y10 0-4-0T	1930	1952	"Super Sentinel"
Sentinel railcar	1925	1948	
Clayton railcar	1927	1937	
J45/DES 1 0-6-0	1944	1967	
DES 2 0-6-0	1949	1962	
Drewry/ Vulcan 0-6-0	1947	1958	A demonstrator purchased by BR

WD and USATC

Class	First Built	Last Withdrawn/ Rebuilt	Comment
WD 2-8-0	1943	1967	Riddles Austerity 2-8-0. LNER purchased 200 in 1946
WD 2-10-0	1943	1946	
S160 2-8-0	1942	1945	US Army Transportation Corps

Ex LMS

Class	First Built	Last Withdrawn/ Rebuilt	Comment
3F 0-6-0 Tank	1924	1967	
3P 4-4-2 Tank	1923	1960	Ordered by Midland Railway. MR version of LTSR 79 Class
4F 0-6-0	1924	1966	
2 MT 2-6-0	1946	1967	
4 MT 2-6-0	1947	1968	

0-6-0 Diesel electric shunter BR Class 11	1945	1972	

Ex Southern

Class	First Built	Last Withdrawn/ Rebuilt	Comment
BB/WC 4-6-2	1945	1967	

Ex GWR

Class	First Built	Last Withdrawn/ Rebuilt	Comment
9400 0-6-0 Panier Tank	1947	1965	Only ex GWR class to work on former GER

BR Steam

Class	First Built	Last Withdrawn/ Rebuilt	Comment
2 MT 2-6-0	1952	1967	Allocated to GE Section in summer 1962
4 MT 2-6-0	1952	1968	
4 MT 2-6-4 Tank	1951	1967	Allocated to GE Section in summer 1962
7 MT 4-6-2	1951	1968	
9F 2-10-0	1954	1968	

Derby Lightweight single, 2 or 4 car	1954	1969	
Metro-Cammell Lightweight 2 car	1955	1981	
Wagon un Machinenbau Railbus Single car	1958	1967	

100 2 car	1957	1988	
101 2, 3 or 4 car	1956	2003	
104 2, 3 or 4 car	1957	1993	
105 2 or 3 car	1959	1988	
109 2 car	1957	1991	
116 2 or 3 car	1961	1995	
125 3 car	1959	1977	
150 2 and 3 car	1984		Still in service
153 Single car Converted from 155	1991		Still in service
155 2 car	1987		Still in service
156 2 car	1988		Still in service
158 2 car and 3 car	1990		Still in service
170 2 car and 3 car	1999		Still in service. Used on the short lived Crosslink service between Norwich and Basingstoke which operated between 2000 and 2002 as well as the short lived through services from Liverpool Street to Peterborough and to Lowestoft via Ipswich. They also supplemented the electric trains on the London to Norwich route for a time.
172 2 car and 3 car	2010		Used on GOBLIN Line Still in service on West Midlands Railway

BR Diesel Loco

Class	First Built	Last Withdrawn/ Rebuilt	Comment
O1 0-4-0 diesel mechanical (dm)	1956	1981	
O3 0-6-0 dm	1957	2008	
O4 0-6-0 dm	1948/1952	1972	
O6 0-4-0 dm	1958	1984	
O8 0-6-0 diesel electric (de)	1952		Still in service
10 0-6-0 de	1955	1972	
15 Bo Bo de	1957	1971	
16 Bo Bo de	1958	1968	
20 Bo Bo de	1957		Still in service
21 Bo Bo de	1958	1968	
24 Bo Bo de	1958	1980/1982	1980 last date in service. 1982 last use in departmental service
31 A 1 A A 1 A de	1957		Still in service
37 Co Co de	1960		Still in service
40 1 Co Co 1 de	1958	1985	
47 Co Co de	1962		Still in service
53 Co Co de	1961	1975	
56 Co Co de	1976		Still in service
57 Co Co de	1997		Rebuild of Class 47. Still in service
58 Co Co de	1988	2002	
60 Co Co de	1989		Still in service
66 Co Co de	1998		Still in service
67 Bo Bo de	1999		Still in service
70 Co Co de	2009		Still in service
D1/1 0-4-0 dm	1954	1967	
D1/3 0-4-0 dm	1956	1968	
D2/11 0-4-0 de	1958	1967	

BR/PRIVATE CO's EMU

Class	First Built	Last Withdrawn/ Rebuilt	Comment
302 4 car	1958	1999	First in service in 1969. Some rebuilt with internal gangways. Others rebuilt by having partitions of compartments removed.
304 4 car	1960	1996	On loan from London Midland Region to Eastern Region in early 1960s.
305 3 and 4 car	1959	2001	Some 4-car units built for LTS line had a motor brake luggage van instead of a motor brake second. GE section 4-car units rebuilt with internal gangways. Equipped with GEC electrical equipment as opposed to English Electric electrical equipment fitted on other first general emus.
306 3 car	1949	1981	Original dc current, then converted to ac. First six body shells built 1940.
307 4 car	1956	1993	Original dc current, then converted to ac. Further rebuilt by being fitted with internal gangways.
308 3 and 4 car	1959	2001	4-car units rebuilt by being fitted with internal gangways.
309 2 and 4 car	1962	2000	Some 4-car units originally had a griddle car in their formation.
310 4 car	1965	2002	First built for LMR. Originally gangwayed within pair of coaches. Later ganwayed throughout unit.
312 4 car	1975	2004	
313 3 car	1976	2023	First built for GN section inner suburban services. Dual ac oh and dc 3rd rail. In services on GE used on Liverpool Street to Watford survive and Colchester to Clacton and Walton locals.

315 4 car	1980	2022	
317 4 car	1981	2022	Built for Midland main line suburban services out of St Pancras and London and North Western and Great Northern suburban services out of Euston and of King's Cross. On GE mainly use on Cambridge line services, but also on some Colchester line services. Were not used on services to Southend.
321 4 car	1988	2023	In 2010s 31 were refurbished and given air conditioning.
322	1990	2022	Primarily for Stansted Express service but also found on other services including to Southend.
357 4 car	1999		Still in service. Built for c2c. Five loaned National Express East Anglia 2004-6. Generally used on Liverpool Street to Southend services.
360 4 car	2002		Still in service on East Midlands Railway.
365 4 car	1994	2021	Used on services out of King's Cross.
379 4 car	2010	2022	Used on Stansted Express and Cambridge services Now in storage.
387 4 car	2014		Still in service
416 2 car	1955	1995	3rd rail dc. Only SR emu used on GE.
720 5 car	2018		Still in service
745 12 car	2018		Still in service
755 3 car and 4 car	2018		Still in service Bi mode

BR Electric Loco

Class	First Built	Last Withdrawn/ Rebuilt	Comment
86 Bo Bo	1965	2021	
90 Bo Bo	1987		Still in service

LT Steam

Class	First Built	Last Withdrawn/ Rebuilt	Comment
Kerr Stuart 0-4-2 saddle tank	1922	1947	Used in construction of Central Line extension.
H2 4-4-4T Ex Metropolitan Railway	1920	1947	Taken over from London Transport in 1937. Used by Stratford depot after servicing at the works.
L2 2-6-4T Ex Metropolitan Railway	1925	1948	Taken over from London Transport in 1937. Used by Stratford depot after servicing at the works.
M2 0-6-4T Ex Metropolitan Railway	1915	1948	Taken over from London Transport in 1937. Used by Stratford depot after servicing at the works. The Railway Observer for March 1947 reported Class M2 0 6 4 side tank No 9076 *Robert H Selbie* had been seen at Liverpool Street station on empty stock workings.

LT/DLR EMU INCLUDING ELIZABETH LINE AND OVERGROUND

Class	First Built	Last Withdrawn/ Rebuilt	Comment
Standard Tube Stock 7 or 8 cars	1923	1966	
1935 Tube Stock 2 car	1935	1966	Worked in 3-car units used Standard Tube Stock trailer car.
1938 Tube Stock 4 car	1938	1988	Used Standard or 1938 Tube Stock trailer cars.
1959 Tube Stock 4 car	1959	2000	
1960 Tube Stock 2 car	1960	1994	Worked in 3-car units used Standard or 1938 Tube Stock trailer cars.
1962 Tube Stock 4 car	1962	1999	
1992 Tube Stock 8 car	1993		Still in service
1996 Tube Stock 8 car	1997		Still in service
345 9 car	2015		Still in service
378 5 car	2008		Still in service
710 4 car and 5 car	2017		Still in service Some dual ac oh and dc 3rd rail. Some ac oh only.
P86 2 car	1987	1995	
P892 car	1989	1995	
B902 car	1991		Still in service
B923 car	1993		Still in service
B2K 2 car	2001		Still in service
B07 3 car	2009		Still in service
B23 3 car	2023		Still in service

Visitors – some were allocated to the section for a short time

Class	First Built	Last Withdrawn/ Rebuilt	Comment
A1 later A10 4-6-2	1922	1948	Used on Newmarket race trains
A1 4-6-2	1945/1948/2008	1966	First member of Class rebuilt from original A1. A new locomotive named *Tornado* was built in 2008. It hauled the Harwich to Liverpool Street leg of the 50th anniversary train of the Kindertransport.
A3 4-6-2	1927	1966	Used on Newmarket race trains
C1 4-4-2	1902	1950	Used on Newmarket race trains
C2 4-4-2	1898	1945	One for a time worked over the GN&GE Joint Line in 1929. Allocated to March.
D2 4-4-0	1898	1951	Worked to GE Section on excursions from GN Section.
J3 0-6-0	1912	1954	Worked to GE Section on excursions from GN Section.
J4 0-6-0	1873	1951	Included rebuilds of earlier engines. Some ex M&GNJTR. Worked to GE Section on excursions from GN Section. M&GNJTR locomotives confined to M&GNJT section Worked to Stratford for servicing.
N5 0-6-2T	1891	1960	Ex GCR Had short periods on GE Section n 1935, 1954 and 1955.
LMS 2 MT 2-6-2 Tank	1946	1967	In the summers of 1949 and 1950 No 41200 was loaned to Ipswich shed to work the Aldeburgh branch.
LMS 4MT 2 Cylinder 2-6-4 Tank Fowler	1927	1966	

Class	First Built	Last Withdrawn/ Rebuilt	Comment
LMS 4MT 2 Cylinder 2-6-4 Tank Fairburn	1945	1967	
LMS 4 MT 3 Cylinder 2-6-4 Tank	1935	1962	
LMS 5 MT 2-6-0	1926	1967	
LMS 5 MT 4-6-0	1934	1968	
BR Class 4 4-6-0	1951	1968	
BR Class 5 4-6-0	1951	1968	
BR Class 6 4-6-2	1951	1966	
'A' Rebuild 4-4-0 Ex M&GNJTR	1882	1941	Mainly confined to M&GNJT section. Only one No 025 was overhauled at Stratford.
Ex M&GNJTR No 16 0-6-0 ST	1877	1937	Confined to M&GNJT section.
Ex M&GNJTR C17 4-4-2 T	1904	1944	Confined to M&GNJT section Worked to Stratford for servicing.
Ex M&GNJTR D52 4-4-0	1894	1945	Confined to M&GNJT section. Worked to Stratford for servicing. No 038 on its way to Stratford in May 1940 was used as station pilot at Ipswich on 27/8 May.
Ex M&GNJTR D53 4-4-0	1894	1943	Small Belpaire firebox Confined to M&GNJT section. Worked to Stratford for servicing.

Class	First Built	Last Withdrawn/ Rebuilt	Comment
Ex M&GNJTR D54 4-4-0	1894	1945	Large Belpaire firebox. Confined to M&GNJT section. Worked to Stratford for servicing.
Ex M&GNJTR J40 0-6-0	1896	1944	Round topped firebox. Confined to M&GNJT section. Worked to Stratford for servicing.
Ex M&GNJTR J41 0-6-0	1896	1943	Belpaire firebox. Confined to M&GNJT section. Worked to Stratford for servicing.
Ex M&GNJTR J93 0-6-0T	1897	1949	Mostly confined to M&GNJT section. No 098 was stationed on GE Section at Kings Lynn from September 1939 to June 1940. Worked to Stratford for servicing.
Graz 0-4-0 diesel Hydraulic (dh)	1924	1924	Experimental. First diesel locomotive on GER Section.
D0226 0-6-0 de	1956	1960	In service 1957-60
D0227 0-6-0 dh	1956	1959	In service 1957-60
23 Bo Bo	1959	1971	Used on Newmarket race trains. Also for a time on Cambridge Buffet Expresses extended to Ely.
33 Bo Bo	1960		Still in service. Only one known internal workings on GE – on 10 January 1986.
45 1 Co Co 1	1960	1989	Tried on GE section in 1974.
55 Co Co	1961	1982	Only worked internal GE services when in preservation.
87 Bo Bo	1973	2006	Worked a rail tour in 2005.

Class	First Built	Last Withdrawn/ Rebuilt	Comment
AM1 3 car	1914 – rebuilt 1952	1966	Rebuilt from dc 3rd and 4th rail to ac o/h. Ran on Fenchurch St to Bow Junction in March 1956 used to test ac power.
EM1 Bo Bo	1941/1950	1981	Prototype only 1941 – rest 1950-53. Some rain trials on GE Section in November 1950.
1967 Tube Stock 4 car units	1968	2011	Tested on Woodford-Hainault section.
LEV1 4 Wheel railbus	1978	1987	
ACV/BUT Lightweight Railcars	1952	1963	Ran trials on Ongar branch in 1952 and Southminster branch in 1953.

Proposed locomotives that were not built and would have worked on GE Section.

Class	Date of design	Comment
L2 2-6-4T	1927	A design of 2-6-4 side tank for the Southend service of a power approximately equal to that of a B12. Cancelled because of the derailment of a River Class 2-6-4 side tank on the Southern Railway at Sevenoaks on 24 August 1927.
L3 2-6-4T	1941	Design prepared just before the death of Nigel Gresley in April 1941. Edward Thompson's L1 Class 2 6 4 side tank was built for the same purpose.
K6 2-6-0	1947	A light 2-6-0 intended for freight and passenger work on lightly laid branch lines. Designed just too late with Nationalisation taking place the following year. LMSR Ivatt 2MT 2-6-0s performed the same role on the GE Section in BR days.
341 ac emu	1991	Original proposal for units for Crossrail.

Carriages and wagons

In LNER days a variety of carriages including five coach articulated suburban sets were built from 1924. High roofed non-corridor compartment stock for Southend services. Standard LNER coaching stock – both corridor and non corridor. In 1937 some new stock was built for the East Anglian and in 1925 and 1938 new stock for the Hook Continental. Post war new corridor and non corridor stock was built. In addition stock from other constituent companies of the LNER also appeared on the GE Section.
In BR days both corridor and non-corridor Mark 1 stock saw service on the GE Section. Mark 1 stock was built between 1951 and 1963. Mark 2 stock was built between 1963 and 1975 and first entered service in 1964. This was all corridor stock. There were seven varieties – Mark 2 and Mark 2A to F. Mark 2D tranche built in 1971-72 were the first carriages to have combined pressure ventilation/air-conditioning fitted and so there were.no opening windows in the seating area, whilst Mark 2F built in 1973-75had full air conditioning fitted. This stock saw service on the GE Section as did Mark 3 stock which was built between 1975 and 1988.
In regards to goods wagons these followed normal British standard design. On the train ferries both British and Continental types were used. The latter being constructed to the British loading gauge.

Ships

Name	Entered service	In Service	Comment
Accrington	1910 – for GCR	In 1946 transferred to Harwich to Antwerp as a cargo/passenger ship and remained in that role until when it became a cargo ship before being scrapped in 1951.	
Amsterdam 1	1894	Scrapped 1928	
Amsterdam 2	1930	In early 1944 the ship was converted at North Shields to a Landing Craft (Infantry), able to carry 420 troops and 6 landing craft, and landed American troops on the notorious Omaha Beach on 6 June 1944. The ship was then immediately withdrawn and converted at Glasgow into 'Hospital Carrier No.64' and was back in Normandy in this role by July. On 7 August 1944 shortly after leaving Juno Beach with 258 patients it was sunk by two mines. Of the 419 people on board, 323 were saved.	

Amsterdam 3	1950	1967	
Antwerp	1919	1951	From 1945 as troop ship
Archangel	1910	1941 whilst on war service on a trooping voyage from Kirkwall to Aberdeen it was bombed and beached and broke up 5 miles south of Newburgh.	
Avalon	1963	1974	
Brightlingsea	1925	1964	Still in service in private ownership
Bruges	1920	In June 1940 the ship was allocated to move British troops from Le Havre to Cherbourg, as the German army advanced from the east. Whilst anchored off Le Havre on the morning of 11 June, the ship received a direct hit from an aircraft bomb and was beached as a total loss.	
Cambridge Ferry	1963	1987	
Cromer	1902	1934	
Dewsbury	1910 for GCR	1946 transferred to Harwich to Antwerp as a cargo/passenger ship and remained in that role until 1959	
Duke of York	1935 for LMSR	Transferred in1948 to Harwich for Hook of Holland service and remained in that role until 1963	
Epping	1914	1964	
Essex Ferry 1/ Train Ferry No 1	1917	1957	Renamed *Essex Ferry II* in 1956
Essex Ferry 2	1956	1981	Named *Essex Ferry*
Felixstowe	1918	1951	
Frinton	1903	Acquired by GER in 1919 – sold 1926	
Hainault	1914	1964	

Koningin Beatrix	1986	1997	Zeeland Steamship Navigation Company
Koningin Emma	1939	1968	Zeeland Steamship Navigation Company
Koningin Juliana	1968	1984	Zeeland Steamship Navigation Company
Koningin Wilhelmina	1960	1978	Zeeland Steamship Navigation Company
Malines	1921	In late 1940 it was requisitioned by the Admiralty and commissioned as a convoy escort HMS *Malines*. The ship sailed to the Mediterranean via the Cape, where it operated as a troopship for much of the time. On 19 July 1942 the ship was torpedoed by German aircraft and beached near Port Said, but was refloated in January 1943. It was then transferred to the Ministry of War Transport, becoming a training ship at Kabret in early 1944. On its arrival back in the Tyne under tow in November 1945 it was laid up unrepaired and broken up at Dunston on Tyne in April 1948.	
Norfolk Ferry	1951	1983	
Norfolk	1900	1931	
Pin Mill	1910 acquired by GER in 1912	1925	

Prague	1930	1948	
Princes Beatrix	1939	1968	Zeeland Steamship Navigation Company
Roulers	1894	1930	
St Denis	1908	1940	
St Edmund	1974	1982	
St George 1	1906. Acquired by GER 1919	1926	
St George 2	1968	1983	
St Nicholas	1983	1991	
Sheringham	1926	1958	
Speedlink Vanguard	1981	1987	
Stena Britannica I	1991	1994	
Stena Britannica II	2003	2010	
Stena Britannica III	2010		Still in service
Stena Discovery	1997	2006	
Stena Europe	1988		Still in service on the Irish Sea Fishguard to Rosslare route
Stena Hollandica I	2000	2010	
Stena Hollandica I	2010		Still in service
Suffolk	1895	1931	
Suffolk Ferry	1947	1981	
Train Ferry No 2	1917	1940 sunk off France	

Train Ferry No 3	1917	In May 1944, the ship was fitted with a ramp to permit the landing of railway equipment where no shore facilities existed, crossing to Cherbourg and then from September in regular service to Dieppe. On 17 March 1945 it was damaged by a mine off Dieppe and sank the next day.	
Vienna	1929	1960	From 1945 as a troopship
Zeeland	1984	1986	Zeeland Steamship Navigation Company

Buses

Make	Registration No	In service	Comment
Thornycroft J 28 single deck rear entrance	DX2173-5 GER Fleet Nos 17-9	1919 -1923	Last GER BUSE. Sold to Thames Valley Traction

Sources and Acknowledgements

Newspapers periodicals and websites
British Newspaper On-Line Archive
Harwich and Dovercourt, org
I was a London firefighter
LNER Encyclopedia
British Railways Eastern Region Magazine
Great Eastern Journal
Great Eastern Railway Magazine
Locomotive Magazine
London and North Eastern Railway Magazine
London Railway Record
North Eastern Railway Magazine
Railway Magazine
Railway Observer
Railway Pictorial
Railways
Railway accident reports

Books

Allen Cecil J., *Great Eastern* – Ian Allan 1959
Allen, Cecil J., *The London and North Eastern Railway* – Ian Allan 1966
Allen, Cecil J., *Titled Trains of Great Britain* – Ian Allan 1967
Allen Dr Ian C., *East Anglia Album* – OPC 1976
Allen Dr Ian C., *East Anglian Branch Line Album* OPC 1977
Allen Dr Ian C., *Diesels in East Anglia* OPC 1980
Bonavia, Michael R., *A History of the LNER* – George Allen and Unwin 1980
Bradley, D.L., *Locomotives of the Southern Railway Pt 2* – RCTS 1976
Brown Paul, *The Fighting Branch* Author 1975
Brown, F.A.S. *Nigel Gresley – Locomotive Engineer* – Ian Allan 1961
Bruce, J. Graeme, Croome, Desmond F., *The Twopenny Tube: The Story of The Central Line* – Capital Transport 1996
Chackesfield, John E., *Richard Maunsell: An Engineering Biography* – Oakwood 1998
Chackesfield, John E., *Sir Henry Fowler: A Versatile Life* – Oakwood 2000
Chackesfield, John E., *Sir William Stanier: A New Biography* – Oakwood 2001
Cooper, J.M., *East Suffolk Railway* – Oakwood 1982

Cowley, Ian, *Anglia East – The Transformation of a Railway* – David and Charles 1987
Crawley, R.J., MacGregor, D.R., Simpson, F.D., *The Years Between – V1 and V2* 1979 V1 OPC 1985 V2
Crump, Norman, *By Rail to Victory* – London and North Eastern Railway 1947
Darwin, Bernard, *War on the Line – Southern Railway 1946*
Doggett, Maurice, *Eastern Counties: The First 50 Years* – Eastern Counties Omnibus Company 1981
Fiennes, Gerard, *I Tried to run a Railway* – Ian Allan1973
Glover, John, *Eastern Electric* – Ian Allan 2003
Gordon, D.I., *A Regional History of the Railways of Great Britain Volume 5 V Eastern Counties* – David and Charles 1968
Grafton, Peter, *Edward Thompson of the LNER* – Oakwood 2007
Green, Chris and Vincent, Mike, *The Network South East Story* – OPC 2014
Greenaway, Ambrose, *A Century of North Sea Passenger Steamers* – Ian Allan 1986
Groves Norman, *Great Northern Locomotive History Vol 2 1867-1895 The Stirling Era* (RCTS 1991
Hands, Peter, *B.R Steam Shed Allocations Part 4 Eastern Region Sheds* – Defiant Publications 1985
Hardy, H.N., *Steam in the Blood* – Ian Allan - 1971
Higgins, R.N., *Over Here: Story of the United States Army Transportation corps Class S160 Locomotives* – Author 1980
Hitchman, Harry G. and Driver Philip, *Parkeston – A Century Of Service* – Authors 1982
Horne, M.A.C., *The Victoria Line: A Short History* – Douglas Rose 1988
Hughes, Geoffrey, *London and North Eastern Railway* – Ian Allan 1996
Hughes, Geoffrey, *Sir Nigel Gresley – the Locomotive Engineer and His Family* – Oakwood 2001
Hughes, Geoffrey, *The Gresley Influence* – Ian Allan 1983
Jackson, Alan A., *London's Local Railways* – David and Charles 1978
Jackson, Alan A., *London's Termini* – David and Charles 1969
Joby, R.S., *Forgotten Railways: East Anglia* – David and Charles 1985
Kay, Peter, *The London, Tilbury and Southend Railway Volumes 1-8* – Author 1996-2020
Klapper, Charles F, *Sir Herbert Walker's Southern Railway* Ian Allan 1973
Lee, Charles E., *East London line and the Thames tunnel* – London Transport 1976
Lee David, Taylor Alan, Shorland-Ball Rob, *The Southwold Railway* Pen and Sword 2019
Lombardelli, Carl, *Branch lines to Braintree* – EARM 1980
Lovett, Denis, *The North London Railway 1846-2012* – Irwell 2012
McCall, A., *Green Line* – New Cavendish 1980
Northern Line Extensions – LURS 1981
Paye Peter, *TheMid Suffolk Light Railway* Wild Swan 1986
Peacock, Thomas B., *The Mistley. Thorpe and Walton Railway* – Author 1946
Phillips, Charles, *The Great Eastern Railway in South Essex* – Pen and Sword 2019
Phillips, Charles, *The Great Eastern Since 1900* – Ian Allan 1985
Phillips, Charles, *The Tendring Hundred Railway* – Connor and Butler 1989
Quayle, H.I., *The Felixstowe Railway* – Oakwood 1978
RCTS, *The Locomotives of the LNER*, 1963 to 1994
Rowledge, W.P., *Heavy Goods Engines of the War Department Volume 3 Austerity 2-8-0 and 2-10-0* – Springmead 1978

Smith, Peter, *Footplate over the Mendips* – OPC 1978
Smith, Peter, *Mendips Engineman* – OPC 1972
Smithson, S.E., *Diesel Multiple Units: Eastern England* – Becknell 1981
Swindale, Dennis, *Branch line to Southminster* – EARM 1981
Swindale, Dennis, *Branch lines to Maldon* – EARM 1978
The British Gazette – reprint with The British Worker – David and Charles 1972
Tourret, R., *United States Army Transportation Corps Locomotives* – Author 1977
Tourret, R., *War Department Locomotives* – Author 1976
Walsh Bernard, *The Stour Valley Railway* Connor & Butler 1987
White, H.P., *A Regional History of the Railways of Great Britain: Volume 3 Greater London* – Phoenix House 1963
Williams, David. L., *Glory Days – British Ferries* – Ian Allan 2003
Wrottesley, A.J., *Midland and Great Northern Joint Railway* – David and Charles 1970

Index